Approaching Urban Design

Series: Exploring Town Planning

Series editor: Clara Greed

Approaching Urban Design

The Design Process

EDITED BY MARION ROBERTS & CLARA GREED

With contributions by Bill Erickson, Tony Lloyd-Jones, Ali Madanipour, Chris Marsh, David Seex, Mike Theis and Tim Townshend

LONGMAN

Pearson Education Limited
Edinburgh Gate, Harlow
Essex CM20 2JE, England
and Associated Companies throughout the world

© Pearson Education 2001

ISBN 0 582 30300 1

British Library Cataloguing-in-Publication Data
A catalogue record for this book is available from the
British Library.

Set by 3 in Times and Melior
Printed in Malaysia, LSP

Contents

Contributors

Bill Erickson is a Senior Lecturer in Urban Design at the University of Westminster, London, and an architect.

Clara Greed is Reader in the Faculty of the Built Environment, University of the West of England, Bristol, and is series editor for *Introducing Town Planning*.

Tony Lloyd-Jones is a part-time Senior Lecturer in Urban Design at the University of Westminster, London, and an advisor to the Department for International Development.

Ali Madanipour is Reader in Urban Design and Director of Postgraduate Research at the School of Architecture, Planning and Landscape, University of Newcastle-upon-Tyne.

Chris Marsh is Principal Lecturer in Surveying and Planning at the University of Westminster, London.

Marion Roberts is Academic Subject Leader in Urban Design at the University of Westminster, London.

David Seex is a Senior Lecturer in Urban Design at the University of Westminster, London, and a conservationist.

Michael Theis is Director, Max Lock Centre and Archive at the University of Westminster, London.

Tim Townshend is Lecturer and Degree Programme Director, MA Urban Design, at the School of Architecture, Planning and Landscape, University of Newcastle-upon-Tyne.

Acknowledgements

First and foremost the editors would like to thank the publishers for their patience and support in producing this book. The University of Westminster has also provided some time for its production. We have some practitioners to thank for their willingness to let us use examples of their work. Terry Farrell and Partners, Andy Karski of Tibbalds Monro and Urban Perspectives have all been generous both with time and material. David Lock of David Lock Associates kindly permitted us to use his masterplan for Ebbsfleet. Former students at the University of Westminster have also supplied us with some fine examples of their work and we must thank them for their diligence in producing it and for their willingness to let us expose it to public view. We are especially grateful to Caroline Lwin, Jane Fowles, Mike Martin and Martin Evans in this regard. Hugh Barton of the University of West of England has kindly allowed us to draw on his standards for catchment areas. Graham Shane of Columbia University in New York provided us with a redrawn diagram of his now famous analysis of the 'great estates' in London. Finally, may we take this opportunity to state that all of the student projects illustrated are hypothetical and have no relation to any real proposals, past or present.

Every effort has been made to trace the owners of copyright material; however, in a few cases this may have been impossible and we take this opportunity to offer our apologies to any copyright holders whose rights we may have unwittingly infringed.

Preface: Putting theory into practice

The purpose of this book is to provide a primer that will enable the application of sensitive design principles to urban form. The wider conceptual basis of urban design was discussed in the preceding companion volume, *Introducing Urban Design: Interventions and Responses* (Greed and Roberts 1998), in which key principles, considerations and concepts were introduced. In this volume we will seek to show how these might be applied and implemented within a range of real-world settings.

Manuals providing guidance for students of urban design have been relatively sparse until recently. While there have been many good examples of design guidance produced by local authorities for developers and planners (see Carmona 1998 for a discussion), students have had less choice. *Responsive Environments*, produced in 1985 by Alcock, Bentley, McGlynn, Murrain and Smith, a team based at Oxford Brookes University, proved to be a ground-breaking text. It provided help for students who were completely new to design tasks by explaining principles and techniques, while at the same time promoting the team's view of a desirable approach to urban design.

The strength and usefulness of *Responsive Environments* was demonstrated by its progress into a new edition in 1996 and its pre-eminence in the field (Bentley 1996). By the mid-1990s urban design had continued to flourish as a field of activity and as an academic discipline (Urban Design Group 1998). Many more higher education institutions had established postgraduate courses in urban design, or with urban design as a specialisation for other postgraduate courses in subjects such as architecture, landscape architecture and regeneration. Some planning courses had made urban design their 'specialist' area of study under the Royal Town Planning Institute's accreditation scheme. Within the professions, urban design practitioners were working for public authorities and private interests, at both home and abroad.

The field was in a state of flux and it seemed appropriate to produce an alternative student text that would reflect a different design approach and another temporal and geographic context. *Responsive Environments* had been based on the authors' own expertise which had been geographically based in 'middle England'. Urban design, by the mid-1990s, was being practised in a variety of contexts in Britain and overseas which were throwing up different sets of problems and issues. This book has been produced mainly by a team from the University of Westminster, with contributions from academics based at the University of Newcastle upon Tyne and within the overall series editorship of Clara Greed at the University of West of England. At the University of Westminster students are coming to grips with the problems of complex inner city sites in a highly pressurised development context, and it seems timely to share this metropolitan experience, since the approach that evolves through tackling these design tasks can be applied equally well to less pressurised and rural settlements. In addition, as levels of expertise and knowledge grow, it is also important to set out the theoretical basis for a design approach, since such theoretical principles would and should be subject to constant re-assessment and revision. This manual sets out to do this, by providing a discursive first part which discusses the origins of the authors' approach, before proceeding to a second part which provides guidance on 'how to do it'.

Since starting on this book other agencies have commissioned design manuals that are intended to provide national standards of guidance for practitioners. Urban Initiatives, in an extensive study for the Department of Environment, Transport and the Regions, has produced a guide for planners and developers (DETR and CABE 2000). This, together with an Urban Design Compendium, commissioned by the regeneration agency, English Partnerships and the Housing Corporation and produced by Llewelyn-Davies will provide good, well-illustrated guidance for competent practitioners. This volume, by contrast, is directed at students and is based on the authors' extensive experience of teaching at postgraduate and undergraduate levels. The distinguishing features of this volume are as follows:

- it is directed at undergraduates in planning, architecture, landscape architecture and postgraduates from 'non-design' disciplines;
- it provides 'hands-on' guidance in tackling a range of urban design tasks;
- it explains the theoretical basis for an approach to design and relates it to 'hands-on' guidance;
- it provides background information and a glossary of 'jargon' terms.

Contents

The book is intended as a design manual. It is divided into five blocks: background; an explanation of approaches; carrying out the urban design project; the project in practice; and information. The first two blocks are more discursive, the third block diagrammatic, the fourth discursive and finally the last block provides a series of notes, guidelines and references. Each block is related to the other, but it is anticipated that readers may wish to 'dip' into and out of different blocks and units as they use the book.

The first block, Understanding the City in Terms of Design, sets the scene. There are obviously many ways in which cities can be understood, for example in terms of sociology, economics, as cultural artefacts, as the products of planning policies; the list is long. This block sets out some basic ideas about design and urban design which form the background to our suggested approach to what urban design is as an intervention into towns and cities (Figure P.1). Towns and cities can and do develop without the explicit attention of professionals who style themselves urban designers, but this is not to say that towns and cities are not designed. Furthermore, in order for urban designers to

make beneficial proposals, it is important for them to understand the forces or factors that influence city development in design terms. Some brief introduction is also made to urban design as a process.

In Block II the authors' approach to undertaking an urban design project in a practical hands-on sense is set out. In Unit 3, the significance of movement systems, public and private space, and scale are explained in terms of their importance for analysis and design. The concept of the armature is set out, both as a tool for analysis and as a structuring device with which to approach an urban design task. Unit 4 recounts what are now rapidly becoming mainstream ideas for creating convivial spaces at a local scale and explains their origins.

Block III provides practical advice on how to tackle a project. Readers should use the information part of the book as a supplement to the advice given here. Design is a process that is often shrouded in mystique by its practitioners. Unit 5 clears up some misunderstandings by offering alternative descriptions of the design process and a discussion of the process itself. Unit 6 deals with making an area analysis and deriving an urban design framework from it, using an inner city area and site in London. An inner city area and site has been chosen because its complexity throws up most of the urban issues that students may have to grapple with. Moving from area appraisal to the problems of a specific site demands a different level of analysis and some understanding of buildings and their requirements; Unit 7 deals with these issues. Unit 8 provides an explanation of how to move from analysis to concepts and a rationale, and illustrates this with five worked examples. Case studies from urban and rural Britain and Hong Kong are explained to inspire students with a variety of possibilities and to demonstrate how urban design principles and methods may be applied to differing situations and tasks.

Block IV provides another level of iteration, or repetition, to the design process in making the relation between projects and practice 'in the real world' more explicit. In Unit 9, basic concepts of development economics are explained and applied to the inner city worked example. The argument for this unit is that in real life, designers have to engage with development economics and produce positive proposals within the constraints of finance and profitability. Unit 10 offers some ideas for evaluating urban design proposals from the perspective of the 'user', i.e. people who might be affected by the proposals. Urban design is an iterative, collective process and it is hoped that reading these units will encourage readers to return to and refine their proposals after the first draft. Unit 11 provides a further

(a)

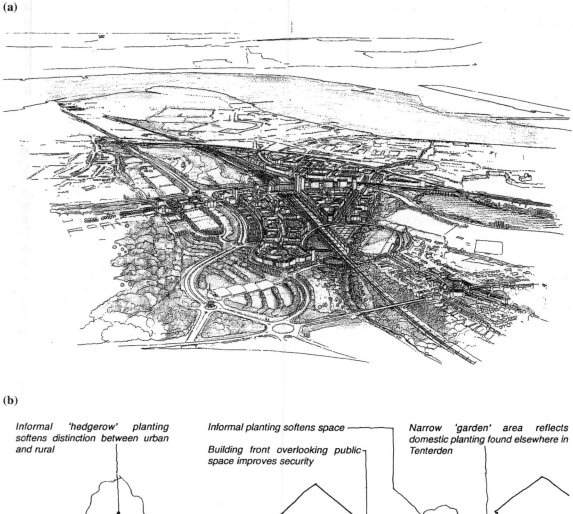

(b)

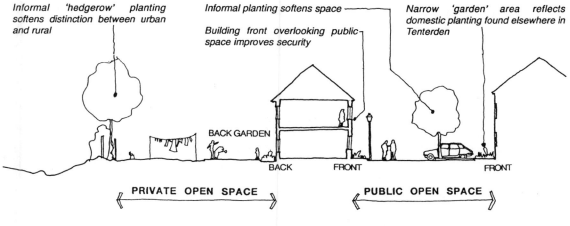

Informal 'hedgerow' planting softens distinction between urban and rural

Informal planting softens space

Building front overlooking public space improves security

Narrow 'garden' area reflects domestic planting found elsewhere in Tenterden

BACK GARDEN

BACK   FRONT   FRONT

PRIVATE OPEN SPACE   PUBLIC OPEN SPACE

SHARED SURFACE ACCESS ROAD OR PRIVATE DRIVE

Figure P.1   Urban design operates at a range of scales from masterplans for new regional centres to design guidance at the intimate scale of the back garden. Both of the examples shown here come from the same county in England. **(a)** Masterplan of Ebbsfleet, Kent (David Lock Associates for Whitecliff Properties). **(b)** Design guidance for Tenterden, Kent (Tibbalds Monro Ltd).

explanation of the ways in which urban design is carried out in practice: who it is carried out for and why. The final unit makes the links between urban design and planning practice in an English and an international context. Planning authorities are making greater use of design guidelines and urban design studies and it is likely that this area of work will grow in the future.

Block V sets out some information and 'tools' for assisting readers in tackling design projects. In Appendix 1 there is advice on getting started and on practical issues such as which scale to use. Appendix 2 gives advice on what are literally the 'building blocks' of urban design: grid patterns, block sizes, street sections, and the requirements of different building types. Appendix 3 tackles the practical issues of spatial planning at a larger scale and provides information on catchment areas for facilities, the relationships between numbers of facilities and density, the relationship between transport systems and density, and a guide to the measurement of density itself. In providing this information and advice, principles of sustainability have been incorporated. Attitudes to what are deemed to be acceptable living conditions vary internationally and some international comparisons are sup-

plied. Appendix 4 acknowledges that over the past 10 years there has been an increased recognition of the needs of those whose movement suffers temporary or permanent impairment – not only the physically disabled but also people pushing prams, elderly people, and those suffering from temporary injuries. This appendix directs the reader to some relevant literature for guidance.

Finally, one of the key problems urban designers face in teaching and in communicating with the public is that of professional jargon. It is difficult to avoid this, for as knowledge and understanding evolve, it is inevitable that new terms and expressions are coined. The glossary provides explanations for key terms in urban design with some forays into relevant areas of planning and architecture. Limits have had to be placed on its extent, but we hope that readers will refer to it as they read the book. There is no formal conclusion to this book as it is a practical manual rather than an overview. Working on it has been an exhausting but salutary process; we hope that it will be of use.

Clara Greed and Marion Roberts
Bristol and London, 2001

BLOCK I UNDERSTANDING THE CITY IN TERMS OF DESIGN

Unit 1 Design problems

Bill Erickson and Tony Lloyd-Jones

Introduction

Urban design, like any other design process, involves method as well as inspiration. This book investigates the challenge of the design problem; where to start and how to proceed. This unit will explain design as a process and how that process can be applied to an urban situation. In simple terms, design attempts to make the future better than the present (Figure 1.1). This involves planned change in the material world. The design process seems easy looking backwards. When a projected design is implemented one can usually look back and evaluate if it has been successful, whether it has improved things or not. If all designers had the benefit of hindsight surely the world would be a better place. The challenge and skill of good design requires not only that one envisages the future but also that one imagines change and its likely impact.

Consider the design of a car, for example. Designers start by asking what makes a good car. Then they look at what is already known: the existing car. The design task can be defined quite accurately – perhaps the car needs to be cleaner, faster, safer, quieter, etc. As each aspect of the car is worked on it can be assessed against these particular criteria. Some aspects may be more difficult to improve – the car may need to be more stylish or fashionable – but this too can be tested by using models and testing consumer reactions. Every single detail of the car is considered and once the new car is designed, tested and perfected it can be put into production. The design task is over.

The first task is to identify the existing condition ('where we are'), and evaluate if it could be improved ('where we want to be'). These design objectives may be quite general but will guide the process. To help, a detailed analysis of the existing condition is undertaken from which it is possible to list opportunities where improvements could be made. Analysis may also enable benchmarks to be set, against which improvements can be measured. Taken together these give a set of design criteria which identify need. This first stage is sometimes known as the design brief; it sets the agenda for change and defines the design problem.

Designers are always asking questions. The second step is to posit new design scenarios, to 'try on' new ideas and 'see if they fit'. This involves the generation

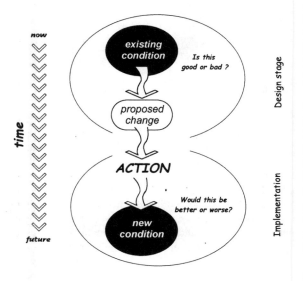

Figure 1.1 Design process: outline.

of a range of new 'what if' ideas. Each new scenario is tested against the design criteria. Those scenarios which appear to satisfy these criteria are retained while others are discarded. Thus an important part of the design process is the generation of new ideas; this is the creative part of the process. Frequently, however, the design criteria are numerous and at times conflicting. For instance, in the example of the car, the criteria of faster, safer and cheaper may be difficult to reconcile. This leads to a process where design scenarios are combined and developed or improved to meet one and then another of the various criteria. Sometimes several solutions may emerge and in this later stage the importance of the testing phase becomes crucial in selecting which ideas are the best.

Seen like this, design is not a simple linear process but an open-ended process where there is always room to introduce innovation. The design solution emerges from this iterative process normally when most of the criteria have been met to some degree. The design solution can be seen as the synthesis of several scenarios and forms the basis for action. Each design solution is unique and one of many that could possibly fit the problem. The basic diagram of the design process can be redrawn to include this cyclic process (Figure 1.2). In the design process the design problem itself is constantly revisited and refined. The activity of exploring design solutions requires a constant re-evaluation of the design criteria and design objectives. Where the design problem involves numerous and perhaps conflicting criteria, design testing can be extremely useful in determining the relative importance of various criteria and may even expose new ones.

This highlights several important aspects of the design process:

- It is cyclic and open-ended; there is always room for improvement.
- Proposing design solutions leads to a redefinition of the design problem.
- Because criteria are often conflicting there is no right or wrong solution but rather solutions that are more or less for the better.
- Design requires us to be inventive in creating new scenarios but rational in testing them against criteria.
- The analysis phase is an integral part of the design process. To get the right answers we need to pose the right questions.

Some design tasks are simple and anyone can undertake them, e.g. deciding what clothes to wear on a cold day. In an age of technology, design is an important activity. Specialist designers develop skills

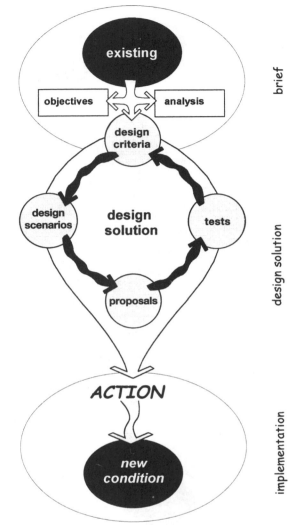

Figure 1.2   Design process: stages.

in a particular field which enable them to become experts. For example, a computer designer needs to know a lot about electronics and a little about plastic boxes, while a musical composer needs to know about sound and instruments. We associate these people with the things they design and group them into distinct professions. Associated with each profession is a body of specialist knowledge and a variety of methodologies that have been found useful in particular design problems. In the built environment the range of professional designers tends to be distinguished by the scale at which they work (Figure 1.3). At one end of the scale we have objects smaller than people such as

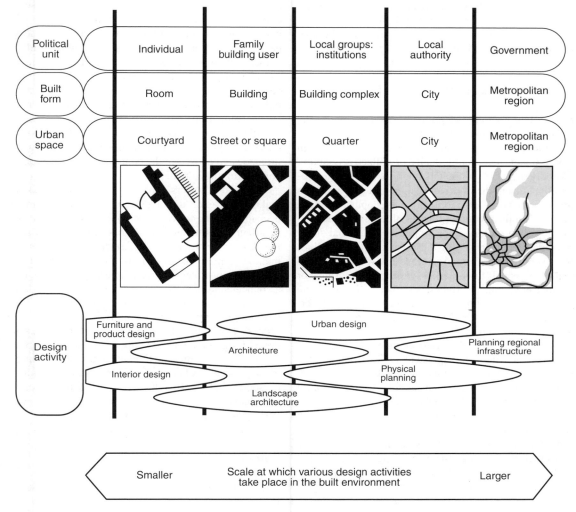

Figure 1.3   Scale of design activity in the built environment.

furniture, consumer products and clothes. In the mid range are buildings and spaces within which we can move around. At the large scale, cities and urban regions also involve spatial planning. We can see that urban design is undertaken within the context of other design activities operating at differing scales and in differing time frames.

Cities are difficult to design. Rather than being replaced with a new model, existing ones are adapted. Cities are complex and constantly changing, and the simple question 'what makes a good city?' is always difficult to answer. Most important of all, a city can never be designed in every detail. This is not to say that the urban environment is not designed in detail; it

certainly is, e.g. each building is designed in turn. Most features of the urban environment are designed by someone. Even the location of lamp-posts and the positioning of natural features such as trees is determined by a design process. Many of these decisions are made within a loose framework by people who may know only a little about what is going on in the rest of the city. Many design decisions lie beyond the scope of the urban design project, and may be made years later by various architects, builders, planners or developers and in a variety of ways. It is clear that for urban designers not only is the substance of the design process, i.e. the fabric of the city, complex, but so too is the professional context in which design takes place. We will return to the substance of urban design in later units where we will investigate methods for both analysis and design. However, first we will introduce the professional context in which urban designers operate.

Urban design as a decision-making process

With a few notable exceptions, cities are seldom the work of a single individual designer but are the product of a myriad of particular decisions about the urban environment, taken individually or collectively and at a variety of scales. While this book focuses on the professional discipline of urban design, as a process it can involve all types of people. Local people making a decision on the location of a school; engineers designing an urban motorway or architects a regional shopping mall; planners setting out urban design guidelines for a suburban conservation area; landscape designers planning a small town park – all are in some sense or another engaging in urban design since all contribute to the developing urban form of the city. Very different sets of actors and decision-making processes are, however, involved in each case.

Since it involves decisions about the allocation of resources to shape the physical environment, urban design is inevitably an economic and political, as well as an aesthetic and functional process. In this book, it is assumed that decision-making takes place in a contemporary planning and development context, within which urban design, as a recognised discipline, has an important and central role. As we have seen, we are concerned with a range of scales, from the city district to the individual site or local urban element. In certain instances, we may be looking at the form of the city as a whole, or even urban form and activity at the larger metropolitan scale.

Within the planning system as it is in the UK and in most other countries, however, there is little opportunity for exploring urban design and spatial planning at the wider scale since the means of implementing policy at this level does not currently exist. Our concerns, therefore, will focus mainly on urban design interventions within an existing urban context, simply because that is where most urban design effort is currently directed. However, the design approach of this book is equally applicable to the design of new settlements or to new extensions to existing towns and cities, as in the more economically dynamic and rapidly urbanising parts of the world.

Urban design can take place in a variety of development contexts – public, private and community contexts as well as contexts that combine all these elements. Urban designers can find themselves employed by any one of a number of 'stakeholders' – parties with a direct interest in a particular site, street, neighbourhood or larger urban area. A client could be a local authority, a regeneration agency, a housing association, a private developer or landowner, or a community organisation. In working for one stakeholder, an urban designer will nevertheless need to take account of the outlook of others with an interest in a particular development issue. In Unit 11, we explore these matters, and their influence on how and where urban design is used in the contemporary development context, in more detail.

This book offers two tools or approaches for making sense of urban design within this complex decision-making process. Unit 3 introduces the idea of an urban armature as a framework or primary structuring device for the city. The armature sits within our method framework, as a basis for establishing larger urban design strategies since our stress is on the city as a connected system of movement spaces. Unit 5 introduces the notion of a *method framework* for urban design, drawing on the idea of design as a cyclic process. However, it is also possible to follow the same urban design process and adopt a strategy that is based on prioritising other factors: land use, landscape or other physical, economic, political, aesthetic, cultural or social factors. In other words, the framework is quite general in its application and can encompass a very wide range of urban design approaches.

Summary

The main points of this unit can be summarised as follows:

- Urban design, like any other design process, combines rational method with inspiration. Design involves planned change in the real world and involves envisaging the future and the likely impact of change.

    The starting point is an analysis of the existing situation and the design 'problem'. In the design process we try out ideas to see if they fit the problem – a process that is cyclic and open-ended. As there are many criteria for a successful solution, and some of these may conflict – no perfect solution is possible.

    Urban design is taken within the context of other design activities operating at different scales and different time frames.

- We can never design the city in every detail and both the fabric of the city and its decision-making context are complicated. Urban design is an economic and political, as well as an aesthetic and functional process, often involving a shifting cast of players.

- We will refer mainly to the UK planning and development context although the principles outlined in this book apply across a range of urban development contexts including areas of rapid urbanisation.
- Urban design can take place in a variety of development contexts – public, private and community, and in contexts that combine all of these elements.
- Urban designers can find themselves employed by any one of a number of 'stakeholders' and needing to address the interests of those who are not their employers.
- Our main tools for dealing with the complexity of decision-making in urban design are a method framework and the concept of the urban armature (structure).

Unit 2 Urban generators

Marion Roberts and Tony Lloyd-Jones

This unit discusses the principal factors that, we would argue, shape the form and substance of towns and cities. We have called these 'urban generators'.

Movement systems

When a tourist goes to a new town the first item they need in order to start exploration is the street map. The map of a city provides the basic information about that city and illustrates the movement system which defines the 'structure' of that place, i.e. how the whole relates to the parts.

Movement systems and urban development

Whereas nowadays movement can be undertaken by a number of means or modes of transport, up until a century ago walking or being carried or pulled by a horse provided the only options. Most cities still have the street network as their primary arteries of movement, or hybrids of them as in the urban motorway. The technologies of movement systems inspire different types of urban form. For example, the winding back alleys of medieval towns are really only passable on foot or with one other animal such as a horse or a mule. By contrast, the ornate central boulevards of Paris are best appreciated at a smart trot behind a horse and carriage. Finally, cities such as Houston in the USA are best appreciated when approached from an urban motorway; here the glittering sides of the tower blocks almost seem to draw the car in at an exhilarating speed.

As can be seen from each of these examples, each mode of transport has inspired a different scale of urban form:

- three- to four-storey height medieval lane (pedestrian, horse and cart);
- seven- or eight-storey Parisian apartment block (pedestrians, carriages);
- multi-storey American skyscraper (motor car).

Interestingly the first two examples involve the buildings being closely packed together so that a continuous façade appears to be formed as the traveller moves through them. In the case of the skyscraper, the car moves so fast that it is possible for the skyscrapers to be spread out and yet still give the impression of a continuous wall of building (Figure 2.1).

Another important aspect to notice is the loss of transferability from one type of movement system to another. It would be impossible to run a two-way highway with modern parking standards down a medieval lane. Similarly, although Parisian boulevards are wide, they are still not wide enough to accommodate an urban motorway. Conversely, travelling on foot by the side of a busy urban road is a distressing and uncomfortable experience unless there is screening by trees or some other type of landscaping device. Hence not only are movement systems important to the definition of an urban area, but the scale and type of movement system also has an influence on the type of urban form and the pedestrian's experience of it.

Many ancient urban settlements evolved from movement systems forming a crossroad or from two systems crossing each other. In the era of the fortified city, the city walls defined the limits of the urban structure, i.e. the extent of the city itself. Nowadays the

Figure 2.1 A Frankfurt street (Bill Erickson).

movement system performs this function in a more ambiguous manner. Roads and railways can form barriers to movement that are as powerful as a wall. Tamed, they can also form a 'seam' which joins one part of the city to another so that the districts or neighbourhoods are formed around the movement system. Cities that have grown over a longer period of time have a less clearly articulated structure, but nevertheless the systems of movement have a clear and close relation to the districts, parts of the centre and sub-centres.

Types of movement systems

The number of patterns of movement systems in urban areas is potentially large, but three major types tend to dominate. The first is the radial system, which tends to develop as routes are made from a centre that is formed by a crossing point. The roads which diverge from this central point are often referred to as arterial routes – the analogy being with a body or a tree. In London some arterial routes date back to the period of the Roman occupation of Britain and, as Mike Hebbert (1998) notes, still form important mixed-use corridors to the centre.

The second system consists of concentric roads. Many ring roads have historical origins, such as those that originate from when the city walls were torn down, as happened most famously in Vienna with the development of the Ringstrasse at the end of the nineteenth century. The Ringstrasse was created as a broad street with many monumental buildings along it when the city walls were demolished in the nineteenth century. Nowadays the undesirability of forcing heavy traffic and major new roads through existing city centres has led to the construction of ring roads around many urban centres (Figure 2.2a). Paris forms an interesting example of this, where the Périphérique, formed at the boundary of the ancient arondissements or boroughs in Paris, forms a sharp edge with the poorer suburbs or *banlieues* excluded beyond it. Gridded systems have been particularly important as organis-

ation patterns for cities in both the eastern and western hemispheres (Figure 2.2b). Further information about grids is given in Appendix 2.

Movement systems and urban regeneration

Increasingly, movement routes are being used to encourage urban development. In the 1930s the building of the Metropolitan line of the Underground helped to spawn that whole north-west sector of London. Whilst building on virgin territory is currently more constrained in most European countries, in the USA Garreau (1991) has noted the development of new peripheral settlements, which he calls 'edge cities' around the junctions of major highways just outside existing cities. These 'edge cities' tend to consist of housing estates for middle-income families, shopping malls and business parks, all connected by roads in a manner in which one bears no formal relation to the other.

In Europe the hope is that the insertion of new transport systems within urban areas will lead to the regeneration of those desolate areas either in the inner city or at its periphery, boosting residential property prices and increasing access to employment. Whether regeneration can always be achieved by such means has still not been proven and more research needs to be carried out. Cowan (1997) argues that neighbourhoods have to be well-connected by infrastructure such as transport and through physical connections such as

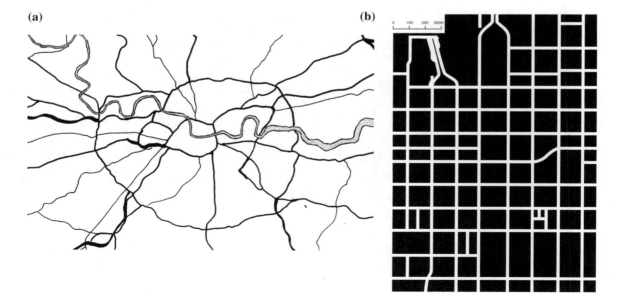

(a)

(b)

Figure 2.2   (a) Road network of London; (b) the grid pattern of Raleigh, North Carolina (Donna Turnbull).

streets and pedestrian routes to achieve successful regeneration.

The retrofitting of new transport and movement systems can cause huge problems in design terms. Cuttings and underpasses are often both ugly and dangerous and the insertion of a new fast road can literally 'cut' away the urban fabric like a gash in skin. Even benign measures such as pedestrianising previously trafficked areas can produce unexpected effects. For example, rents in South Molton Street, off London's fashionable Bond Street, rose fourfold once it was pedestrianised, driving all but the most specialised and high-class shops out.

The analogy between movement systems and the arteries of a body is both useful and descriptive. It has been amplified in the past few decades because, as buildings have become more complicated and more dependent on services to them, such as water, gas, electricity, telephone wires and, for specialised functions, fibre optic cables, these services have tended to follow the roads. This means that the 'lifeblood' of the urban system (people, heat, light, water) is literally travelling through these movement systems. Without movement, cities would not exist. Growth and change are dependent upon movement systems, but as with the body, controlling the effects of change and the ability to conduct major surgery sensitively are still not fully within our capabilities.

Sustainability

Movement is intimately connected to the 'environmental sustainability' of particular urban structures. Over the past two decades concern has been rising about the use of the car and its harmful effect on the environment. In North America, the New American Urbanism movement, spearheaded by Peter Calthorpe, Andres Duany and Elizabeth Plater Zyberg (DPZ) (Calthorpe 1993; Murrain 1993; Katz 1994), has proposed new types of urban structure for new settlements and for infills to existing settlements which are based around mass public transport systems.

In Western Europe, calls have been made to return to the traditional form of the European city in an attempt to curb and reduce the need for the motor car. Currently there is much activity in exploring this issue at all levels of government. In Britain, research and guidelines have been drawn up for the planning of sustainable new settlements (Barton *et al.* 1995; Aldous 1992) and for providing housing at higher densities (Llewelyn Davies 1998). A comprehensive approach to achieving sustainable urban development was set out in the Urban Task

Figure 2.3 Grenoble: tramway system retro-fitted into the heart of the city (Peter Jones).

Force Report – *Towards an Urban Renaissance* (Urban Task Force 1999). Planning policy guidelines have also been revised and produced to reduce incentives for car use by curbing the growth of out-of-town developments and promoting existing town centres. Continental Europe provides more radical instances of reducing use of the private motor car and promoting attractive urban design solutions, as for example in the introduction of a light rail system into the city of Strasbourg in France and in the Dutch planning system with its three levels of permissible development which are related to transport nodes (see also Figure 2.3).

As has been hinted at above, sustainable development raises issues of density and use, in that the higher densities of nineteenth- and early twentieth-century settlements are proposed, as well as a greater mixing of uses (Coupland 1996). Urban designers have long been arguing for these principles to be included as part of planning practice. In this design manual, it will be assumed that the principle of reducing car use is a desirable objective that should run through urban design interventions at all scales of development. In some cases this may mean contesting existing planning standards and norms, e.g. in terms of parking provision. This places a challenge upon designers to think through standards for themselves and to be able to justify any guidelines which they produce. Appendix 3 of this book provides further information on the connections between density, urban form and transport systems.

Summary

- Different types of urban form have been supported by technological changes in movement systems (i.e. from horse-drawn carriages to cars).

- Movement systems have been associated with urban development historically and are now being used as a tool for urban regeneration.
- Major patterns of movement systems are radial or arterial routes, ring roads and grids.
- Movement systems are important for issues of sustainability and regeneration.
- Infrastructure systems, such as telephone lines, water and gas are often routed under roads and hence are closely connected to movement systems.

Natural features

Environmental sustainability, as a concept, is difficult to define. It is not only about reducing pollution, but also incorporates the idea of conserving and maintaining the biodiversity of species on the planet. This is of importance to the generation of urban forms within cities and for the urban structure of a city as a whole. It is a commonplace to note that cities have often formed around natural features: around ports and harbours, at river crossings, or in the natural 'bowl' of a range of hills. In addition, many cities incorporate natural features that form an integral part of their identity, such as Table Mountain in Cape Town, South Africa. The protection of these natural features from inappropriate development through the evolution of design strategies is becoming increasingly important.

The transformation of natural features into a used landscape often forms a key part of a town or city's evolution and provides an explanation for the development of a particular type of urban structure. In Berlin, for example, the one-time royal hunting park, the Tiergarten, forms an important green area within its urban core. The canals in Amsterdam and Venice are themselves integral to the cities, which have developed in conjunction with them. At times, the influence of natural features may be hidden and only legible to those with a deep knowledge of the city. In a particularly intriguing diagram, the urban designer Graham Shane has shown how the 'great estates' built by wealthy landowners in eighteenth-century London were built on the more solid, higher ground above the tributaries of the River Fleet which flowed into the Thames (Figure 2.4). The tributaries of the Fleet were eventually built over, with a more haphazard form of development.

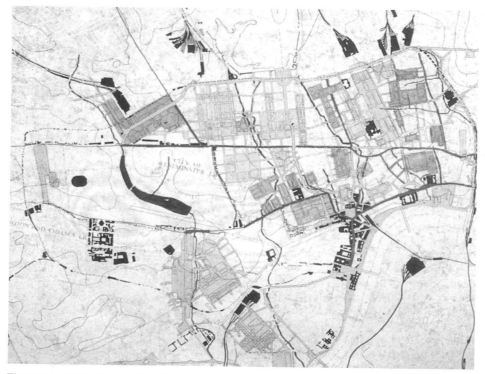

Figure 2.4   Field diagram of London (drawn by Graham Shane).

Urban designers then, have to pay attention to natural features for their generative properties. This is not to imply that natural features are awkward elements to be built round or bulldozed; green vegetation, indigenous flora and fauna, water, trees and clean air all have restorative and structural properties that can and should play an important role in design proposals. Methods for the incorporation of natural features into urban design solutions merit an entire volume on its own. Throughout this manual, suggestions will be made for how natural features might be incorporated in the light of the examples used. Reference can also be made to Thompson (1998).

A problem for designers is that green landscaped features do not of themselves generate value in terms of return to the landowner. Indeed they often may carry a considerable cost in terms of maintenance. In a sense, urban development and the natural world can sometimes seem at loggerheads: where land values are high, then there is pressure to build on all available space. This leads on to the next generator, which is development economics.

Summary

- Towns and cities are often formed around natural features, such as ports or river crossings.
- Urban designers need to pay attention to the manner in which natural features have played a part in a city's evolution.
- Open spaces are often vulnerable to development pressures.

Development process

Places are formed through the development of buildings and other structures. Since buildings involve highly complex and valuable arrangements of materials, services and spaces it is not surprising that their form is heavily influenced by relationships of ownership and control as well as political processes and cultural practices.

Because many settlements in the western and eastern hemispheres have grown around ancient routes, past relations of power and politics have had a profound effect. Kostof (1991) describes how field patterns often formed the initial template for a street layout that is described as 'organic'. The term 'organic' has come to be connected with planning layouts that are low density and often picturesque and it is unfortunate that they also carry connotations of an instinctive, vegetative process which takes place almost without human agency. Kostof (1991) reminds us that all developments have in some sense been planned: whether it be the sinuous curves of a quiet road in Hampstead Garden Suburb in London, the formal layout of the Rue de Rivoli in Paris or a *favela* (squatter settlement) in São Paulo, each of these settlements has some set of rules, of agreements covering their shape, orientation to the sun, or relationship to their neighbours or to the road, however simple or rudimentary such arrangements might be.

It is perhaps in the cities of rapidly developing countries that we see the most stark exposition of the relationships between land values, political control and urban form. In the centre of cities such as São Paulo and Mexico City where land prices are high, tall skyscrapers dominate the horizon. Because these buildings are owned and used by the most wealthy of its inhabitants, the semi-private spaces of these buildings – their foyers and internal courtyards – are highly controlled and policed. On waste-land sites around the periphery of the city are the informal settlements housing the poorest of the country's inhabitants (Figure 2.5). These

Figure 2.5 The high towers of Jakarta's commercial centre contrasted with nearby 'informal' squatter settlements (Mike Theis).

are normally one-storey-high dwellings, rudimentary and crudely built, with almost no control over the spaces around them. In Unit 9 of this book, Chris Marsh explains the development process in more detail, with a worked example to illustrate how designers can work within the constraints of the property market in Britain to achieve a more liveable, humane urban form. From the discussion above it can be seen that development economics is not an add-on to an understanding of urban form and urban design, but an essential part of it.

As has been hinted at above, the relationships of ownership and control of land and buildings also affect the public realm, i.e. the spaces between and around buildings to which the public has access. There is increasing concern nowadays about the privatisation of public space, i.e. the way in which 'public' spaces inside shopping centres and large public institutions have been taken into strict systems of private management and control (Punter 1990; Davis 1992). Historically, there has always been a shifting set of controls over the public realm, dependent upon the current social and political structure. For example, the district of Bloomsbury in London was originally developed as a private venture and gates across the entrances kept out *hoi polloi*.

While urban designers cannot change the significant power relations of wealth and ownership that are generators of urban form, they can help to influence the shape and use of the public realm to be of widest benefit. They can also propose design controls and guidelines which can regulate and shape development decisions. In Unit 12, Tim Townshend and Ali Madanipour discuss the types of design control that exist in Britain and in other countries at the moment and the arrangements that it would be desirable to have.

Summary

In short, the economics of the development industry largely control

- what is built and for which purposes, and
- who owns it and manages it.

The development process also influences and is influenced by

- the division of public and private space and its management, and
- local and central government intervention.

Urban types

Although certain biological functions are common to all human beings, such as eating and sleeping, the manner in which even the most basic activities are carried out varies between societies and cultures. Eating and drinking, work, and familial relations vary significantly between states and continents. Societies and individuals may differ, but to function at all as cohabiting beings, a certain degree of order and organisation is required. Patterns of order are played out through spatial organisation, inscribed into the design of buildings and into the layout of towns and cities. Since many types of organisation are repeated and there is a benefit in repetition in terms of economies of thought, materials and labour, each society tends to evolve a series of urban types of which building types are an element.

Building types

The definition of a building type can be difficult in terms of making precise categories for particular historical influences, but as a general concept, the notion of type is useful. Perhaps the most common type to notice in a global context is that of the high-rise tower. This is now found throughout the world, can accommodate offices, educational institutions and other public services, housing, shops and other commercial activities. Some architects have even suggested building vertical cities in tower blocks. Clearly, tower blocks belong to different categories of type dependent upon their use.

Other building types are less adaptable. Suburban low-density, single-storey housing is a form that is found throughout Europe and North America. This building type is less readily adaptable to other uses, partly as a result of its construction at low densities and partly due to the inflexibility of layout. Whereas in pre-industrial times, building types were closely related to their locality and dependent on local customs and materials, in the current age of globalised functions, types are no longer place-specific. This presents both a problem and an opportunity for the urban designer. The problem is that everywhere can look like everywhere else (Relph 1976; Zukin 1998). Some prototypes – types of city, city neighbourhood or district, types of street or urban place, types of building – combine both spatial and functional characteristics. Particular activities, and the way these are managed, are associated with particular forms. The nature of this relationship can change over time but this is normally a gradual process. More information on building types within a British context is given in Appendix 2.

Urban types as urban 'fabric'

Some urban designers find it useful to consider urban types as 'urban fabric', making an analogy between the background of an urban structure and the warp and weft of a piece of cloth. Others make an analogy between urban types and the flesh or tissue of a body. 'Tissue studies' involve the analysis of some common urban types in order to establish their characteristics. These might be formal properties such as street widths, plot widths, building heights, building shapes or footprints and the degree of repetition of these units. Such studies of shape and form, i.e. of the urban morphology, can fulfil a number of purposes.

At the level of training, by studying existing urban types, urban designers can learn more about size and scale, which can add to their skills as designers. Drawing a space which one has experienced and properly understanding its dimensions and proportional relationships is a direct method of learning. Often the scale of a problem can be assessed by superimposing a known urban area on a new site, as in the example shown in Figure 2.6, where an area the size and shape of the Greenwich peninsula, which is the site of the Millennium Dome, is illustrated by superimposing areas of other cities onto it. Studies of the urban fabric can also be used in conservation work, where, by studying the morphology of an area in its original

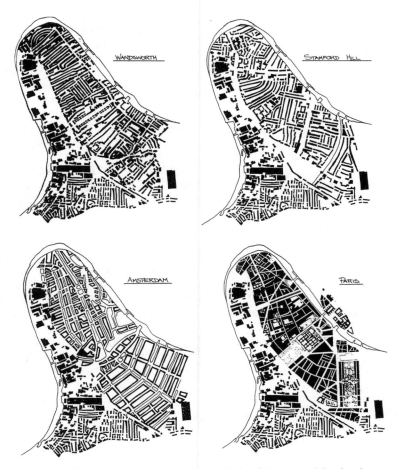

Figure 2.6 Tissue study: a comparative analysis of site potential using known examples imposed on the Greenwich peninsula (John O'Leary).

form, proposals can be made for its improvement in a manner that enhances the original intention. This type of study has been pioneered by architects and designers in Italy, France and England (Moudon 1994) and has now become an accepted tool in urban design analysis (see Unit 6 and Appendix 2).

New urban types

New urban types are emerging all the time as a result of technological and social change, and through a process of evolution, invention, purposeful adaptation and combination. The twentieth century is particularly rich in them, from modernist skyscraper office blocks and plazas and high-rise housing estates to out-of town shopping centres, and from underground railway systems to urban motorways. The urban designers that are being trained today will be expected to help develop the urban types of the future. They will need to consider what building types, systems of transportation and arrangements of urban space and form would be appropriate to life in the future city, and how these would be managed. This does not mean that existing urban types may not be used; often it is useful to draw on existing types but to consider them in new configurations.

Summary

- Sense may be made of urban developments by using the categories of both building and urban types.
- The study of urban types as 'tissue' provides benefits to the urban designer in terms of adding to their knowledge and skill base.
- The notion of urban type may be used to develop strategies for conservation and in assessing the scale of new developments.
- New types are emerging and present a challenge to the urban designer.

Social and cultural meanings

So far, space and buildings have been considered as physical, functional entities, whose existence depends on quantifiable measures, such as property values and traffic flows. The notion of type brings the idea of culture to the fore – that buildings might not only be shaped by the ritual relationships between members of society at a particular chronological time, but also that

a building typology is imbued with meanings that are emblematic of that region or strata of society. It is not only buildings which carry these properties; the configuration of urban areas and urban spaces also has deep layers of social and cultural meaning. These meanings are not clear and transparent, but may be various and contradictory (Franck and Schneekloth 1994; Massey 1994).

A prime example of this is provided by the social housing built during the 1950s to 1970s, especially those dwellings which are composed of blocks of flats. The imagery of such estates in the media, in fictional representations on TV and in films, is generally appalling and suggests that drug dealing, burglary and assault are commonplace activities. While some badly neglected and badly managed estates undoubtedly suffer from the excesses of poverty, which includes criminality, this imagery might be unrecognisable to others on different estates of the same era (Figure 2.7). Here the tenants might have fond feelings towards their flats, wry memories of the escapades of their children and a feeling of camaraderie towards some of their neighbours.

Urban geographers have grappled with the different meanings that are invested in parts of the urban fabric and have noted that it is not simply that these different interpretations exist, but that they also have an influence on the way that urban space is thought about, lived in and acted on by professionals and politicians. For example, if people have to walk in a place which they have learned to think of as threatening, they are less likely to linger and more likely to move quickly through it, trying always to be out of it as soon as possible. Furthermore, if there were a proposal to demolish the area and rebuild it, objections would be less likely. In contrast, if a place appears to be friendly and beautiful, as in a favourite street with some charming buildings, people are not only more likely to take the opportunity to spend time there, but are also more likely to object to any drastic changes to it.

At the present time, it is difficult for urban designers to do more than note that differential meanings of space exist. Such a recognition has the implication that even though a designer might produce a design that seems logical and has elements of charm, it could provoke quite hostile responses in another person, particularly a non-professional who does not share the same values or jargon. One way around this difficulty is to consult widely on any design scheme (see for example, Cowan 1998). This is not always possible, particularly when the people who are going to inhabit the space may be transient or come from very different circumstances. Another way of avoiding potential problems is

Figure 2.7   What may seem a hostile environment to some will be liked by others: social housing, London (Marion Roberts).

by trying to anticipate expected responses. By being aware of popular imagery, designers may be in a position to challenge certain development decisions that are based on prejudice. For example, in Britain during the 1960s and 1970s, whole areas of by-law terraced housing built at the end of the nineteenth century were torn down as 'slums'. Eventually, through the action of campaigners, the positive attributes of these areas were recognised and policy was changed towards rehabilitation.

In Unit 10, Marion Roberts and Clara Greed consider some of the problems different types of individual might have in moving around towns and cities. Although these may be functional requirements, such as the need to avoid steps for people with certain types of disability, they can also be connected to the idea of ritual, meaning and management. The option of what is appropriate behaviour in any given place depends partly on internal controls which individuals learn through their upbringing, but also on external controls such as policing.

To end on a more optimistic note, it is important to affirm that changing the image of a place can often have wholly beneficial effects. The city of Glasgow took this approach on a city-wide basis when they adopted the slogan 'Glasgow's Miles Better'. By combining the slogan with positive design interventions, such as an urban design strategy for the city centre, the revitalisation of the Merchant City and the regeneration of the Gorbals, Glasgow's status has improved and events such as the Year of Culture in 1990 and the Year of Architecture in 1999 have raised levels of civic pride generally (Booth and Boyle 1993).

Summary

- Spaces and places are imbued with powerful meanings by different groups of people.
- Urban designers need to be aware of the range and depth of these meanings.
- Meanings can vary between social groups and individuals, and be fragmented and contradictory.
- Meanings and associations change over time.
- Design interventions can and do change perceptions.

BLOCK II APPROACHING THE DESIGN TASK

Unit 3 The 'armature' and 'fabric' as a model for understanding spatial organisation

Bill Erickson

Introduction

The previous units have looked at urban design as a process and at the forces which shape the built form of cities. This unit will investigate how these can be brought together. The aim is to find a method of describing the city, in particular those parts of the city that are the province of urban design. As discussed in Unit 1, an important part of any design process is analysis and problem definition, especially as so much of urban design is concerned with existing situations. However, the same method must also help us arrive at design solutions so it needs to be flexible and adaptable. Two such methods are investigated here: the use of the *grid* and the *urban armature*.

The task of urban design is not to design everything in detail but to create a framework that will influence subsequent decision-making. Where, then, do urban designers need to place their energy to be effective? Obviously they need to have objectives, an idea of where urban development will lead, and how to improve the city for those who live in it. While these aims may be social, urban designers' goals are physical. They need to concentrate on those components in the city that will have the maximum influence on the subsequent development. The task of urban design is to create the spatial patterns that will encourage people to use and develop the city in a particular way.

A practical first step towards a design method is to distinguish two sets of urban elements:

1   The principal elements are those that will have a
significant influence on the form, structure or use of the city.
2   The second group is much larger and consists of the bulk of urban elements whose detailed configuration will not dramatically influence the overall pattern or use of the city.

The principal elements are those features to which the urban designer needs to give special attention while the second group can be more properly left to individual developers and designers. A simple way to distinguish these two groups would be to define the first group and describe the second as everything else. In Block I the movement network of the city was compared to the arteries of the body. If this analogy is expanded to include, along with the arteries, the other 'vital organs' as well as the skeleton and nervous system, we might arrive at a description of the principal elements of the body.

Definition of the armature

What features might be included in a list of the principal elements in urban design terms? One would start with the main public spaces, the squares and main roads together with other transport arteries. To these one would add other places where people come together, such as community or religious buildings, and perhaps shopping areas and places of recreation also. Finally one might add the features that have a strong shared meaning and give local identity, such as monuments, landmarks and cultural institutions. Taken together these elements form a core around which the pattern of public activity revolves. That is not to say the principal elements include all the buildings and spaces in public ownership or control but rather those with a large section of the public as stakeholders. The term *urban armature* will be used to describe this core, which can be thought of as a series of physical objects, buildings, spaces, roads, trees, monuments, etc., with a particular configuration or arrangement.

The features of the urban armature are those of particular concern to the urban designer. If the emphasis of design activity is placed on the armature, what of the second group of urban elements – the broad mass of the city? Large areas of cities are often formed by districts where the nature of the buildings, spaces and streets have a high degree of consistency. This is especially common in residential districts, e.g. suburban districts of single-family houses in cul-de-sac roads, rows of terraced houses or apartment blocks formed into grids. Here it is useful to return to the notion of urban fabric described in Unit 2. Through the study of urban types and morphology these broad areas can be understood in a generic way without the need to describe everything in detail. This suggests that from an urban design point of view it may be that the design of the urban fabric requires a differing process to that of the armature.

Establishing design criteria

The initial stage of the design process is to set design objectives and establish design criteria so that reasoned decisions can be made. Design objectives are normally determined within the larger planning/development context and at the urban scale have a strong political and economic dimension. Differing parties may have conflicting objectives and the reconciliation of these may be controversial. For example, the design objective for property investors may be to maximise return on investment while other groups may place greater emphasis on reducing social exclusion or ensuring environmentally sustainable development. While most people agree that urban movement systems should be efficient, differing objectives may place more or less importance on, say, public versus private transport. Less tangible objectives may also be important; for example, should the built environment be familiar and reassuring or new and stimulating? Designers may also determine objectives that are more general such as the need to create environments people like and feel comfortable in, or a desire for the built environment to respond to the natural environment.

Once broad objectives have been outlined they can be translated into more specific design criteria against which particular design scenarios can be tested. By way of example it is useful to take the series of urban generators set out in Unit 2 and examine the types of design criteria they may suggest for a particular urban design project. This is an indicative list only and specific criteria need to be established in the light of particular circumstances and objectives.

- *Movement*
  - enables efficient movement of people and goods;
  - encourages environmentally sustainable transport modes.
- *Natural features*
  - encourage life-styles that minimise the impact on the natural environment;
  - integrate natural and built features into a unified system.
- *Development process*
  - provides spaces for a diverse range of economic activities;
  - creates demand for investment.
- *Building types*
  - provide appropriate built forms for modern life-styles;
  - promote the development of built forms people understand with a proven market.
- *Social and cultural meanings*
  - create an environment that is easy to understand;
  - generate a rich local identity.

Design criteria are necessary but design projects need design solutions as well. This requires method. The more numerous and diverse the criteria, the more difficult the design process becomes. The design of cities has a long history and while a broad range of urban design techniques have been developed over the years many criteria have remained remarkably similar. This has led to the evolution of a number of long-established models for urban design which remain informative today. An example of such a model, which can accommodate both armature and fabric, is given below.

Gridiron plan

One of the most enduring and reliable urban design techniques is the gridiron plan. One of the most famous and spectacular examples of this plan is New York, where the gridiron pattern was laid out nearly 200 years ago, and has proved an efficient basis for the development of one of the world's most successful cities. The advantages of the grid are that it is quick to design, simple and provides properties that are easy to subdivide and to sell. These are the very design criteria that have made the gridiron plan a popular design method for at least 2,500 years (Figure 3.1).

The form of many cities is similar despite the differences in the manner in which they came about. In ancient times cities were often established as colonies. A group of people arrived at a chosen site and set about the task of laying a settlement, for which the simple gridiron plan provided an admirable tool. The basis of the method was similar and simple. It consisted of two series of straight roads crossing at right angles to form rectangular blocks. Most blocks were built on but some were omitted to form public spaces. All that was needed was a more or less flat area of land and a labour force. The plan could be laid out quickly using simple technology and most importantly it was easy to describe, record and remember. Despite its relative simplicity, the gridiron plan was robust and has produced places with a varied and vivid character. The overall size can be adjusted as needs dictate and it allows particular buildings and spaces to be given a privileged location by locating them on the main cross axes or around the forum. Finally, the rectangular block is well suited to most common building types and it proved a simple but equitable method of dividing land among new settlers (Mumford 1961).

Specifying the fabric

The grid plan coupled with the use of standard building types is an effective method for the layout of urban fabric. It has been adapted over the last century or so to include more irregular patterns, as for example at Milton Keynes. The classic grid has all but been

replaced in some instances by a new urban type – the cul-de-sac – in an attempt to soften the relentless form of the rectilinear grid. However, culs-de-sac are connected together at more or less regular intervals to form a road pattern that can be thought of as a highly deformed grid.

The grid form itself provides a movement system. The designer might set out the grid or may describe the typical block. These blocks can be subdivided into standard plots aimed at particular sections of the real estate market. Particular building types are frequently associated with certain cities, e.g. the New York brown stone apartment building, the London terraced house or the Hong Kong apartment tower. Given that the urban designer can never design every aspect of the city, the use of urban types, particularly building types together with street and block types formed into more or less regular grid forms (Figure 3.2), is a useful way to set out the nature of development one would expect to see in a particular area. However, there is a problem. The endless repetition of similar units can appear banal and can be confusing because each street looks much like another. What is needed is a method to activate parts of the urban fabric, to create foci, and channels of activity that will make special places. This is where the urban armature can be a useful model, both as a way of understanding the city and as an aid to design.

Urban armatures

All settlements have an armature of some sort. In some cities the armature evolves over time while in others it is designated by those who first lay out the plan. In most cases it is a combination of planned and unplanned events that lead to the creation of the urban armature. In the example of the gridiron layout of a Roman colonial town one can see how the armature was envisaged, if not designed in detail, when the town was set out. The main roads which enter the city

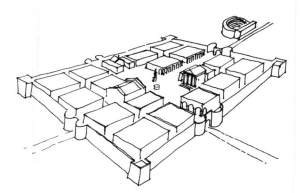

Figure 3.1   A typical Roman town.

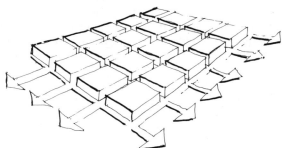

Figure 3.2   Grid form shown as the repetition of blocks.

through its gates lead directly to the forum. These streets are the busiest, they are the broadest and they connect the city to its hinterland. Both citizens and visitors are likely to travel along them to reach the heart of the city. It is on these busy streets that shops will flourish. Dominating the vistas down these streets are large religious and civic buildings, many of which surround the open space to which the streets lead. This is the forum. It is the economic, social and symbolic heart of the city. It is a space the people share in their daily lives in trade, religious ritual and governance. It is the space in which together they, or their forebears, shared in the founding of the city.

Such a city would have been meaningful to the inhabitants, comprehensible to visitors and an efficient place to live, work, trade and if needed defend. The key to this success is that the symbolic form, the legible features and the movement structure of the city reinforce one another. In fact they are, for the most part, made of the same physical features. The principal streets, temples, civic buildings and public spaces form a core of the city. This core, which is the locus of civic life, economic activity and public utility, gives the city its identity. MacDonald (1986) refers to this core as an *urban armature* (Figure 3.3). Beyond the core lie the domestic buildings within which individuals live and work in private. Thus while at first sight the gridiron plan appears uniform, it allows the principal elements of the city to gather together to form an armature.

As cities became larger, people found it difficult to understand the city as a single entity. What became increasingly important was the experience of the city as one moved through it and how one developed an image of the city as differing urban features were revealed. By creating an ordered experience rather than an ordered plan it was easy to reconcile imperfect geometries or awkward sites and to allow gradual development or rapid expansion. Movement through the city became the key to its understanding. The city was not to be understood as a single entity; rather it was revealed to the pedestrian like a narrative. This approach was not a single device but, as Kostof (1991) puts it, a 'rich bag of tricks' that was rediscovered several times during the subsequent centuries as a powerful technique for urban design and remains so today.

Axes and movement

The armature is an urban structure that is experienced through movement. It is composed of spaces (streets and squares) and of objects (buildings and monuments). The juxtaposition of elements and their

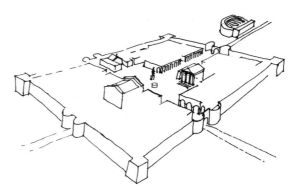

Figure 3.3   Features of an urban armature.

relationship to the movement system is important. The papal restructuring of Renaissance Rome shows how the interventions in an existing but rather chaotic city were designed to make the armature more vivid and efficient. The restructuring was designed with movement in mind and it created a new experience of the city at the same time as making the movement system more efficient and easier to comprehend. The new streets became the favoured sites for palaces and retain to this day the city's most fashionable shopping. This is one of the most important lessons that can be drawn from this type of intervention: if the structure is strong and appropriate (i.e. vivid, legible, meaningful and efficient) it will generate activity and will be long lasting.

The approach adopted in Rome was adopted across Europe during the seventeenth and eighteenth centuries, not simply because it was fashionable but because it could function at the metropolitan scale of the expanding capitals. This enabled large numbers of people to live, trade and move about the city while creating a very vivid public impression. This approach, sometimes known as the 'Grand Manner', reached its most dramatic in the nineteenth-century restructuring of Paris (Figure 3.5).

The technique can operate at a variety of scales from the metropolitan to the local. The basic principles are straightforward and for the most part concerned with making a vivid armature:

- Large public spaces are created at strategic points.
- These spaces are connected by broad straight roads (boulevards) which enable movement as well as visual connections.
- These visual connections are reinforced by the erection of monuments on the axes of streets which leads to the use of radial patterns.
- The main squares and streets are the favoured sites

Papal interventions in Rome

Between about 1550 and 1650 a number of 'interventions' were undertaken in Rome by the powerful popes in an effort to make Rome the most beautiful city in Christendom. The most dramatic was the construction of the new St Peter's Cathedral with its sweeping colonnades enclosing the vast Piazza. However, a number of other projects were undertaken as well. Many took the form of new streets opened through the existing congested city (Figure 3.4).

The various projects focused on principal churches but created new public spaces around them so they could be seen. These spaces were linked together by a series of new axial streets. These streets allowed efficient movement in the city and connected undeveloped land into the city network, allowing the city to expand as well as creating new routes through the city. Monuments were erected to articulate the arrangement and to act as signposts. These urban interventions dealt almost exclusively with improvements to the urban armature, and some, such as the famous Spanish Steps, were very dramatic. The less public areas were allowed to develop in their own way but this development was given new impetus by the creation of the new and efficient urban structure. It embraced undeveloped areas, drawing them into the urban core and enabling the city to expand. At the same time the structure reinforced the symbolic understanding of the city and bolstered the political and economic power of the church.

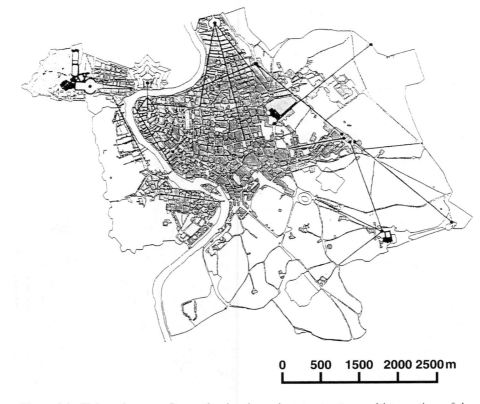

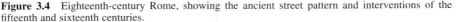

Figure 3.4   Eighteenth-century Rome, showing the ancient street pattern and interventions of the fifteenth and sixteenth centuries.

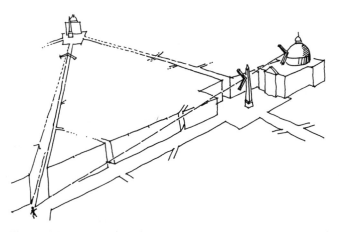

Figure 3.5 Features of the 'Grand Manner' design method (Bill Erickson).

for public buildings which tend to be formal and grandiose.

- The spatial containment of the public space is codefied; building lines and heights are controlled by law.
- The architectural treatment of buildings is controlled and co-ordinated to create a consistent urban image.
- The resulting urban structure (the armature) gives scale to the city as a whole and enables smaller local developments to relate to its parts.

As a result of the restructuring of nineteenth-century Paris, much of the city was completely rebuilt, requiring the forced displacement of large populations which would be unacceptable today. However, the resulting urban image has given Paris a reputation as one of the most beautiful cities in the world with an extremely robust structure that guides contemporary urban projects. The monuments and boulevards form an integrated public structure which operates at the metropolitan scale across the entire city, making it 'legible' and connecting individual districts (Figure 3.6).

The plan of a typical nineteenth-century district demonstrates, however, that the plans of the individual blocks and houses are contorted and cramped. The 'Grand Manner' seems at odds with the obvious advantages of the gridiron, such as regular and convenient building plots. This highlights one of the central dilemmas of urban design: spatial structures which may be effective at one scale, say that of the armature, may not be suitable at another, say that of the development of the individual plot. An obvious answer might be to combine the two methods as an

efficient connective structure for the armature with a simple block pattern for the remaining secondary areas (Figure 3.7). We can see such an attempt in the

Figure 3.6   A boulevard in Paris with a vista (Bill Erickson).

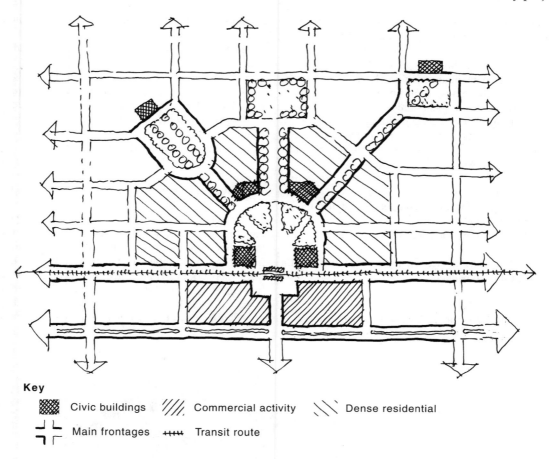

Key

▨ Civic buildings   ⁄⁄⁄ Commercial activity   ＼＼ Dense residential

⅃ ⌐ Main frontages   ┿┿┿┿ Transit route

Figure 3.7 Features of a 'transit oriented development'.

design of relatively new cities, such as Washington and Canberra for example. At a smaller scale, a similar approach has been advocated more recently by urban designers such as Raymond Unwin (1920), Leon Krier (1992), Ricardo Bofil (Broadbent 1990) and Peter Calthorpe (1993). Here an axial composition of streets, public buildings and open spaces is used as an armature, around which the more private areas are established, using a more regular grid-like composition.

Urban armatures and the evolutionary project

Today much of the work of urban designers is concerned with interventions in the existing city rather than the creation of new settlements. Further urban projects need to be flexible in terms of time and content. Generally the spatial patterns of the city, the streets and the public spaces survive far longer than any particular building and the use of an individual building may change several times during the lifetime of the building. The urban design task can be seen as that of shaping the core around which this urban activity can evolve in the future rather than a finished project with fixed and final detail in every respect. This is the main difference between the urban project and the traditional architectural project: the need to accommodate change. Here it is useful to return to the notion of the urban armature as a way of defining the core from which the urban project will evolve. The armature can be thought of not only as a descriptive technique but also as a design tool.

The components of the urban armature in the

modern city will vary from place to place but a first attempt at a definition can be made from the analysis of the historical models described above. An urban armature will include those principal elements of the built environment involved with movement, activity and cultural meanings. It is possible to distinguish arterial roads from local streets, shopping centres from housing districts, civic buildings from privately owned ones (Figure 3.8). A more complex definition of an armature for the modern city might be summarised as follows:

The armature as a public structure
1 encompasses the main components of the movement structure;
2 distinguishes and privileges those parts of the city in collective use;
3 is a structuring device for the urban fabric within which it is embedded.

The armature in relation to locality and activity
4 is articulated giving metre and scale to the city;

5 gives identity to individual localities within the city;
6 reconciles differences between specialised and collective uses.

The armature as a reinforcement of image and identity
7 includes the artefacts that render the city legible, imageable and memorable;
8 persists over time;
9 links the city to its landscape and ecology.

1   Movement structure

The armature encompasses the main components of the movement structure: the arterial roads, the nodes of the public transport and key pedestrian routes (Figure 3.9). It has been shown that the shape of the movement network will influence the configuration of movement (Hillier 1996). The main roads are not always the quickest route. We all know the example of the 'rat run', i.e. a shortcut that makes a journey

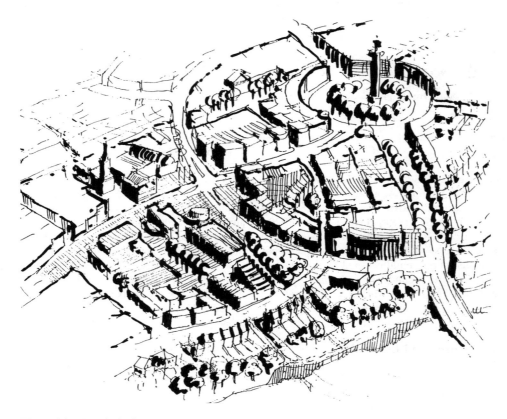

Figure 3.8   A typical urban quarter.

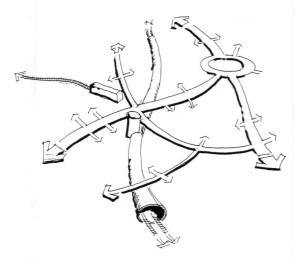

Figure 3.9   Elements of the armature: movement.

easier. Traffic planners react to it by controlling traffic and forcing it onto designated routes. This can be described as *configured movement*, i.e. movement patterns that are channelled into particular routes. The other important type of configured movement is public transport. The location of railway lines and stations is obviously fixed and the route a local bus takes is also configured. Channels of configured movement (freeways, railway lines, etc.) connect the city at the large scale but locally may act as a barrier. What become significant are the points of interchange: bus stops, metro stations, airports and traffic interchanges.

If dependence on private transport is to be reduced then a range of local activities need to be within walking distance. However, if designers want pedestrians to take a particular route they need to encourage them rather than force them. Pedestrians follow a pattern of *natural movement*, i.e. they take the route that is the most obvious. We can distinguish four types of movement and should seek to design for each in an integrated manner:

- *Pedestrian movement*. This remains the most basic way many people experience the city. However, for most of us the range of pedestrian movement is constrained and this is one way of defining an urban district (Figure 3.10).
- *Private automated movement*. The private car enables natural movement but at speed. This speed allows space to be stretched to the point where pedestrian movement is no longer possible, which distorts the nature of urban districts.

Several urban types have evolved, such as suburban residential development, where pedestrian movement has been replaced by vehicular movement and the life-styles involved become dependent upon the car.

- *Public transport*. This is configured and is highly nodal in that it forms a network with access at specific points. It may be by different modes such as bus, tram or rail, but the stopping points or stations become significant in structuring the armature. This nodal transport is combined with pedestrian movement to form radial zones around the stops.
- *Rapid transport*. This connects one centre to another. We can think of these centres as making termini rather than stops in a network. Termini such as major rail stations form key nodes in the armature and are the points at which scale is changed. Often large volumes of pedestrian movement are associated with these nodes. They may form significant elements in their own right, often as specialised zones. An airport is one such example: it generates a large amount of activity but may not be experienced as being part of the city.

2   Public spaces

The armature distinguishes and privileges those parts of the city in collective use. The principal elements are buildings, spaces and institutions of public interest. They will include the main streets and squares together with the public buildings and institutions but may also

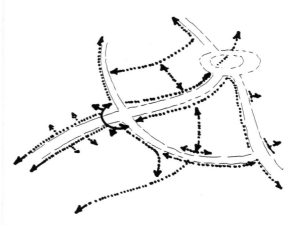

Figure 3.10   Elements of the armature: pedestrian movement.

LOOK FOR *Busy routes (vehicular, pedestrian, transit); pedestrian shortcuts; public transport nodes.*

TIP *It may not be surprising but the most direct routes are the most used. People tend to walk along routes with a clear visual destination. In design terms, if a particular space or street is to attract pedestrian activity it needs to be placed on an obvious and well-connected route. A short cut is more useful than a big attractor.*

include privately owned buildings such as shopping centres (Figure 3.11).

Simple definitions of public and private are no longer easy. Issues of ownership, responsibility and control when conflated with access, mobility and safety make complex and plural understandings of the notion of 'public realm'. At this stage it is useful to attempt a working description of the public realm, bearing in mind that the aim is to distinguish those primary elements which form part of the urban armature.

Here 'public' should not be thought of as public ownership but rather places of collective interest or shared activity. To this end several components of the public realm can be identified and dealt with in turn. They are as follows:

- movement space
- places of transaction
- places of assembly
- public and cultural buildings

Movement space   The first component of the public structure is open space of the public realm. The most basic function of public space is to allow access to private buildings. This simple function is usually performed by streets that have one of a variety of forms – alley, boulevard, cul-de-sac, crescent, etc. Generally the movement spaces conform to a loose hierarchy that is usually determined by natural movement rather than size.

Places of transaction   In addition to its function as a place of movement the street is a place of transaction (MacCormac 1987). A typical high street retains its identity as a place of movement but is also lined by shops. In this case the street retains its physical containment but there is a much higher degree of interaction between public outside and private inside. Some authors refer to these spaces as having *active edges* (Figure 3.12; see Unit 4 for more discussion). In any urban area, while all the streets may be public, some are sites of far more intense transaction and these can be thought of as being of greater public interest. This gives us a second attribute of the core: the streets with a high level of transaction as well as arteries of movement. We could add to this the buildings themselves (the shops, markets, etc.) which people use in their daily lives.

Places of assembly   A third component of public realm is the space of assembly: the square. This is a place of congregation rather than movement and is more suited to transactions of various types. It is a space of community; the space of markets and infor-

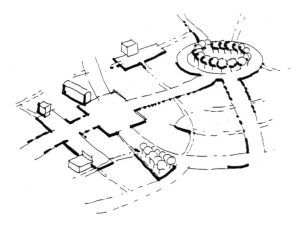

Figure 3.11 Elements of the armature: public spaces.

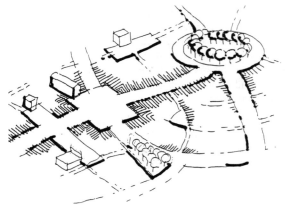

Figure 3.12 Elements of the armature: transactions, active edges.

mal meetings; the place to promenade or to sit and observe, an opportunity for display, a place in which to see and be seen.

Public and cultural buildings   Since ancient times there has been a trend for civic activities to take place in specific public buildings, e.g. parliaments and council chambers, courts of law, libraries, schools. As the institutions they house come to be thought of more as services, these buildings are losing the significance they once had as symbols of social cohesion. It may be more useful to think of cultural buildings, which could include the local schools, discos, clubs, fitness centres and football grounds as important sites of social activity. These buildings and spaces, together with sites of 'high culture', such as museums and art galleries, are shared by the community and should be given pride of place not only to reinforce their symbolic function but to ensure they are easy to locate and use.

3 Urban structure

The armature provides a structuring device for the urban tissue within which it is embedded. It will divide the urban tissue into districts and provide the connective infrastructure between them. It will have a hierarchical relationship to the features that structure these districts.

When defining the urban armature it is useful to remember that it excludes the bulk of the urban fabric. The remaining mass is frequently homogeneous and is formed by the repetition of similar elements, most frequently rows of houses or blocks of apartments (Figure 3.13). These districts can be thought of as a predominately private realm. The form of this type of fabric is often best understood from a study of its elements and their typologies, the pattern of blocks, streets and typical buildings. It can be thought of as large 'patches', each of which has particular physical and social characteristics.

The armature gives this mass form as well as structure. Here one might use the analogy of a tree and liken

Figure 3.13 Elements of the armature: fabric.

the system of branches and trunk to the armature, and the leaves to the urban fabric. We can recognise the form of a tree when it is denuded of its leaves but the leaves without branches are no longer a tree. In describing or designing the armature we need to be aware of the points at which it might 'bud', i.e. how the pattern of blocks, streets and plots and buildings will relate to the armature.

4   Scale and articulation of parts

The armature is articulated giving metre and scale to the city. The armature will break the experience of the city into pieces, or localities, each of which has its own scale. It may also be experienced at differing speeds, e.g. both as a commuter and as a pedestrian, the features of these movement systems interlocking together.

The armature can operate at a variety of scales. As one moves across the landscape of the city from one district to another, a distinct rhythm is established. Each district has a centre and a character of its own. The process for defining the armature will be similar at differing scales. Each district will have its own armature and the dominant features of these will combine to make the city-wide armature. Likewise, the features of a district armature will form the focus of a smaller armature at the neighbourhood scale. The urban armature is to a degree fractal, i.e. the form is similar regardless of the scale at which it is studied.

As discussed in Unit 2, the mode of transport will also affect one's experience of the city. The various scales of the armature are to a large degree dictated by the speed and type of movement. For example, at the local level the route to the transport stop will be a key feature in the local armature; it will generally include a cluster of local shops and be oriented to pedestrian movement (Figure 3.14). The route of the bus or train will itself form a key route of the armature at a larger scale, not only because it channels movement and activity but because it is the way in which the passengers experience and remember connections between districts. In this way the nature of the transport mode will influence the configuration of the armature. The combination of pedestrian and public transport tends to form an armature similar to beads on a string while movement based on private cars will be more dispersed.

5   Locality and identity

The armature gives identity to individual localities within the city. The armature will not be uniform but

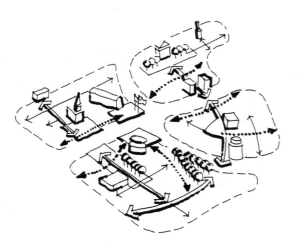

Figure 3.14   Elements of the armature: local armature.

will have localised points of intensity which will provide foci for individual districts.

As we move through the city we move from one district to another. Each district may have its own centre and hierarchy as well as subtle differences in its building typologies, perhaps brought about by changes in topography or the age of the buildings. Each district will have its own special landmarks and memorable features that give it its own identity. These features form the main elements of the armature at a local level (Figure 3.14).

LOOK FOR *A pattern of district centres.*

TIP *Differing scale is often associated with the form of movement: think of neighbourhood features as those within walking distance, local features as a short ride or a long walk away, and metropolitan features as requiring a special journey. (See Appendix 3 for further information.)*

LOOK FOR *Particular activities and urban types which distinguish one district from its neighbour. (See Mental Mapping overleaf for definitions of a district.)*

TIP *Seek to cluster features together to form areas of intensity linked by distinct connections.*

Mental mapping

Mental mapping is about understanding how and why people perceive a place in the way that they do. Everyone remembers places that they have been to and uses those memories to orientate themselves spatially and psychologically and to find their way around. Although there has been considerable debate among urban geographers about the validity and significance of mental mapping, urban designers have found it a useful method of both heightening their awareness of the environment and attempting to understand others' perceptions.

The aim of mental mapping is to understand which are the significant features of the urban environment for orientation. This method of enquiry came to the fore within the field of urban design in the early 1960s, when Kevin Lynch (1960) published a study of people's perceptions of the city, entitled *The Image of the City*, using a method derived from environmental psychology. His aim was to develop a structure within which individuals' mental maps could be classified and used as a means of developing design ideas on the city scale. Although the extent to which people use the structure for navigation is debatable, Lynch's categories are useful because they enable designers to categorise the environment in a manner that is not dependent on their specialist knowledge and provide a rough accordance with the categories that non-professionals are likely to use. Lynch devised his method in order to encourage public participation in policy and was disappointed to find it used primarily as an 'expert tool'.

Lynch found that his interviewees categorised the urban environment into five different elements. These categories have been reproduced in other experiments. The graphic notation system is that proposed by Alcock *et al.* (1985).

Paths

Paths are routes through which the observer moves, e.g. roads, footpaths, railways and walkways. They are the means by which people can view the city and form their mental maps of it. Paths can often be the strongest organising element in people's mental maps.

Landmarks

Landmarks are usually a defined simple physical object, such as a church spire, a tower, a dome or a hill. They are not entered into but serve as a point of reference. They may be either distant or local. The more familiar a journey is, the more frequently local landmarks are noticed and used.

Edges   − − − − ⌐

Edges are linear elements not used or thought of as routes. They may either join two recognisable areas as a 'seam', or may act as a barrier between recognisable areas. Edges may take the form of intensely busy roads, railway lines, cuttings and canals.

Districts

Districts are medium to large elements of a city which the observer walks into and which have an identifiable set of characteristics. These might be related to use or architectural style. A district may be defined by what is exterior to it. Some people organise their mental maps around districts rather than nodes.

Nodes   ◌

The term 'transport node' is now commonly used and carries some of the meanings of Lynch's terminology. A node is a point to or from which an observer might be travelling and provides an event on the journey. It is characteristically a major junction or interchange. It can also be a meeting of paths. Its key feature, unlike a landmark, is that it must be entered. In some districts a node provides a concentration of activities, such that the node is the core of that district.

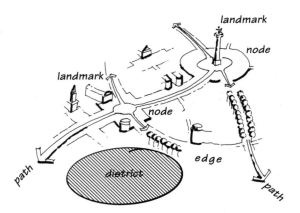

> **LOOK FOR** *Large single-use activities and their*
> *interface with the local area.*
>
> **TIP** *These areas frequently have a large*
> *perimeter with a low level of activity. Treat these*
> *perimeters as backs and bury the zone within*
> *other activities. Treat the entrance as an active*
> *front and try to combine it into the armature.*

Figure 3.15   Elements of the armature: urban image.

6   Single-use activities

The armature reconciles differences between special-ised and collective uses.

Within a city there are large areas of specialised activity which differ from the urban fabric and often form gaps or large impermeable blocks within it. They may be sites of a particular activity, such as factories, sports stadia or hospitals. The entrances may present an opportunity to create some interaction with local districts but frequently high levels of traffic can make this difficult. They may constitute elements of the armature at a large scale but not at the local scale.

7   Legibility

The armature includes the artefacts that render the city legible and imageable. The armature will include not only the features of utility but also those unique features that are memorable, including landmarks and objects of shared meaning such as monuments.

By adopting Kevin Lynch's definition of city image (Lynch 1960), several obvious elements present them-selves as candidates for inclusion in the armature (see box). The importance of movement spaces, or paths as Lynch would call them, has been addressed above, as has the importance of nodes. Here the features people use to navigate through the city are at issue, in particu-lar those features which they distinguish as being memorable or significant. These may include land-marks along with paths and nodes (Figure 3.15) .

As people dwell in places, they come to associate themselves with particular features of the environment. Likewise there are features they associate with their neighbourhood and with their city as a whole. Around these features group identities are formed and shared. Famous examples include New York's Statue of Liberty, Sydney's Harbour Bridge and the Eiffel Tower in Paris. These monuments are inseparable from the identity of the city but may or may not have a prac-tical use. These landmarks are obviously key features in the urban armature.

8   History

The armature persists over time. All the elements of the armature will alter over time but many will persist and form permanent features in the cultural landscape, linking the city to its history. The city records traces of its own history, including its origins. Throughout the city are echoes of decisions people have taken in the past. While the buildings may have gone, the bound-aries between them may survive. Buildings may out-live their usefulness and be reused or replaced. However, new buildings will be constrained by the shape and size of the plot that accommodated the orig-inal buildings and the alignment of the street they face. A road may bend around a tree long ago felled or a city gate long ago demolished. Rivers and shorelines may be infilled and city walls demolished but their influ-ence persists in the pattern of urban development around them. Significant features of the armature may in fact be absent but manifest themselves in the historic effect they impose.

> **LOOK FOR** *Local landmarks; streets, buildings*
> *and spaces with unique qualities.*
>
> **TIP** *Use features to reinforce each other, place*
> *landmarks at nodal points or at the end of main*
> *paths. Locate places of assembly such as public*
> *buildings and public squares near actives streets*
> *and transport.*

9   Landscape and ecology

The armature links the city to its landscape and ecology. The armature can reconcile the city within its natural landscape by combining key features of the landscape with the urban image.

The urban landscape is dominated by the artificial, but this human-made environment is imposed across a much older natural landscape. Monuments, landmarks and districts can as easily be natural features as human constructions. In designing cities it is easy to retain the view to the distant mountain, or the riverside walk. These provide opportunities for people to experience the physical terrain in which they dwell. For example, in the design of Canberra, Walter Burly Griffin located key buildings on the crests of small hills and provided broad avenues whose axes aligned with the peaks of surrounding mountains (Figure 3.16). At the centre of

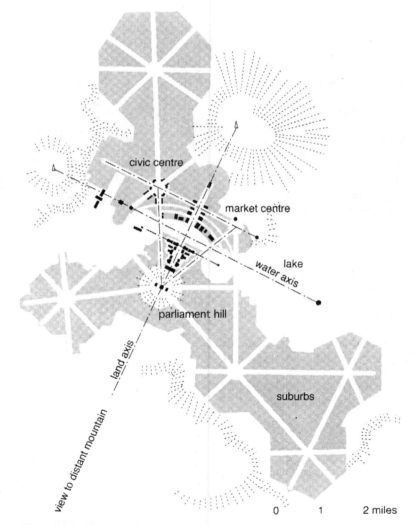

Figure 3.16   Plan of Canberra.

the city he created a lake which provided the setting for public buildings and recreational spaces. The result is an urban composition that is well placed within its natural setting.

The city is located not only in the physical landscape but also within an ecological system. The manner in which the city interacts with its local ecological system is of increasing importance. The urban armature may articulate this relationship in a similar manner to that in which it articulates the urban fabric. One response is to develop a network of 'green spaces' throughout the city (Turner 1996). Other ways in which urban design can interact with the natural environment include responses to climate. Design can improve local microclimates both internally and externally, perhaps by catching the sun or providing shelter from wind, thereby making places more user-friendly.

> **LOOK FOR** *Natural features which may form landmarks; water courses and wildlife corridors.*
>
> **TIP** *These networks can be likened to separate 'green armatures' accommodating parks, waterways, natural reserves, and even waste land. The points of interaction between these networks and the urban armature are vital as each has the potential to revitalise the other.*

Conclusion: the armature as an urban design tool

The urban armature is a tool that may be used both for analysis and in design. By helping to distinguish the key elements of the city that are of special interest, its use enables the designer to give emphasis to particular features and to structure the urban project. While developing the urban armature as a structuring device the designer also needs to remember the nature of the urban fabric in which the armature is embedded (Figure 3.17). As shown above, the use of urban types can be used to develop an urban morphology that will be an adaptable method of specifying the urban fabric while designing the armature in more detail. Because the armature can be thought of at a range of scales it can be used on projects of differing sizes and complexity, both in new conditions and within an existing urban context.

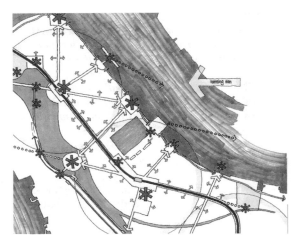

(a)

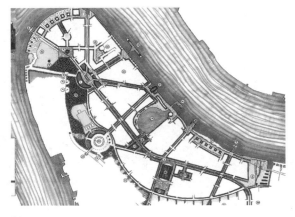

(b)

Figure 3.17 Student project for a development at Port Greenwich (courtesy Justine West). (a) Local structure; (b) features of the local armature; (c) detail of the proposed urban form at a local scale (opposite).

Design can be divided up into two activities:

1 the design of the urban fabric;
2 the design of the armature as an integrated system within the fabric.

Urban types can be used to describe the typical morphology of the urban fabric. This is likely to result in aspects of an urban project being resolved to differing levels. Particular aspects, such as those features that are in the public realm, may be specified more pre-

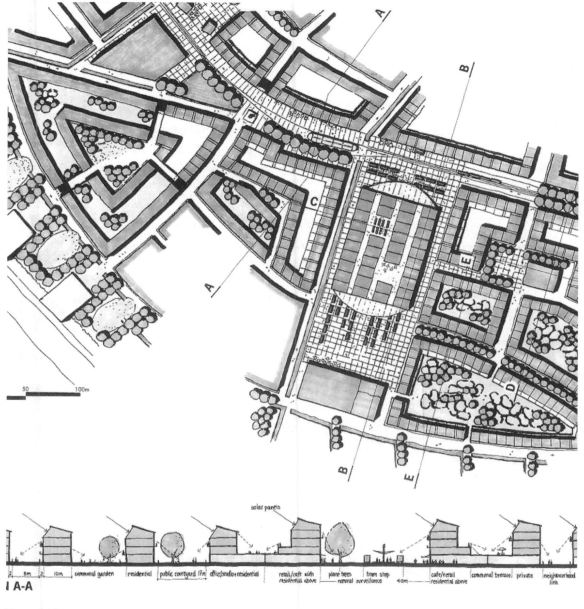

Figure 3.17 (c)

cisely. As one moves away from the key features in the design, less detail will be given, allowing more freedom to individual developers. As we have seen, control of some aspects remains essential, but this might be achieved through the use of guidelines and codes rather than detailed design. The task is to provide the minimum of prescriptive design guidance to establish the maximum effect. The object is to encourage and to foster a particular direction rather than to enforce or prohibit. In this way the notion of the urban armature can assist in deciding where to place emphasis and where the designer can stand back.

Check-list of design objectives to make a strong armature

The armature as a public structure

1 *The armature encompasses the main components of the movement structure*
   - Aim for a strong hierarchy of movement spaces.
   - To be effective the movement pattern should be simple and direct.
   - Develop a typology of movement spaces, each associated with particular type of movement.

2 *The armature distinguishes and privileges those parts of the city in collective use*
   - Places of transaction such as shopping areas and places of assembly, e.g. public squares, should be well integrated into the movement network to form a chain of active spaces.
   - Buildings in collective use should be accessible, visible and, where possible, associated with public spaces.
   - Active uses should be gathered together to form intense areas of transaction.

3 *The armature is a structuring device for the urban tissue within which it is embedded*
   - Ensure that the components of the armature have a compact and clear structure.
   - An understanding of the pattern of urban fabric within which the armature will become embedded will enable an effective connection between the two to be achieved.

The armature as a locality and activity

4 *The armature is articulated giving metre and scale to the city*
   - Provide a system of nested structures which act as armatures at differing scales determined by the mode of movement.
   - Ensure the armature is structured so that experience of it as one moves through the city is broken into identifiable segments.

5 *The armature gives identity to individual localities within the city*
   - Collect elements of the city into a compact core to reinforce one another.
   - Create a clear distinction between differing districts of a similar scale.

6 *The armature reconciles differences between specialised and collective uses*
   - Treat large specialist elements as districts in their own right and integrate them at the larger scale.

The armature reinforces image and identity

7 *The armature includes the artefacts which render the city legible and imageable*
   - Provide vivid objects and places around which collective meanings can be built.
   - Combine paths, nodes and landmarks to reinforce other aspects of the armature.

8 *The armature persists over time*
   - Look for historic monuments and traces of historic morphology that have persisted over time.
   - Provide new features which can be used flexibly over time and can contribute to a long-lasting image.

9 *The armature links the city to its landscape and ecology*
   - Identify key features of the natural landscape which could form a 'green armature' and link it to the built one.
   - Where possible, retain features based on natural systems such as water courses.

Unit 4 Making convivial places

Marion Roberts

Introduction

Unit 3 introduced readers to the concept of the armature, both as a device for analysis and as a design tool for structuring urban areas. Although it has been argued that the armature can operate across a range of scales, as a design tool it provides limited guidance for the creation of lively, convivial places at a local level. This unit will address this issue, drawing on the ideas of a number of authors (e.g. Jacobs 1992; Cullen 1988; Bentley 1996; Montgomery 1998). The unit will provide a brief pointer to some key ideas for design strategies rather than an in-depth exploration; readers who require more explanation are recommended to return to the authors cited in the text.

The pedestrian experience

One of the reasons why car driving is attractive is because the pedestrian experience has become unpleasant in many towns and cities. Some features that contribute towards a hostile environment for pedestrians are:

- close proximity to heavy traffic with fumes and noise;
- open, exposed routes with indeterminate spaces which are neither public nor private;
- lack of other people and activities adjacent to the route.

At the local scale, urban designers can intervene to eliminate some or all of these problems. It should be noted that there is no preferred design configuration or style that provides the ideal solution. Designers need to consider the relationships between activities, buildings and spaces in order to promote convivial experiences.

Copenhagen provides an example of a city that has achieved a great pedestrian conviviality. Advised by the Danish urban designer Jan Gehl (1987, 1995), the City of Copenhagen produced policies that are hostile to cars and friendly to pedestrians and cyclists, and traffic has remained stable in the city for the last 30 years. Eighty per cent of all journeys undertaken in the city are now on foot. The population of the city centre has risen. Gehl confounds his critics with images of people sitting in parks, streets and squares, looking at each other, and looking at the view (Figure 4.1). He even shows people sitting outdoors at café tables in the

Figure 4.1 People sitting, waiting and generally 'hanging out' in a square in Stockholm (Marion Roberts).

middle of winter with blankets wrapped around them, thereby refuting the proposition that a lively street life is only possible in a warm climate.

> **LOOK FOR** *Narrow pavements; excessive traffic; obstructions of various kinds.*
>
> **TIP** *Imagine walking the streets of any masterplan or proposals for design guidance that you make. Take measures to provide pedestrians with a comfortable environment.*

Active frontages

Unit 3 has already emphasised the importance of active edges or frontages in making a place 'people friendly'. The term 'active frontages' implies a relationship between the ground-floor uses of the buildings that frame a space or a street and the people walking through or generally 'occupying' it. The term 'transactions' (also explained in Unit 3) is important here. An active frontage is one that allows some kind of movement or visual relationship between the person outside and the activity inside. At its most minimal, this might be one of simple observation, e.g. a window display or people working. Even in a single-function housing estate it is possible to have more active frontages by, for example, including gables and bay windows, or positioning windows so that a glimpse of the interior can be given without an invasion of privacy. At the next level of interaction, an active frontage could encourage the pedestrian to come in and make a purchase, view an exhibit, come in to worship or pay a bill, for example. The most interactive frontages are those which spill out into the street or the space in front of the building, as in cafés or bars, or shops that put some of their merchandise outside (Figure 4.2).

It is not possible to arrange for highly interactive frontages in all locations. They are most likely to come into being at points along the 'armature' of the urban structure at different scales. As Bill Hillier (1996) has pointed out, cities have their own 'movement economies' whereby people make journeys from origins and destinations everywhere and it is at the points where most journeys coincide that active frontages are most vital and will be self-sustaining. These are the 'hot spots' within the town or city. Providing for active frontages is particularly important in making new public spaces, or in re-animating existing ones. The encouragement of cafés and bars has been important for the revitalisation of many public spaces, for as Montgomery (1997) notes, cafés provide 'a space to be

Figure 4.2   This street in west London may appear untidy and has too much traffic, but it has many active frontages (Marion Roberts).

Figure 4.3   The green areas in this inner city housing estate are devoid of life and meaning (Marion Roberts).

private in public'. However, a 'cappuccino culture' is not the only way to create good places. Street stalls give life and vigour to a public place, as do places where children can play safely, benches where people can sit and watch each other, or the provision of art works and sculptures that everyone can sit on or touch; the possibilities are endless.

An important ingredient in the creation of animated spaces is an overlap and congestion of activities. Very few people will sit on a bench on a green space in the middle of a housing estate (Figure 4.3), but people will be sitting jammed next to each other and on the walls of flower beds in the middle of a lively square that is surrounded with life and activity. Labelling one urban plot 'café' in a block of otherwise mono-functional space will not ensure that the animation sought for is achieved.

Thinking about the active frontages of buildings has a further implication. If the public realm is to be public, then, by definition, some spaces are definitely not public. Examples of these might be back gardens and the service yards of buildings. This means that the 'fronts' and 'backs' of buildings need to be distinguished. Many problems have arisen on housing estates of the post-war era where it is not clear where the front of the dwelling is and whether the space that surrounds it is 'public' or 'private'. Some of the most unpleasant streets in city centres are those which surround what are essentially the 'backs' of buildings, such as the exterior of an inward-facing shopping mall. To create a lively public realm, it is important to ensure that the 'backs' of buildings do not address it.

> **LOOK FOR** *Examples of existing 'active' edges; fronts and backs of buildings.*
>
> **TIP** *Check design proposals for uses and activities around public spaces and for fronts and backs of buildings. The simplest arrangement is for backs to face backs and fronts to face fronts.*

The importance of mixed uses

Jane Jacobs (1992) was the first of the new wave of urban critics in the 1960s to decry the scientific approach to planning prevalent in the Anglo-Saxon world at that time which parcelled out land in single-use zones. Her position was supported by Christopher Alexander (1966) and later by other critics of the modern movement. The arguments against dividing land up into areas that have one land use such as housing or offices are as follows:

- Single-use zoning encourages car use because there are long distances to travel between different functions.
- Large areas of mono-functional zoning cause difficulties for people in carrying out the different tasks they have to combine in a day – typically working mothers with children who have to combine working, child-care and shopping in order to survive.
- Single-use zoning encourages low densities with consequent inefficiencies in public services (lack of public transport, shops, etc.).

- Single-use zoning encourages crime because areas are only used at particular times of the day (e.g. offices during working hours), making it easier for burglars to operate.
- Single-use zoning lends itself to boredom and monotony in aesthetic terms.

In the discussion of active frontages in the last section, it was seen that a mix of uses is a necessary prerequisite for the provision of activity. It is rare that a cafe or restaurant can occupy more than the first two floors of a building and a similar argument applies to many smaller retail outlets. This implies a horizontal layering of activities throughout a street or urban block in certain places, rather than having each block or blocks of building allocated to one use. This is not to suggest that all parts of the urban fabric should contain an intense variety of mixed uses. Some areas need to have a predominance of one use, but even so would be more pleasant places if there were at least a sprinkling of other uses. Jacobs and Appleyard (1986) describe the ideal zoning map as being a constellation of coloured dots, where each colour represents one use. In some areas of the map, one colour would dominate but others would be present. This means that in a housing area, for example, there would still be space for start-up businesses and services, small shops, eating places and bars, and some discreet backyard industry. Along the main armatures and in the central districts there would be a greater mixing of uses and the colours would be spread out more evenly.

Urban designers cannot prescribe mixed-use development in a British context (see Coupland 1996 for a discussion of the difficulties). Other countries have different planning controls and regimes and the development industry is more comfortable with funding mixed-use development. Government policy in Britain is now moving towards the promotion of mixed-use development and, in this sense, urban designers, even at the level of student projects, need to challenge fixed ideas and make proposals for lively, pedestrian-friendly spaces.

LOOK FOR *Existing land uses at a fine-grain scale in the study area/site, e.g. small offices over shops; 'backland' industry.*

TIP *Establish constellations of uses that can easily be combined in close proximity, e.g. small shops, offices and residential use at a local level; major transport nodes, headquarter offices and services, large shopping centres and major leisure services at a district level.*

Scale and grain

Pedestrian-friendly environments are those that have a scale to which human beings can relate. There is nothing more dispiriting than being confronted by a cliff of massive buildings on either side of a wide street with what seem like endless spaces between them. This is not an argument against high-rise or large-scale building forms; rather it is an argument for ensuring that the scale of development at pavement or walkway level is one in which pedestrians can feel comfortable. Shopping mall designers understand scale and grain very well. They typically place large department stores at the end of their malls. These large stores act as 'magnets' to which pedestrians are drawn, past a number of smaller-scale retail outlets, often on two levels. Here the large scale is configured so that it complements the smaller, 'finer-grained' façades of the specialist shops.

Many people find shopping malls claustrophobic and this may relate to the feeling of being in a tightly packed, intense space with no obvious exit routes. Similar feelings can be experienced in outdoor shopping streets as well, where the size of the blocks is large and the pavements are very crowded. This is an argument for adopting a modest 'grain' of development, even in densely-built city centre locations (Figure 4.4). While no hard and fast standards can be given, students would do well to think hard about the width and depth of the urban block which they are proposing and about the way in which this might be let out in plots or lots at ground-floor level. Here the issue of street sections is relevant as an over-wide street with a lack of enclosure can feel as oppressive as a narrow street with high buildings (Figure 4.5). Appendix 2 gives some suggested guidelines for street sections in different localities.

Figure 4.4 A traditional 'fine-grain' shopping street, now pedestrianised, in Durham (Marion Roberts).

Figure 4.5 A street in the Olympic village in Barcelona which has been designed as a 'super-block'. This is possibly too large a grain to support a lively public culture (Bill Erickson).

> **LOOK FOR** *The size of adjacent blocks and street sections at the appraisal stage.*
>
> **TIP** *Draw sections through your proposed blocks/ streets which include the pavement, road and human beings. Check against existing sections of places you know/feel comfortable with.*

Densities

Achieving lively streets and spaces with a fine-grained mix of uses sets requirements for a critical mass of people. Even a modest level of appropriate shops in a predominately residential area, such as a dry-cleaner and a newsagent, requires a significant number of people to be able to walk past it or to be able to stop at it every day for it to remain viable. In low-density areas, there are still places in which a higher density will be both necessary and desirable. This might be around significant railway or tram stations, along local high streets or around key public spaces. Relatively high densities can be achieved with only three stories of building and, at this scale, it is possible to fulfil a family's requirement for a house with a garden as well as providing flats and many other small-scale uses. In thinking about density it is often worthwhile to study existing desirable areas which are of medium to high density and to analyse which elements of their form and configuration are capable of reproduction and adaptation. Appendix 3 gives some guidelines on appropriate catchment areas required to support different facilities, appropriate densities for different areas and types of uses, and densities that will support public transport systems.

> **LOOK FOR** *Areas that are active and lively; analyse their densities and building heights.*
>
> **TIP** *Raise building heights and densities near your designated 'armature' and transport nodes.*

Space and time

It has been suggested that it is a certain congestion of people and activities that provides the basis for a convivial urban life. These elements have temporal as well as spatial attributes. People move through space and time and activities are generally time-limited. Jane Jacobs (1992) suggested that the best city areas were those which followed a 'dance' of time, with a ritual of morning, afternoon, evening and late night movement and activities occurring in the same space (Figure 4.6). Since the early 1990s, these ideas have been taken up in the 24-hour city movement. Experiments have been carried out in a number of cities to re-introduce residential use back into town centres and to provide evening entertainment and recreation for different sections of the population (Comedia 1991; Greenhalgh et al. 1997; Heath 1997).

Attention needs to be paid to the time-relatedness of movement and activities when carrying out urban design projects. This does not only apply to town centres; it is also relevant to the design of routes and green spaces. It is as important to imagine their use at night as it is their use during the day. It is also critical to consider these issues from the point of view of the most vulnerable sections of the population, such as elderly people, people from ethnic minorities, women, and young, single men who are particularly likely to suffer attack.

Issues of safety are particularly important at night, because people feel safer if there is a sufficient critical mass of other people present. In Britain, the Home Office has run a Safer Cities project which has sought to reverse the decline in British town centres, taking measures to attract people back during both day and night (Oc and Tiesdell 1997). Urban designers can contribute to this process through consideration of both daytime and night-time uses of places and through paying attention to issues raised in Unit 3, such as configured and natural movements along routes and paths.

Figure 4.6   People enjoying sitting outside in a public square in Barcelona at night in April (Bill Erickson).

LOOK FOR *Daytime uses, night-time uses and those uses which fall in-between, such as sports centres, libraries and some cafés.*

TIP *Avoid forcing people to walk through or alongside unsupervised or unlit green spaces at night; group night-time activities adjacent to transport nodes or stops; pay careful attention to routes to and from car parking areas; provide permeability for daytime use and concentrated, configured movement routes for night-time use.*

Determinate and indeterminate spaces

So far this unit has considered spaces in terms of their uses and activities, examining the physical factors that can influence both. Use and activity can transform spaces that are not in themselves pleasing, but in an ideal world one would hope to create places which are attractive to the senses *and* which are well-used and liked. Trying to define qualitative factors is difficult,

but one idea which helps in this consideration is that of drawing attention to the object and the field. Most people have come across the type of psychological test in which one is asked to 'read' a black and white picture where, on closer examination, it becomes apparent that the picture can be read in two ways – one where the black shapes are the 'figures', with a white background, and the other where the white shape itself becomes the figure and the black forms the background (Rowe and Koetter 1978). 'Reading' space as an object in itself is one of the key lessons of an urban design approach to shaping the built landscape (Trancik 1986). In a sense, one can move through the urban landscape, seeing it as a series of solids and voids. As Arnheim (1977) points out, in a strongly defined street that is enclosed by buildings, the void that is the shape of the street itself becomes almost a 'figure'.

This is not to imply that it is only clearly defined and contained spaces which are pleasant. The approach of the modern movement in architecture and town planning was to create an urbanism with objects placed in spaces which literally flowed around them. Good urban design can encompass both of these categories: the space as figure and the figure in space, e.g. the defined character of the medieval street, with its strong enclosure of walls and buildings, and the free-flowing space of the business park, with its buildings set in a landscape of water and vegetation. Both these types of space can provide comfortable and stimulating environments (Figure 4.7).

Problems arise when a space is neither a 'figure' nor free-flowing, but is an uncomfortable mixture of the two. This frequently occurs in a European setting, where an established street becomes partially redeveloped so that one side of it consists of a strong line of buildings facing directly onto the street and the other side has buildings set back from the street and separated from each other. The resultant space is neither one thing nor another; neither a conventional street, nor a suburban layout. It often feels uncomfortable to walk along because it is ill-defined and exposed. Urban design, in this situation, can become a task of urban repair, putting back or mending a shattered street pattern. Often public spaces become ill-defined too; for example, in a square that remains unfinished with only two sides built, the space which should have been a discernible geometrical shape, instead just 'leaks' away. Again the job of the urban designer might be to rebuild the square, to increase its definition. In this sense we would argue for determinate spaces that can

be readily understood, as either defined voids within surrounding solids, or as a 'field' or background, within which objects are placed.

> **LOOK FOR** *Solids and voids, figure and background; establish zones of continuity and those where continuity has been broken.*
>
> **TIP** *In an established area look for historic maps. Assess where patterns of streets and spaces have been disrupted by later development. Assess whether the restoration of previous patterns is desirable.*

Sense and stimulation

The beauty of Gordon Cullen's (1988) work on townscapes was the extent to which he was able to record and analyse the different types of sensory pleasure that it is possible to derive from the urban landscape. Cullen's genius was to recognise that such pleasure is not dependent on architectural style, but rather accrues from the qualities of a given place, both in terms of its spatial qualities and in its colours, textures and surfaces. Issues of colour, texture and surface are connected with architectural style, but in many ways it is not

Figure 4.7   Stockholm: a modernist space which people enjoy (Marion Roberts).

helpful to consider stylistic categories. We would rather suggest that the issue of order and chaos be considered as a response to the creation of places. Too much order creates a boring, unstimulating environment and chaos is equally uncomfortable. Pleasure is more likely to be derived from a situation in between.

Without delving into the area of design control, which is considered in Unit 12, it seems appropriate to draw readers' attention to noting the contribution which the visual, sensory aspects of built surfaces can bring. Further, an important role which urban designers can play is by proposing guidelines that suggest, say, a certain palette of materials, or the locations of landmark buildings which can provide variety in an established townscape.

While individual responses to particular areas are subjective, nevertheless it is possible to build up a case for particular guidelines through careful contextual analysis and argument (Punter and Carmona 1997). Turner (1996) suggests that in nature, species gather together in 'patches' and 'corridors'; our proposals for an 'armature' with 'patches' of local identity and consistency mirrors this approach to contextualism. Moughtin *et al.* (1995) provide further elaboration and

suggestions on how to approach the issues of ornament, materials, decoration and features in urban design.

Water, vegetation and art

Of the enjoyable experiences on offer in cities, perhaps the most simple is the contrast between the hard surfaces of buildings, streets and roads and the apparent softness of greenery and water (Figure 4.8). A tree, a fountain or an attractive planter can make a small space memorable and provide a marker for the seasons. Incorporating art works into the urban landscape also

> **LOOK FOR** *Use of materials, textures, colours, architectural features.*
>
> **TIP** *Define districts with particular identifiable characteristics and then propose variations within or beyond them. Suggest locations for landmark buildings.*

Figure 4.8   Children enjoying themselves, despite prohibition, in the fountains at the Parc Citroën, Paris (Marion Roberts).

can enhance meaning and identity. As noted earlier in this unit, such features can provide a focus for activities or for gathering. A fountain may make an identifiable meeting place, while a bench that is also a work of craft or art can provide a place to sit and watch other people. These ideas might be a development of a 'green' strategy, as referred to in Unit 3, or they might arise from thinking about the spaces themselves. In any case, to work, they need to be incorporated into the design thinking from the start, rather than being applied later (Arts Council for England 1996).

LOOK FOR *Existing water courses, trees, green spaces.*

TIP *Think hard about the green areas, water courses, art works which you are proposing. What relationship do they have to the spaces? Are you simply placing them at random? Will they be sat on or looked at, or simply ignored?*

Summary

The following list is not a formula for creating convivial, well-used spaces. Experience suggests, however, that the following ingredients are helpful, if not essential. Each will require interpretation to fit circumstances:

- Ensure that densities are sufficiently high to create diversity and vitality.
- Encourage mixed uses.
- Provide a diversity of active, ground-floor frontages and activities to engage and attract a critical mass of pedestrians.
- Pay attention to the scale and grain of development.
- Encourage pedestrians to walk, gather and linger.
- Ensure that spaces are as welcoming at night as they are in the daytime.
- Create spaces with a sense of definition either in containment, or in a free-flow of space.
- Provide visual pleasure, order and contrast.
- Enhance sensory enjoyment with greenery, water or art.

BLOCK III UNDERTAKING THE DESIGN TASK

5 The design process

Tony Lloyd Jones

Understanding the urban design process

This block introduces the notion of a *method framework* for urban design, drawing on the idea, set out in Block I, of design as a cyclic process involving analysis and synthesis, or composition. Readers should note that this is meant as a guide rather than a formula that can be rigidly applied to any situation.

Artistic inspiration versus Geddesian analysis

To those unfamiliar with the process, design is rather mysterious, driven by artistic inspiration and primarily concerned with visual aesthetics rather than practical purpose. This view of design as inspiration is also shared by many designers who see themselves as (and sometimes actually are) gifted artists. In urban design, this view is represented in the '*beaux arts*' approach, where the stress is on beautifying the city through grand and often formal street layouts and landscaping interventions. A similar motivation underlies the 'big architecture' approach to urban design, where it is the visual and spatial impact of the large-scale development, as a 'statement' of the individual architect, that is seen to count.

Design as a problem-solving activity

The contrary view is of design as a problem-solving activity, concerned with the issue of spatial organisation to meet functional needs. This approach has its roots in the engineering outlook of the nineteenth century, with its railways, bridges, buildings and new structures of concrete, iron and glass. In town planning, the city was also seen in engineering terms, with increasing problems of public health and traffic circulation addressed by planning new urban infrastructure and garden cities. Out of this movement emerged the idea of 'functionalism' or 'form follows function'. The functionalist approach suggests that if we analyse the problems that the design sets out to address in sufficient detail and in a scientific manner, a spatial solution will emerge from this analysis or 'programme'. It suggests that design is a linear process, which, if carried out with sufficient rigour, will lead to a single, optimum solution.

On the surface, there are parallels between this functionalism in modernist architecture and the 'civic diagnosis' of the turn-of-century Scottish biologist and urban theorist, Patrick Geddes – his notion of 'survey–analyse–design'. Many of the modernist architects and planners wished to build the modern city anew according to strict functionalist principles, ignoring the past. Geddes, however, was concerned with learning from history and with understanding the organic and gradually evolving form of the city and the life of its inhabitants. The 'programme' part of Geddes' formula – survey and analyse – sets out to provide a rational framework for understanding the issues that a particular plan seeks to address. This is achieved through a careful 'reading' of the urban context within which a particular intervention is to be made. Each situation requires, alongside a statement of the current economic and social issues to be addressed, an understanding of the particular cultural circumstances in terms of the history of the urban fabric and the lives and life-styles of the people. With its stress on sensitivity to the urban context, this approach provides the basis for much contemporary urban design and, in particular, for the approach adopted in this primer.

The urban design cycle and the importance of types

Taken one way, the Geddesian approach suggests that the collection of sufficient data and its careful analysis will yield a rational solution to a particular set of urban problems. The scientific planning tradition follows this view, i.e. that the solution to any particular planning problem lies in gathering sufficient data. However, it is clear that design does not work in this way and that no amount of information and data analysis will cause a spatial plan or design to emerge of its own accord; rather, urban design follows a cycle. Information is gathered, and concepts are formulated and evaluated against the knowledge that has been accumulated. This suggests where additional information is needed, how it can be structured, where a design concept can be modified or how a new idea can take shape. Any particular urban design development can involve a number of such cycles of analysis, synthesis or composition and evaluation (see Unit 1).

Design also does seem to require leaps of the imagination to proceed. However, there is much that the student unfamiliar with design can do to help the imagination on its way, including following some of the principles set out here. If not from analysis, where do design ideas come from? Is it an entirely subjective matter? While it is true that much of the 'brain-work' that goes on between design analysis and solution is unconscious, few designs are entirely unique. Most solutions to a particular set of problems can be divided up into 'families' that share common features. This suggests that design concepts are shaped by drawing on pre-existing forms or precedents. A clue to what these might be is the idea of urban types – buildings, spaces, infrastructure – introduced as one of the basic 'generators of urban form' in Unit 2. In the design process, it seems likely that we draw on a library of such prototypes or precedents, built up from our experience, learning and memory, combining them in various ways and testing them against the evolving brief. The element of invention and creativity in the way that such types are combined and developed always allows for original designs and new urban types to emerge.

Design as a rational and experimental process

The design process is rational and experimental rather than simply inspirational. It works through a process of deduction rather than induction, where a design solution is an early hypothesis to be tested, drawing on pre-existing models, rather than the end-point of the long accumulation of facts. To map out an urban design solution requires analysing and simplifying the problems to be addressed. This process of simplification and abstraction is necessary before the designer is able to give a physical shape to a solution. With too much detail, this is simply not possible. The aim is to clarify priorities and make explicit future scenarios, dealing with such questions as:

- What are the most important factors? How are these measured and weighted?
- Where there are conflicting requirements, are compromises possible? If not, which requirement takes priority?
- What assumptions are being made about the future situation in which an urban design policy or plan is being implemented?

Since design is a matter of prioritisation and assumption, every solution will be better at dealing with some issues and worse at dealing with others. More efficient design solutions can often be achieved through modifications, but improvements in one area are often coupled with compromises elsewhere. This is a matter of experimentation and students that are new to it will discover design to be an open-ended and time-consuming process.

A framework for the urban design process

To summarise, the urban design in the framework presented here involves a cyclic process of analysis–composition–evaluation. It is an attempt to reconcile factors that relate to client or user needs, factors that relate to the site or area under study and its context, and factors that relate to the constraints of planning policy and local planning regulations. It involves understanding the problems that are to be addressed and refining, abstracting and prioritising the essential issues. In the process of analysis and synthesis or composition, urban types, drawn from the influence of experience or practice, are used to organise information and to shape out a solution.

The particular influences, which techniques are

used and how they are combined reflect the preferences and design of the urban designer or design team. This is a fourth factor in the urban design process. It involves issues of aesthetics and of symbolic and cultural expression on which there is a considerable amount of literature for the interested student. The remainder of this unit is concerned with looking at the design factors and at the different stages of the design cycle in more detail and describing what methods and techniques can be used.

Defining and analysing the problem

Design involves prioritising and reconciling often conflicting aims and objectives and arriving at a strategy or solution that addresses a multitude of different factors. Part of the problem to be addressed will be set out in the statement of client or user requirements that would form part of the commissioning brief for an urban designer in practice, or be described in the project brief in a student urban design exercise. Unit 11 explores what these factors might include in greater detail. Other requirements will emerge in the collection and analysis of data in the initial phase of the urban design process. Some of these will relate to the site and its context, or the area under study, and emerge in the process of urban analysis. Others will relate to constraints of planning policy and local planning regulations (see Units 6, 7 and 12). Yet other factors that will shape the design process relate to the design philosophy or approach being used to shape particular urban design solutions. These will often operate at an unconscious level, an implicit rather than explicit element of the urban design process.

Study area appraisal and surveys

Whether the area that is the object of an urban design study is a development site or a larger district, city quarter or neighbourhood, determining the particular physical and social characteristics of the study area is an essential starting point for the urban design process. How an urban design appraisal is used in local area urban design studies is described in the following sections. This section offers reflections on the appraisal process in practice and a framework for incorporating the appraisal in the larger design process. The appraisal may be viewed as a two-stage process – survey and analysis – although in practice there is considerable overlap.

The survey involves a visual inspection of the study area and the collection of material in the form of anno-

tated maps, written notes, photographs or videos and sketches. These primary data are supplemented with material from other sources: local authority development plans, historical plans and literature on the history of the area, socio-economic surveys, estate agents surveys and so forth. Ideally, students should carry out questionnaire surveys of local residents or users, or interview representative stakeholders. In the scope of the average student project, there is unlikely to be time to carry out surveys in this amount of detail and in this primer we will concentrate on short-cut techniques that allow students to carry out a rapid appraisal of urban form and activity. Additionally, the appraisal stage of an urban design project is most efficiently carried out in teams, with the different tasks being shared out so that more information can be gathered and processed.

The methods outlined in this primer, then, are intended to provide a basis for *rapid area appraisal*. The primer outlines a systematic approach that can be used to help in student urban design projects.

Site planning and the need for context studies

Any site planning exercise should involve a wider appraisal of the urban context in which the site is located. The scale of this exercise depends on the limited time and resources available, but it is important to get some measure of the urban context within which an intervention is being proposed. The scope of a context study depends on how the context is spatially defined. Generally, it is useful to define a series of concentric areas around the site of a proposed development, so that the site can be viewed in its city-wide, district and local context (for more details of how this is done, see Appendix 1). Unit 6 provides a practical example of how to carry out an area appraisal under defined criteria.

Study area analysis

The study area analysis forms the basis of the first level of analysis, which after the survey forms the second part of the appraisal and is described in detail in Unit 6. In practice, much of the basic, unprocessed survey data can be sifted and mapped as part of the contextual analysis, skipping one step in the process. Whether information is mapped in one or two stages depends of the type of notation that is developed for the purpose. Sometimes it is better to have one type of notation to record information and another to carry out an analysis (see Units 6 and 7).

Unit 6 sets out the basic tools that can be used for rapid area appraisal using simple freehand analytical diagrams and drawings. There are other more sophisticated, though less often used, techniques for which computers are either useful or essential, examples of which are as follows:

- *Spatial structure analysis*: graph theory and space syntax (see Hillier and Hanson 1984).
- *Network analysis*: modelling of transport/vehicular links and flows.
- *Computer analysis*: standard Geographical Information Systems computer applications rely on comprehensive data collection and entry, and are generally more useful at the larger planning scale for identifying area features through a 'sieving' or 'hot-spotting' process.

A common feature of the techniques of urban form and activity analysis is their ability to abstract essential factors which are important in developing clear spatial strategies. Unlike the hard-edged and more rigorous scientific analytical methods listed here, they also incorporate a degree of 'fuzziness' which can be useful in allowing the necessary flexibility in developing spatial solutions. What this type of analysis provides is clear cues and clues from which development strategies can be shaped.

Developing a rationale

Following on from the context or study area appraisal is a second level of analysis which generalises and abstracts from the first.

Summary analysis, opportunities and constraints diagrams   The most important features of each of the separate analytical studies are summarised in a summary analysis diagram (or diagrams). From this summary can be drawn the main opportunities for development and improvement that the area offers and likely constraints on development. Where possible, opportunities and constraints should be mapped as a diagram. Sometimes opportunities and constraints involve non-place-specific economic, planning or management factors, which should be listed as bullet points.

Clarifying scenarios   The idea of identifying opportunities and constraints is a little less clear-cut than it sounds, as what is an opportunity and what is a constraint is dependent on what assumptions are made about the likely funds that can be made available to

finance future development. The basic assumption of urban regeneration, for example, is to turn constraints on development, in terms of poor quality land and infrastructure and unattractive buildings, into development opportunities by strategic public investment and incentives to private investors. The important issue here is to be clear about the time-scale being considered and the broader development scenario (what type of development will be economically and socially feasible). It might be useful to list the features of the scenario and to test out the effect of different scenarios, short term and long term, optimistic and pessimistic, on the nature of an area's development opportunities and constraints.

SWOT analysis   Another technique that can be used, in place of or alongside the spatial mapping of opportunities and constraints, is a SWOT analysis. This is a common management technique that considers the strengths and weaknesses of an organisation, and the opportunities offered and threats faced as a basis for developing a planning strategy. While a study area may not have the same sense of identity as an organisation, considering its strengths and weaknesses is a useful exercise. Contrasting opportunities with threats tends to provide a greater focus on who is being affected and lays greater stress on the competitive economic environment that affects area development these days.

Area strategy   It is useful at this stage in the exercise to think in terms of an area strategy (Figure 5.1). Where the exercise is to devise an urban design framework for the area, the purpose may already be set out in the client's brief. In the absence of such a framework or where the study is concerned with a particular development site or sites, an area strategy is a useful device within which to develop site development options. In this case it is being used as a scenario and a way in which the development may be presented to the local authority.

Urban design objectives   What are the objectives that the strategy sets out to achieve? These could be listed as a few important bullet points. They may include the prime objectives that are given in the client's brief or other established user requirements, as well as objectives that have emerged from the area appraisal and SWOT analysis.

Urban design composition   The rationale provides a basis on which to develop an urban design option (or alternative options if time allows), whether these are in

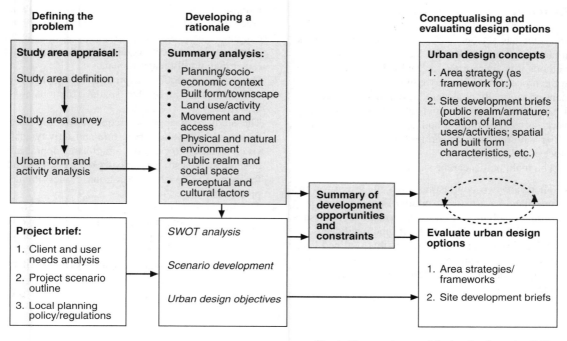

Figure 5.1   Developing an area rationale and strategy/concept diagram.

the form of an area strategy or specific site develop-ment proposals, or both. The examples given in this book show how the summary analysis of an area appraisal can help shape the development of an urban design framework or armature for the area. The approach is visualised initially as a concept diagram (a 'bubble' diagram) which sketches out the broad move-ment and land-use development strategy. This may be sufficient for considering specific development inter-ventions on particular sites. Where the requirement is to formulate an area strategy or urban design frame-work, the public realm, built form and land-use elements are worked out in more detail and the concept diagram turned into a strategic development plan or framework plan for the area.

Alternatively, the intention may be to create an intervention in the form of a site development pro-posal, a planning brief for a development site or a public realm improvement strategy.

Evaluation

In sketching out design proposals, urban designers make quick and often unconscious evaluations of the options they are exploring. Since almost every design involves compromises in certain aspects and few meet all the requirements, it is usually readily apparent which parts of the design do not 'work'. The designer may decide to adjust the proposal, to develop an entirely new one, or to go with the current option as representing the best compromise. Evaluation, in prac-tice, is seldom a formal process in which the design is measured against identified criteria. In Unit 10 of this book, a worked example is given for a set of evaluation criteria, which students may find useful in their own urban design tasks. These criteria have been derived from contemporary work in urban design studies (Punter 1990).

The issue of how performance is measured is tricky in that there are many qualitative aspects of design that do not have simple quantitative measures. Sometimes measurable indicators can be devised or identified which, while not measuring design qualities directly, provide indirect indices of performance. Another useful aid to evaluation is to use the techniques of urban form and activity analysis listed above and carry out 'before' and 'after' comparisons. These can be carried out simply by using figure ground plans or through the use of the evaluation criteria.

Summary

This unit has set out a framework within which the urban design process can be located, indicating which methods it is appropriate to employ at different stages in the process and how they contribute to the development of rationally considered urban design proposals. It has aimed to provide an insight into how the design works as a cyclic process and how those who are unfamiliar with this process can find ways of entering this process and managing it.

The main points can be summarised as follows:

- There are two contrasting ideas of design: on the one hand as artistic inspiration; on the other as a problem-solving activity, concerned with the issues of spatial organisation to meet functional needs.
- A Geddesian approach, such as that outlined here, involves a rational approach to understanding urban design problems, and involves a careful reading of the existing urban context.
- Urban design follows a cycle which draws on precedents and existing models, and adapts and combines them to come up with possible design solutions. This process is rational and experimental rather than purely inspirational.
- Urban design requires a process of simplification and abstraction to enable spatial solutions to be devised.
- The study area appraisal requires two processes: survey and analysis. Urban form and activity analysis can be used to carry out a rapid area appraisal to develop an area strategy or carry out a context study for particular local interventions or development proposals.
- The importance of developing a design rationale has been stressed, both as a basis for discovering workable urban design options and in providing a supporting argument for them.
- Proposals can be evaluated against defined criteria.

6 Area analysis

Marion Roberts

Getting started

Before starting on a design project, it is worthwhile taking the time to assemble the necessary materials. It is also advisable to decide which scale of drawings it would be most practicable to use and to draw a base plan from the official map of the area. Advice on this and some other useful techniques is given in Appendix 1. Those who are new to urban design projects would be advised to read that first before embarking on their area and site analysis.

Clerkenwell has been chosen as an exercise to illustrate the process of developing an urban design framework and an urban design project. As an inner city area in a major metropolis, Clerkenwell provides a series of complex and interesting problems but also offers the potential for varied and creative design interventions. In the Clerkenwell example there are two potential study sites, so the defined area for the context appraisal is large. The worked example for design proposals will be for a disused site in the north.

Movement systems

Location

Since site appraisal information may be presented to people who do not know the area well, or indeed at all, a simple diagram which locates the area within its town or city 'sets the scene' (Figure 6.1).

Public transport

It is always useful to note the public transport movements throughout an area and their connections with

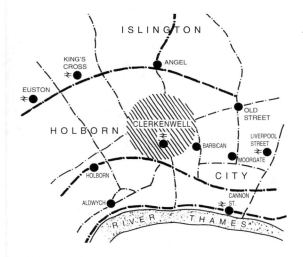

Figure 6.1 Clerkenwell: its location within London and its transport links (Jane Fowles, Saci Gabour, Daniela Lucchese and Caroline Lwin).

the wider city and region (Figure 6.2). In a site at the centre of a major city, national and international connections will also be important. By plotting these connections, judgements can be made about whether the area is well linked or not and about the type of activities which may be supported in an area. Often this analysis needs to be done at two scales: city-wide and area-wide. The frequency of public transport connections is also worth assessing; for example, a good bus link running at frequent intervals may be more significant in some towns than an infrequent rail link.

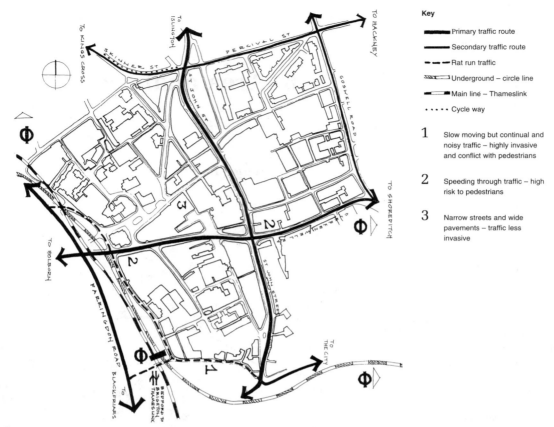

Figure 6.2 Clerkenwell: local connections (Jane Fowles, Saci Gabour, Daniela Lucchese and Caroline Lwin).

Pedestrian movement and cycling

As with public transport, it is useful to plot the routes that are most heavily trafficked by pedestrians and to note the existing cycle routes. It is important to note the most heavily used routes – normally denoting them by using a thicker line. Those that are not part of the 'official' network, i.e. short-cuts across parks or grassy areas, or through housing estates, are particularly important, as they are routes that are not really catered for at the present time.

Vehicle movement

Given that vehicles dominate so much of the environment their presence and absence should be noted. Again density of flow at particular times is worth recording, as is, where appropriate, the type of traffic. In the Clerkenwell case the main vehicular movement has been recorded with the public transport diagram. Clerkenwell, as with many locations in inner London

and other major conurbations, suffers from degradation of environmental quality through excessive traffic movement and parking. This has been recorded using photographs (Figure 6.3).

Permeability

The concept of permeability is derived from the work of Jane Jacobs (1992) and Hillier and Hanson (1984) and was developed in the book *Responsive Environments* (Alcock *et al.* 1985). Jacobs noted that where the block sizes were large, the number of routes around an area diminished. This meant that pedestrians walking through an area would be concentrated on one or two streets and that any enterprises in the back streets would suffer from the lack of passers-by and accessibility, leading to their probable failure. The permeability diagram in Figure 6.4 has been derived from the analysis of pedestrian routes. The points at which pedestrian routes do not 'connect up' have been noted.

The construction of Clerkenwell Road in the 10th century severed the area through its historic heart and it remains a psychological and physical barrier to the use and enjoyment of the area as a whole

St John's Square, once a grand and prominent public space, is now little more than a glorified car park

Winding Cowcross Street and narrow Turnmill Street are used as busy rat runs during weekday office hours

Because Clerkenwell Green still functions as a valuable social space, parked cars are less dominant than in St John's Square

The proliferation of motor cycle couriers in the area provides a busy trade for pubs and cafés in Clerkenwell Green but also means speeding bikes on many of the narrow streets

Figure 6.3 Clerkenwell: degradation of environmental quality by traffic (Jane Fowles, Saci Gabour, Daniela Lucchese and Caroline Lwin).

Infrastructure

The infrastructure of the utilities, such as power, water and drainage, may sometimes be relevant where major new connections are required or where existing infrastructure impedes movement and activity or has a strong visual presence. As Clerkenwell is an inner-city area well-served by such infrastructure, this aspect of the movement system is less relevant. It is also noteworthy that most infrastructure in urban areas is channelled under the road system.

Natural features

Landscape

It is unusual to find an urban landscape that is made up

solely of buildings and 'hard' infrastructure such as road and rail. If it were, such an absence of vegetation would be noteworthy in itself! While urban designers are not required to know the Latin names of trees and shrubs, 'soft' or green landscape and natural features such as rivers, mountains and the contours of the terrain form an important part of the ecology of a place (see Thomson 1998). As advised in Unit 3 of this book, it is important to note the type of landscape and the presence of other natural features, and to form some assessment of their quality, in conjunction with that of the buildings. As with many judgements in site appraisal, this is subjective and in a professional setting the services of a landscape architect could be called upon. Clerkenwell, in common with many inner-city areas, has a paucity of open green space

Figure 6.4   Clerkenwell: permeability.

Topography

Microclimatic effects are accentuated by the topography, i.e. the shape of the landforms in the appraisal area. Walking or cycling up a steep slope into a strong prevailing wind can be daunting, particularly for the elderly or small children. Noting the contours of a place and their convergence and divergence within the built and natural landscape forms an important part of any site appraisal.

Microclimate

Tall buildings can often affect the microclimates around their base, creating unpleasant wind corridors. Conversely, some existing open spaces can be suntraps, with wonderful shelter and winter sun. Noting the incidence of these existing features of the microclimate can give clues about further development.

Pollution and noise

(Figure 6.5). This means that it is all the more important to note what there is.

Noise pollution is an increasingly important issue. Noises may come from various sources:

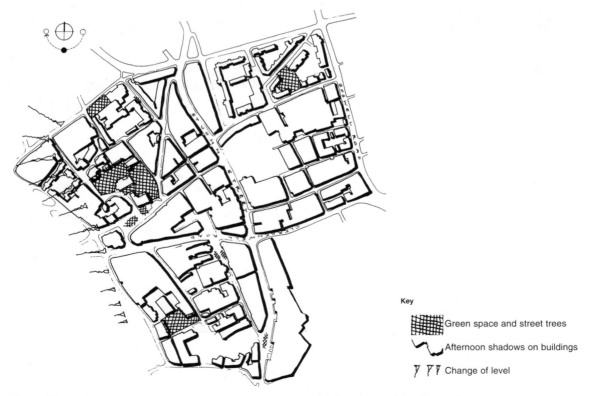

Key

Green space and street trees

Afternoon shadows on buildings

Change of level

Figure 6.5   Clerkenwell: landscape (Jane Fowles, Saci Gabour, Daniela Lucchese and Caroline Lwin).

- traffic
- aircraft
- railways (overground and underground)
- nearby sources (factories, places of entertainment)

While it may be necessary to use the services of an expert in severe cases of noise pollution, it is worthwhile to plot on a diagram the incidence and extent of noise pollution. Other sources of pollution such as industrial plants and contaminated ground should also be recorded.

Flora and fauna: habitats

The preservation of diverse species and the management of surface water have gained in importance over the last decade. In areas that are situated near to rural areas or are in urban areas but adjacent to natural landscape features such as a river or a large existing common, such issues are becoming increasingly important. Here reference to the relevant local authority records can help in establishing whether or not a survey of existing species has been carried out. Similarly noting the presence of ponds, low-lying marshy areas and other potential water runoff areas not

only suggests whether some measures to facilitate the preservation of existing species needs to be incorporated into the design but also might provide design inspiration for other ecological features such as reed-bed drainage systems. In densely built-up central areas such as Clerkenwell, issues of ecological diversity and conservation are generally not key issues. On occasions they may become important – perhaps through interventions in the past – and it is worthwhile being aware of their potential relevance.

Development economics

Land uses

Land uses provide evidence of both activities and property values. Empty properties are also a sign of decline. Recording land use is an essential part of any site appraisal and it should include making a note of derelict or vacant properties. A classification of uses can be generalised into categories that generate different types of activity, rather than using the stricter definitions adopted by planners (Figure 6.6). Mixed uses within one building are also important to note, as these contribute to the vitality of an area (see Unit 4).

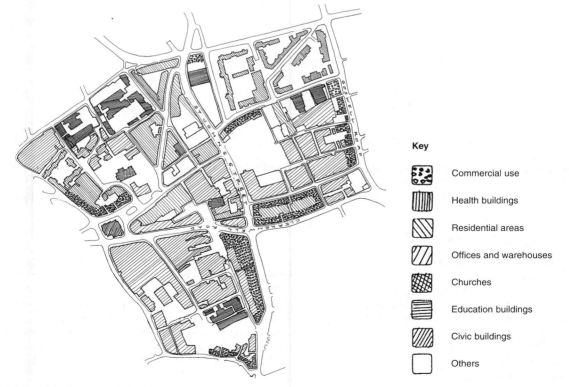

Figure 6.6   Clerkenwell: land uses (Jane Fowles, Saci Gabour, Daniela Lucchese and Caroline Lwin).

Development pressures

The extent to which land uses are changing can be observed by noting new uses coming into an area and existing ones in decline. Other sources of information include the following:

- estate agents' windows and boards;
- articles in local and national newspapers;
- articles in the specialist press, e.g. *Estates Gazette*.

Changes of use should also be noted, such as the transformation of a traditional pub into an up-market wine bar; the conversion of warehouses into loft apartments; the conversion of industrial premises into craft workshops and design studios. All of these changes can be observed in the streets most immediately adjacent to Farringdon Underground Station. Generally, the land-use survey and observations made about the property market in Clerkenwell give an overwhelming impression of a former industrial area, with some medieval enclaves, in a process of transformation. This transformation is taking place along the major traffic arteries and around the underground station. Here former warehouse buildings are being converted into 'lofts' (up-market flats), design studios and specialist craft production workshops, restaurants and bars. The transformation is more evident in the southern part of the study area,

with the northern part being more closely related to the local authority housing to the north of the study site.

Planning policies

Reference should be made to the local authority's planning policies with regard both to the area and to the site. Specific urban design policies or those concerned with physical characteristics such as density have an obvious impact, but there are many other policy areas which have an impact on built form (e.g. parking requirements). Some of these policies may have been formulated without due consideration of their impact upon design, or may not be consistent with current ideas of sustainability in urban development. It may well be necessary to find ways round or even to challenge these policies, if they exist. The Clerkenwell–Smithfield site itself is classified as one of three Special Policy Areas in Islington's Unitary Development Plan (along with Finsbury Park and King's Cross). The designation of this area overlaps with the conservation areas in the study area.

The retention of built form

An important part of an analysis is to find out and note whether any parts of the study area have been desig-

---

Typo-morphological analysis

Typo-morphological analysis has been developed in four main centres to date (Moudon 1994): at the Universities of Newcastle and Birmingham in the UK, in Italy and in Paris.

Morphological analysis can:

- reveal historical changes over time, suggesting which are the most important routes and spaces and buildings;
- demonstrate the most significant building types and their evolution;
- assist in categorising different sub-areas;
- assist in finding typical patterns of spaces, buildings and routes which can be elaborated in a design solution.

Figure ground drawings

A key tool of morphological analysis is the figure ground drawing. In this technique the spaces rather than details of the buildings are revealed. Figure ground drawings are produced by shading in the buildings in plan form in black, thereby revealing the public and semi-public realms as white. An historical contextual study would compare figure ground drawings of an area at different points in its history. Data that can be used to build up historical figure ground plans are normally available in the local history section of the public library, and the local planning office may have useful background information on locally listed or important buildings. The production of figure ground drawings enables the designer to see the urban landscape as a series of solids and voids (Trancik 1986). This level of simplification permits the identification of recurring patterns within the built form (see Figure 6.7).

nated conservation areas, to identify any listed buildings, and to note any spaces or views that should be preserved. There is also a need for the urban designer to come to their own assessment of the value of specific buildings and of types of buildings, as well as noting the local authority's views. Noting buildings of value can be most usefully explored in an analytical diagram. This part of the task involves searches through local authority policy documents and historical research, as well as the designer's own judgement. Within the study area, Clerkenwell Green and Charterhouse Square are conservation areas. Their particular character makes their designation wholly admirable.

Urban types

Historical evolution

Key features in Clerkenwell's evolution can be traced using historical figure ground plans. The four figure ground drawings in Figure 6.7 reveal its early origins as a village outside the city of London. Despite the pressures on Clerkenwell resulting from its close proximity to the City of London, the medieval street pattern and long-established building lines have generally been maintained, and buildings mainly of three to five storeys with narrow street frontages dominate the area. St John Street was a major route to the north from London in former times, linking farmland with Smith Field, while the River Fleet was historically the area's western boundary. The period following the Great Fire of 1666 saw a major expansion of Clerkenwell as a suburb, with narrow alleyways servicing deep urban blocks, many of which were based on the existing field boundaries. At the beginning of the nineteenth century a number of brewers and distillers established themselves in the district, attracted by the natural water. The brewery site occupies the whole of a former enclosed orchard garden that had survived the earliest period of urbanisation.

In the mid-nineteenth century, the Metropolitan Works Board proposed improvements to the road system, replacing slum dwellings and improving the water supply. The result was a new road, Clerkenwell Road, which improved east–west links and which was lined with buildings that paid no regard to the former street pattern or scale of Clerkenwell. It crashed through St John's Square with no respect for its history, leaving St John's Gate, in the southern portion, stranded. Rebuilding to replace slum housing and repair war damage led to further loss of the historic urban morphology, but even in the modernist housing estates of the 1960s some of the original street pattern remains.

Key features to note include the following:

- the presence of Charterhouse Square as a green space and the medieval complex to its north;
- the construction of the east–west route of Clerkenwell Road which cut off northern Clerkenwell from the south;
- the construction of the underground line, which cut off Clerkenwell from the West End of London;
- St John Street, which persists as an important north–south route.

A further level of analysis can be carried out by grouping the urban types into categories – either chronologically (by historical periods) or by more formal properties (e.g. suburban housing, grids of terraced housing, medieval streets). An example is given in Figure 6.8, which helps to simplify our understanding of an area.

Formal and informal spaces

The figure ground plan can also help to reveal the differences between those spaces or areas that have already been consciously designed as 'set pieces' and those which have developed in accordance with more informal rules. A system of informal alleys can be traced in the western side of Clerkenwell. It is also possible to note the characteristic wedge shapes of Clerkenwell Green and the manner in which the formality of St John Square has been cut in half by the Clerkenwell Road.

Fronts and backs

Noting the position of the fronts and backs of buildings can help to establish which streets and spaces are formally defined, and where there are areas of confusion (Figure 6.8). It can also highlight discontinuities, as in the St John Street section of the northern study site.

Street profile analysis

Drawing sections through typical streets helps designers to familiarise themselves with the scales of development around their site or study area. Contrasts between different types of streets help to identify any hierarchy of routes in an area. A hierarchy of routes occurs when there is a gradation between wider streets with taller buildings to narrower ones. More information on street sections is given in Appendix 2.

Building types

Figure ground plans combined with observations made

(a)

- Predominantly residential land use
- Development concentrated along street frontages
- Plan prior to building of Clerkenwell Road

(b)

- Intensification of development and change to include brewery/distilleries, factories and other industries
- Centre of blocks now developed and accessed via yards and alleyways
- 'Middlesex House of Detention' on north edge of district
- Prior to building of Clerkenwell Road

(c)

(d)

- Larger, denser block structure
- Derelict land visible as spaces within urban matrix
- Greater mix of land use although northern districts remain predominantly residential

Figure 6.7 Historical evolution of Clerkenwell: figure ground plans for (a) 1799, (b) 1873, (c) 1914 and (d) 1996 (Jane Fowles, Saci Gabour, Daniela Lucchese and Caroline Lwin).

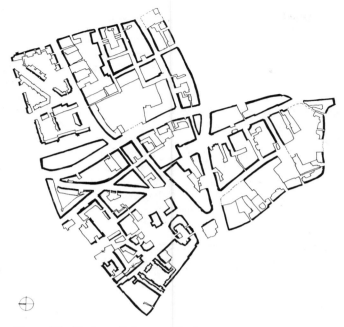

Figure 6.8   Clerkenwell: fronts and backs.

by walking around the area are helpful in assessing the following:

- dominant building types (e.g. terraced houses, warehouses);
- dominant urban layouts (e.g. axial layout, gridded residential streets, 'organic' urban settlement);
- the extent to which the pattern of dominant building/ urban types has been modified or eroded over time.

Architectural characteristics

It is not necessary for an urban designer to be an architectural historian with a detailed knowledge of styles, influences and provenance. It is important for the urban designers to be able to analyse and note the key features of buildings within a local area which contribute to its overall character or which form a key characteristic of a particular type. Now it may be that an area does not have a clearly identifiable character, but that in itself is a valuable observation. In places with a discernible character it is not possible to outline all the features that it may be necessary to note: the list below gives some guidance to the type of topics which may be featured:

- overall proportions
- door/window openings
  - regularity

- projection beyond wall/roof lines
  - proportions
  - special features (e.g. decorative fanlights)
- uniformity of eaves/cornice line
- shape of roof
- range of materials commonly used in different types
- mouldings/decorative features
  - columns, pilasters, pediments
  - string courses
  - quoins
- special features (e.g. corner features)

Social processes

Townscape analysis

Townscape is a method of structuring or analysing the designer's view of a place. It was developed by Gordon Cullen and others writing for the journal *Architectural Review* after the Second World War. Their aim was to bring back concern for the visual experience in architecture and post-war urban planning. Cullen's book *Townscape* was first published in 1961 and became a classic that has been reprinted many times since its first publication. Cullen's own practice provided examples of the manner in which townscape principles could be put in practice (Cullen 1988).

The methodology of townscape derives from basic observational skills and develops a method of noting in graphic format what is seen. This method focuses mainly on what can be seen at an immediate and local level. In this way it allows the observer to pay attention to the many small details that give a place its particular identity and characteristics. As a detailed visual analysis it can record just how a space is shaped, how a tree frames a view, or how the rhythm of the window and door openings guide the eye.

Townscape draws particular attention to the way in which a space changes as the observer moves through it. Cullen calls this experience 'serial vision' and the notation method that he developed allows the observer to record the features of the environment that are important to the view. The point of the concept is to note how effectively the routes so experienced stimulate the observer's interest and enjoyment and, where interest is lacking, to improve them. Incorporated into the notion of moving through a series of spaces – treating the urban landscape as a series of outdoor rooms – are other concepts propounded by Cullen and his successors Tugnett and Robertson (1987), such as 'glimpse views', 'framed views' and other sensory, visual experiences of outdoor space as a series of enclosures.

Townscape notation gives a quick and graphic means of recording information about a place. Richard Guise of the University of the West of England has developed a notation system (Figure 6.9), based mainly on Cullen's work.

Figure 6.9 Townscape notation system (Richard Guise).

A different type of townscape analysis has been applied to Clerkenwell (Figure 6.10). Here key routes, which exemplify the attractive character of Clerkenwell, have been sketched in serial vision sequence. Readers who lack either confidence or practice in drawing from life, may find tracing over a photograph an easier technique.

1. Faulkner's Alley
   Tunnel view, enclosed and narrow.

2. Faulkner's Alley
   Emerging onto Benjamin Street, opening on left allows a view of buildings along street façade.

3. St John's Churchyard
   Rare green space frames buildings to the north.

4. Britton Street/Albion Place
   Street façade running away with building on corner which addresses both streets.

5. Britton Street
   Series of buildings and trees, repeating rhythm and drawing pedestrians along the street. Spire of St James visible above the roofscape.

Figure 6.10   Townscape analysis of Clerkenwell (Jane Fowles, Saci Gabour, Daniela Lucchese and Caroline Lwin).

Legibility

Please see Unit 3 for an explanation of the legibility technique. The legibility analysis of Clerkenwell (Figure 6.11) demonstrates that for the observers, the east side of St John Street was more imageable, with some key nodes, paths and landmarks. The eastern side of the area, which includes the study site, was found by them to be less memorable. It also suggests the extent to which Clerkenwell is cut off from the West End of London by the railway.

Cultural associations

Although Lynch (1960) suggested that people use the key elements (nodes, landmarks, edges, districts and paths) to form their image of a place, his study did not examine their associated meanings. The connection between people and places often exists at an imaginative level where past associations, events and even street names become an important part of the urban fabric. As well as carrying out the more obvious scientific task of morphological and building quality analysis, designers are well advised to delve, even superficially, into local history. Sources of reference are local history libraries, the local public library and the planning office. Normally this task can be carried out simultaneously with the morphological study.

Key features in Clerkenwell are as follows:

- religious and other institutions, e.g. Priory of St John, Charterhouse, Bart's hospital;
- past associations with radical politics, e.g. the Chartists met on Clerkenwell Green, and the Marx Memorial Library, where Lenin's paper Iskra was published, is housed there;
- past associations with skilled craftsmen, clock-makers and watch-makers – a tradition that continues in design studios and printers' workshops;
- the name of the area derives from a spring water well (Clerk's well);
- Clerkenwell later became important for breweries and gin factories, but is now a 'play' area on the fringe of the financial district, with an expanding number of bars and restaurants;
- St John Street was the main cattle drive to the north of England until the mid-1850s;
- the meat market of Smithfield was established in 1878.

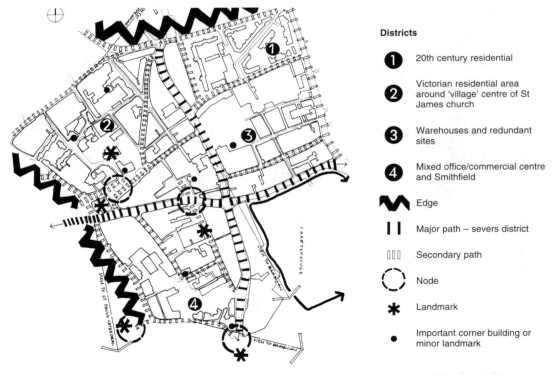

Districts

1 20th century residential

2 Victorian residential area around 'village' centre of St James church

3 Warehouses and redundant sites

4 Mixed office/commercial centre and Smithfield

Edge

Major path – severs district

Secondary path

Node

Landmark

Important corner building or minor landmark

Figure 6.11   Clerkenwell: legibility analysis (Jane Fowles, Saci Gabour, Daniela Lucchese and Caroline Lwin).

Summary: opportunities and constraints

Site appraisal provides an opportunity to:

- assess the character of an area or of the neighbourhood of a site;
- establish current trends in relation to the area or site;
- rationalise and make explicit unconscious observation.

It becomes more forceful as a design tool once the information is analysed and abstracted to another level.

Figure 6.12 provides a summary of the analysis of Clerkenwell. It identifies the key routes, the different morphological areas, key nodes, existing buildings of good quality, significant pedestrian routes, key existing spaces, potential development sites and an area identified as the 'heart of Clerkenwell'.

This summary analysis is taken further in Figure 6.13, which identifies the main constraints and opportunities that will influence the proposals for an urban design framework. Three of the constraints are transport related: the Clerkenwell Road cutting through the site

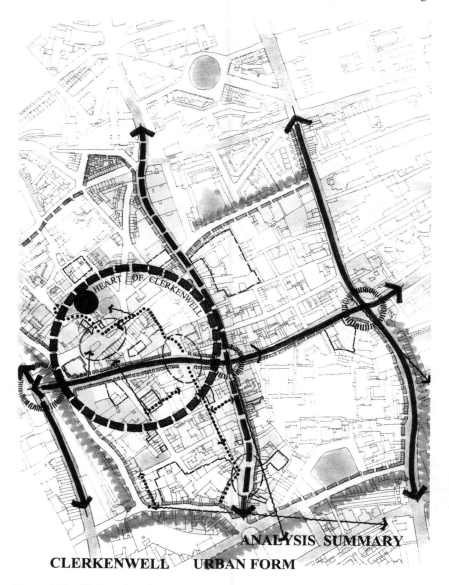

Figure 6.12   Clerkenwell: summary of analysis (Mike Martin and Kamal Chunilal).

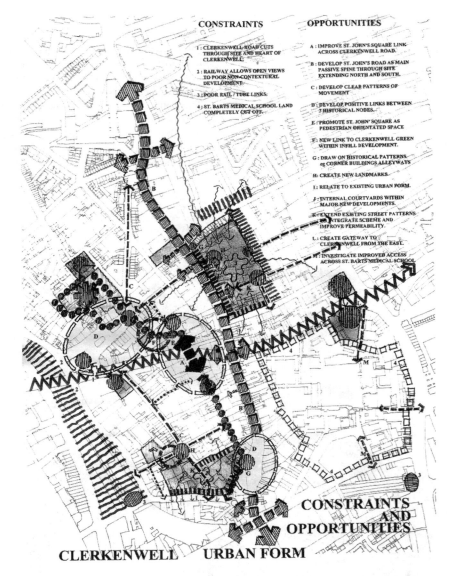

CONSTRAINTS

1 : CLERKENWELL ROAD CUTS
THROUGH SITE AND HEART OF
CLERKENWELL.

2 : RAILWAY ALLOWS OPEN VIEWS
TO POOR NON-CONTEXTURAL
DEVELOPMENT.

3 : POOR RAIL / TUBE LINKS.

4 : ST. BARTS MEDICAL SCHOOL LAND
COMPLETELY CUT OFF.

OPPORTUNITIES

A : IMPROVE ST. JOHN'S SQUARE LINK
ACROSS CLERKENWELL ROAD.

B : DEVELOP ST. JOHN'S ROAD AS MAIN
PASSIVE SPINE THROUGH SITE
EXTENDING NORTH AND SOUTH.

C : DEVELOP CLEAR PATTERNS OF
MOVEMENT.

D : DEVELOP POSITIVE LINKS BETWEEN
3 HISTORICAL NODES.

E : PROMOTE ST. JOHN' SQUARE AS
PEDESTRIAN ORIENTATED SPACE

F : NEW LINK TO CLERKENWELL GREEN
WITHIN INFILL DEVELOPMENT.

G : DRAW ON HISTORICAL PATTERNS
eg CORNER BUILDINGS ALLEYWAYS

H : CREATE NEW LANDMARKS.

I : RELATE TO EXISTING URBAN FORM.

J : INTERNAL COURTYARDS WITHIN
MAJOR NEW DEVELOPMENTS.

K : EXTEND EXISTING STREET PATTERNS
INTEGRATE SCHEME AND
IMPROVE PERMEABILITY.

L : CREATE GATEWAY TO
CLERKENWELL FROM THE EAST.

M : INVESTIGATE IMPROVED ACCESS
ACROSS ST. BARTS MEDICAL SCHOOL

CONSTRAINTS
AND
OPPORTUNITIES

CLERKENWELL   URBAN FORM

Figure 6.13   Clerkenwell: constraints and opportunities (Mike Martin and Kamal Chunilal).

and the intrusive rail links that cut the area off from the west. In identifying opportunities a move is made towards making proposals: the question is how to move on from identified weaknesses to suggestions for improvement. These can vary from the modest (e.g. the suggestion to improve the main north–south route, St John Street) to the more imaginative (e.g. creating links between the three historic 'nodes' in the area). Further links between historic nodes and future development sites are also indicated. Opportunities to develop interior

'courtyards' or small open spaces within the development sites are noted, as are the possibilities of extending existing street patterns into the development sites. Potential places for new landmarks are indicated, as are opportunities to draw on historical patterns.

Moving from analysis to an area framework

The next step following identifying opportunities and

constraints is to develop a series of urban design concepts. These are most easily expressed in diagram form (Figure 6.14). The concepts have been worked up from the urban design objectives that were set out in the written strategy. The strategy illustrates where these objectives might be applied, without working them out in detail.

The final stage demonstrates how the concepts are worked up into an urban design area framework, or development brief (Figure 6.15). Here the importance of the armature as an organising concept is illustrated; existing and new routes are clearly articulated. Each connects new and existing spaces with proposals for new buildings and developments. It is important to note that although these new buildings are shown, and clearly distinguished from the existing buildings on the development sites, only a loose indication of their possible 'footprint' has been indicated. Similarly the use of shading and the depiction of trees and other vegetation in the plan suggests which streets and areas

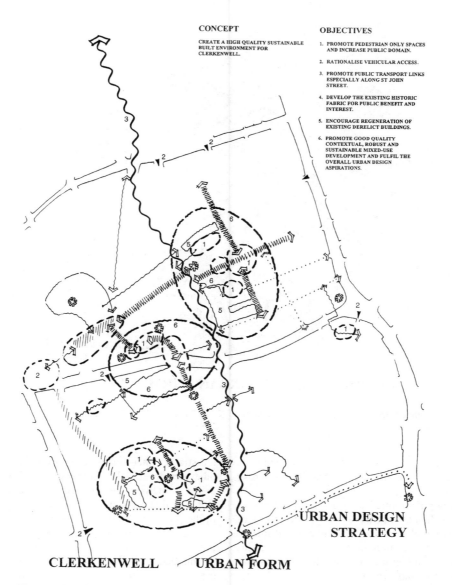

CONCEPT

CREATE A HIGH QUALITY SUSTAINABLE BUILT ENVIRONMENT FOR CLERKENWELL.

OBJECTIVES

1. PROMOTE PEDESTRIAN ONLY SPACES AND INCREASE PUBLIC DOMAIN.

2. RATIONALISE VEHICULAR ACCESS.

3. PROMOTE PUBLIC TRANSPORT LINKS ESPECIALLY ALONG ST JOHN STREET.

4. DEVELOP THE EXISTING HISTORIC FABRIC FOR PUBLIC BENEFIT AND INTEREST.

5. ENCOURAGE REGENERATION OF EXISTING DERELICT BUILDINGS.

6. PROMOTE GOOD QUALITY CONTEXTUAL, ROBUST AND SUSTAINABLE MIXED-USE DEVELOPMENT AND FULFIL THE OVERALL URBAN DESIGN ASPIRATIONS.

URBAN DESIGN STRATEGY

CLERKENWELL   URBAN FORM

Figure 6.14 Clerkenwell: urban design strategy (Mike Martin and Kamal Chunilal).

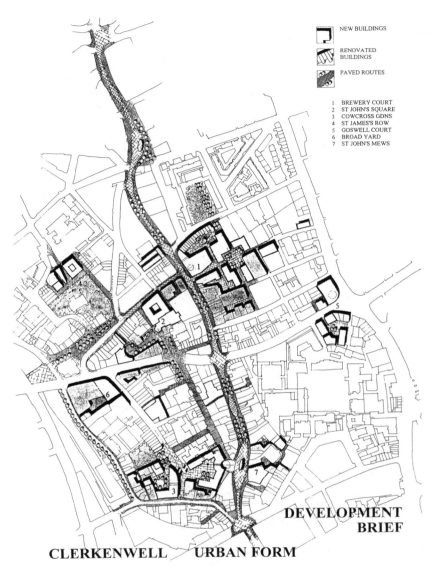

Figure 6.15 Clerkenwell: development brief (Mike Martin and Kamal Chunilal).

should be subject to environmental improvements, but does not specify in precise detail what those improvements should be.

The development brief is excellent in its subtle reworking of themes that have been identified in the site analysis: the character of back alleys and internal space; the opportunity to reunite the two halves of historic St John's Square; the opportunities to strengthen connections to and from the core of historic Clerkenwell. The framework is strengthened by a writ-

ten strategy that makes suggestions for land uses and other design guidelines (Table 6.1). The development of the framework drew on the ideas set out in Units 3 and 4 in that 'armatures' or links between key points in the public realm were used as a basis for the entire strategy. Similarly the framework, in its sensitive proposals to create small, well-linked, urban spaces surrounded by mixed uses, provides the basis for creating the types of conviviality explained in Unit 4.

Table 6.1   Design strategy (to be read with the design brief).

Promote public transport links and develop St John Street as a pedestrian/cycle/tram route	Develop historic qualities; reinforce sense of place; encourage 'usability'; regenerate historic areas for public interest	Encourage renovation of existing derelict and contextual buildings, for uses that address local community business needs	Promote quality contextual, robust and sustainable mixed-use development to fulfil local needs, commercial requirements and to fulfil the urban design aspirations
• New developments to make positive relationship with St John Street • Reduce width of road, introduce light transit system down centre, discouraging cars, encouraging buses and taxis • Create vibrant backbone with incidental sitting, recreation areas associated with pedestrian cross-routes; introduce environmental improvements, paving, trees, street furniture • Promote compatible ground-floor uses • Encourage use of residential apartments on first floor and above to bring life and activity • Intensify restaurant, leisure and cultural uses along route	• Maximise tourist potential, pedestrian routes to include historic trail, renovate historic buildings, develop themed museums, e.g. brewing, watch-making • Co-ordinated street furniture, information boards, direction signs • Introduce policy on façade treatment, painting sign boards to ensure sensitive treatment in historic areas • Introduce traditional art/craft workshops into a proportion of renovated buildings • Ensure new development relates to and respects historic qualities and contributes to the spirit of Clerkenwell	• Establish forum for public debate generating involvement in the future of Clerkenwell • Establish acceptable and compatible uses dependent on building type and location • Improve surrounding infrastructure, etc., to encourage investment • Encourage consolidation of existing street frontages • Promote imaginative refurbishment	• Ensure reasonable distribution of uses and mixed size of development • Ensure all new building and redevelopment contributes to the 'whole' for Clerkenwell • Ensure development always addresses quality as well as economic issues • Ensure each new building creates well-shaped adjacent public space • Ensure street elevations respect mean storey heights and street proportions

Summary

This unit has demonstrated how to:

• undertake an area analysis;
• summarise that analysis into a diagram and a series of statements;
• develop the summary into opportunities and constraints;
• carry the analysis forward into proposing design concepts and developing them into an area framework.

Some projects will stop at the area framework. The area framework can provide the basis for an action planning exercise or may be used as a local development plan. Alternatively it can be used to better inform a series of detailed studies at local level and provide the basis for design guidance for the area as a whole. In the next two units advice will be given about how to make proposals at a more local level.

Unit 7 Design at the local scale

David Seex

Introduction

This unit will outline the scope of urban design at a local scale and the work of the urban designer in creating urban design frameworks, briefs and masterplans; what we might describe as site planning. Together these encompass the two most detailed levels of the 'hierarchy of urban design' guidance identified in Carmona (1998: table 3.7). Site planning is the process of reconciling three distinct sets of requirements in order to produce a suitable layout or urban design brief for the site or area. These requirements are those generated by the site itself and its urban context, those of the landowner and/or developer, and those of the relevant planning policy. The next section will identify and illustrate through case studies those factors relevant to the analysis–composition–evaluation methodology outlined in Unit 5. These factors are not to be taken as a set of absolutes, but simply as indications of what the student may need to take into account. Indeed, as the reader will become aware, every site varies and different factors will assume differing importance according to site conditions. In this and the following sections we hope to provide the potential urban designer with a methodology and a set of criteria that can be applied to most urban development situations. In effect these are a set of tools that the urban designer takes to each job.

The arrangement and interrelationship of buildings and space is fundamental to the design process within our towns and cities. The role of the urban designer is:

- to look forward;
- to understand the dynamics of cultural change; and
- to create an urban fabric that can accommodate differing societies.

While design guides and design codes are primarily intended to provide a framework for development control in respect of individual or small groups of new buildings, design briefs and masterplans are prepared in order to provide a coordinated controlling framework for the development of an urban area or site. Site planning is not simply a question of applying a set of standards; it is an art rather than a science, but an art best created by working within a disciplined framework. In this case the art is to create an environment of human scale with balance, harmony, contrast, interest and meaning. These are values that can create the basis of good design as opposed to style. Site planning at its worst is no more than an entirely speculative arrangement of buildings of one single use with little or no regard for public space or for the wider environment (many housing estates, for example). At its best, site planning can produce a masterplan that creates new public spaces framed by a variety of building types and uses (e.g. Figure 7.1). We believe that the future lies with high-density mixed-use development within our towns and cities, and will demonstrate the process of site planning through such examples, including those that insert new development into an existing urban fabric – what we might call 'urban repair'.

The process of site planning is thus that of arranging a set of buildings and spaces in such a way as to meet as many as possible of the requirements of the landowner and/or developer and of the planning authorities (one of which, as noted in Unit 5, is likely to be the client), as well as the 'urban design requirements' of the site itself. At the same time we should look beyond the site itself and seek to make a contribution to the wider urban environment. The urban design

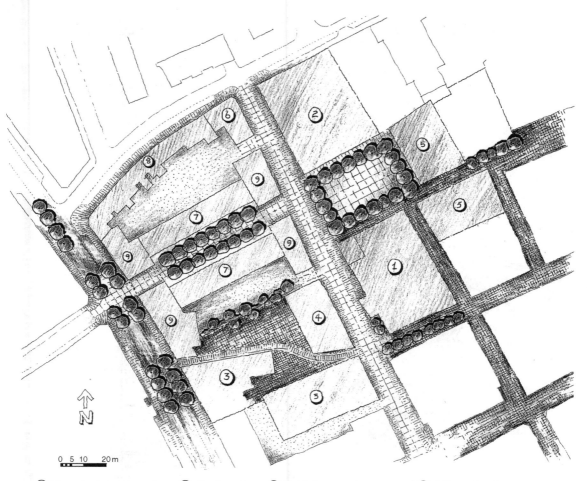

① The school of photography   ② Sports centre   ③ Public house and restaurant   ④ Office and studio space
⑤ Loft apartments   ⑥ Public house   ⑦ Townhouses   ⑧ Converted flats above shops   ⑨ New flats

Figure 7.1   Clerkenwell: masterplan (Martin Evans).

process in many ways parallels the building design process in that it is about the organisation of space and routes and the creation of hierarchies. However, the scale is different. Site planning is effected through the generation of an urban design brief or masterplan, illustrating a set of building 'footprints' and three-dimensional massing, together with some explanation of the qualities of the areas between these buildings. It is not a two-dimensional exercise; the built environment is three-dimensional and should always be considered in such terms. The intention of good urban design is not to usurp the role of the architect or building designer, but to establish a brief or masterplan such that when buildings are commissioned there is information available about the pattern of built form and

how buildings should address the public realm. It should be noted that many buildings, particularly speculative housing, are not designed by architects and the design brief may be the only significant input from a design professional. The brief should comprise requirements for building lines and access points, height and massing, use, location and nature of public space; not producing a building design but saying at a conceptual level 'this is what the building might do'. A good urban design brief will define the public elements of a building without defining its style, such that the brief may be taken forward by an architect or other designer to the stage of detailed building design (e.g. Figure 7.2).

Site planning is only one link in the chain of urban

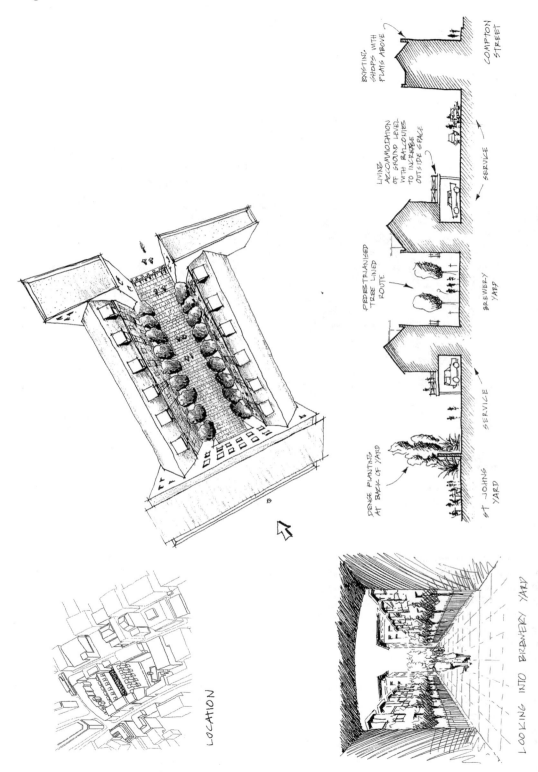

Existing shops with flats above

Living accommodation at ground level with balconies to increase outside space

Pedestrianised tree lined route

Dense planting at back of yard

Compton Street

Service

Brewery yard

Service

St Johns yard

Location

Looking into Brewery yard

Figure 7.2 Clerkenwell: partial axonometric (Martin Evans).

design decisions, although by its very nature it has a key position. Unit 3 explored the main organisational principles that lay behind the urban design process. This and the following unit consider the ways in which these principles may be used to create an urban design brief that an architect or designer may then take forward to the level of an individual building. In site planning, the designer's skill is in the use of the 'toolbox'. This skill may be part community-led, or part client-led, but either way there is a series of techniques that may be used in any site planning exercise. It is in this role that the urban designer is uniquely placed to consider the quality of the public space. As we have seen, urban design is working at the interface between planning and architecture, thus while planning has frequently not concerned itself with design, the architect quite rightly has a primary responsibility to the client rather than directly to the public realm.

Designers utilise a range of techniques to achieve unity in an urban design project: the landscape or ground treatment may be used to link an otherwise disparate group of buildings; the use of geometric shapes for built form may lead to a unified composition; buildings may be arranged around a series of axes and sub-axes; or the urban space itself could form the basis of the composition. Our case studies will use the last three of these techniques. In all the case studies the designers have utilised in some form a combination of the street and the square, the two most fundamental elements of the urban fabric. The street is the quintessential element of urban form: 'streets moderate the form and structure and comfort of urban communities' (Jacobs 1993: 3), while the square provides the highlight in the urban matrix, creating a visual and social focus. 'In any composition there is a need to emphasize some parts and subordinate others; this is the art of design' (Moughtin 1992: 90).

Site analysis

All design work must commence with an analysis of the problem. While an urban design or development framework will flow from the urban analysis outlined in Unit 6, an urban design brief or masterplan for a development site will require a site appraisal. The site appraisal process is broadly the same as that for the urban analysis/area appraisal and deals with many of the same issues but at a more local scale. The site survey and analysis will involve gathering and recording information in respect of the physical characteristics of the site itself, the land uses and urban forms immediately around the site, any constraints imposed

by adjoining property, access and movement, the townscape context, any urban design opportunities that the site presents, and the planning policy context.

Site planning will often follow on from an urban design framework or strategy and/or an area analysis, in which case much of this information may already have been collected, e.g. the built form characteristics of the area. However, it may be wise to confirm this analysis for yourself when you are undertaking the more detailed site survey. It is of course vitally important for the designer to familiarise him/herself with the site. Some of the survey will be undertaken through desk study – the urban morphology of the area can be obtained from historical documents, and the policy background and planning history of the site from planning documents; but much will require visiting the site itself, usually on more than one occasion. The following are the main categories of information to be gathered, preferably in a notebook that can be continually added to throughout the course of the project:

- *Site characteristics*:   We will need to accurately record the site boundaries, which should have been provided by the client, and consider (either at this point or more likely when we have further information) whether these actually represent – from an urban design point of view – the best development site. We must also record and make notes about levels and slopes; trees, landscape or surface materials of interest; any existing structures or buildings on the site; and any rights of way across the site.
- *Adjoining sites*.   We need to look at the adjoining sites for any constraints that they might impose upon our site and consider the following questions: is the site open or enclosed by adjoining buildings? If the latter, do any of these overlook our site? Do any adjacent buildings have requirements for daylight, sunlight or privacy? Do any of these have party walls abutting the site? Do any of the adjacent uses generate noise or other forms of pollution? Are there any apparent requirements for pedestrian desire lines to/from adjoining sites?
- *Access*.   We need to record existing pedestrian and vehicular flows to and around the site and any existing access points to the site, and note the local provision of public transport.
- *Visual qualities*.   The townscape character of the surrounding streets, the form and scale of the buildings and the nature of the spaces between buildings may have an impact on the way in which we make proposals for site development. An area analysis may have enabled us to deter-

mine which townscape elements (if any) form important parts of the character of the area. An historical study of the area's development may help us to understand how this townscape has evolved and identify which are the most important elements. Of particular importance is any townscape element on or immediately adjacent to the site. This analysis may point to a range of urban design opportunities, possibly including the opportunity to repair the effects of earlier unsympathetic developments.

- *Land-use context.* Just as the location, form and design of adjoining buildings will influence our proposal, so will their uses. Furthermore the mix of uses or dominant use in the vicinity should influence our thinking; the implications of use and form being intertwined in urban design. We must also of course consider land-use policies in any development plan(s) that may affect our site. Apart from the obvious fact that such policies may have a very strong influence on the mix of uses that we propose, many land-use policies have an indirect effect on design and built form (e.g. policies on density or on dwelling mix). This leads us onto the last set of issues: the policies that may affect our design.
- *Policy context.* Whichever country or part of the country we are working in, there will be a range of physical policies that will influence or control the design and form of new urban development. Design codes or guidelines and conservation policies will set out clear criteria for the design of new buildings and may control what may be demolished or removed (see Greed and Roberts 1998: 74–78). Specific urban design policies or those concerned with physical characteristics such as density will also be directly relevant, but there are many other policy areas that have an impact on built form (e.g. space between buildings, parking requirements; see Greed and Roberts 1998: table 3.2; Unit 11). Some of these policies may have been formulated without due consideration of their impact upon design, or may not be consistent with current ideas of sustainability in urban development. It may well be necessary to find ways round or even to challenge such policies.

Most of this information will have been recorded graphically as a series of sketch plans and diagrams, in order to highlight those characteristics which are most likely to influence the development of our site. In other words, the designer must analyse the information he or she has gathered in terms of impact on

use and *form*. The result of the site analysis can be presented as an 'opportunities and constraints diagram' and used as a starting point for the generation of the design layout. However, before work can commence on this layout, further information is needed; in particular, both a basic knowledge of the spatial requirements of different building types and how people use them, and an awareness of the issues affecting the relationships between buildings and urban spaces (see Appendix 2).

Buildings provide protected space for defined activities by means of walls and a roof and internal subdivisions of rooms or 'cells'. As urban designers we need an appreciation of how these cells relate to each other and to the outside world. This has an impact on, for example, where the external doors and windows of a building are and how close or distant they should be from other buildings or public spaces. Thus the designer must be aware of the constraints that lead to the sizes and arrangement of rooms and buildings, e.g. the requirement for natural light or the maximum distance to a fire exit. The urban designer also needs to appreciate the ways in which activity and access are related to public and private space. Without this awareness the designer would be unable to produce a workable site layout or 'footprint' of buildings and spaces. The built envelope or structure of the building provides a controlled environment within the building. This control can be considered under two categories – control over the natural environment and control over human activity:

- *Environmental control*: this includes the provision of shelter from the elements (the walls and roof of the building), natural lighting (windows) and natural ventilation (windows).
- *Activity control*: this includes (i) physical access to and from the building (front doors, emergency exits), the different requirements for public, private and service access, horizontal and vertical movement within the building; and (ii) visual access, including the requirement for clear visibility from the public realm of certain entrances and for views into or out of buildings.

As previously noted, the art of site planning (creating an urban design brief or masterplan) is to establish information about the proposed pattern of built form and how buildings should address the public realm. There are a range of issues that will affect the positioning of the intended new buildings, relative both to one another and to the existing urban environment. These are discussed briefly here and will be explored in the case studies.

Issues influencing the arrangement of buildings

Orientation

We need to consider orientation both in terms of the site itself and of the individual buildings that we propose. The orientation of the site, and the presence of closely adjoining buildings, will affect which parts are sunny and which are shady, and for how long. This in turn will influence the type and location of buildings we can propose and their positioning and orientation on the site, and possibly also have an effect on the spacing of buildings. The most important consideration is to identify which spaces – both outdoors and indoor (rooms) – require sunlight or daylight, and whether or not this is more critical at certain times of the day. A simple sun path diagram is a useful tool in terms of site layout, assisting us in considering orientation of facades, shadowing, aspect and prospect. Large buildings should be located and oriented so as to avoid overshadowing of public space or residential gardens, so even at an early stage it is necessary to consider the buildings in three dimensions and the appropriate height:width ratios of the open spaces. We must also bear in mind the nature of the locality: some compromises on ideal orientation are inevitable in a dense urban environment but should rarely be necessary in a suburban one.

Topography

A slope or gradient may affect views and the likelihood of buildings being overlooked by others, while providing opportunities to maximise or minimise these as appropriate. A steep slope may also present opportunities for split-level floor plans, which may be useful in separating uses or different types of access. Slope may have an impact on the way we consider orientation, the gradient perhaps resulting in an area receiving more or less sunlight than it would if flat. We must take this into account and look for any possible advantages when positioning the buildings and spaces.

Privacy

While the front door is a boundary between public and private space, the degree of privacy required within buildings varies both between types of buildings and between different rooms within the same building. Some parts of 'private' buildings require full public

access for much of the day (e.g. the trading areas of shops or restaurants), whereas other parts of the same buildings need protection or privacy. The most sensitive building type is the private dwelling, but even here there is variation between the more private bedrooms and living rooms, and kitchens and dining rooms which can accommodate being seen from public areas to a certain extent. Furthermore, privacy can be time-sensitive: a dwelling that is overlooked by an office which is only occupied from 09.00 to 17.00 hours may be more acceptable than being overlooked from another dwelling. Privacy between dwellings is often achieved by means of physical separation, and most UK development plans include standards for distances between dwellings. Separation by distance is, however, a crude way of achieving privacy, and there are other design solutions which may be more appropriate in urban settings. We may also need to consider unbuilt space in terms of privacy. Urban designers traditionally distinguish between public and private space, partly because private outdoor space also requires privacy or seclusion. This may be to protect the users of the space from observation, as in the case of a domestic garden, or it may be because the activities that take place there are unsightly or dangerous and users of the public realm should be protected from them.

Design procedure

The analysis will have given an idea of the movement patterns around the site and of appropriate land or building uses. Together these enable the designer to form a view as to the nature and form of the buildings and spaces desired. Having gained a broad idea of proposed land uses and having collected the necessary data for appropriate building 'footprints', the designer can make a first attempt at site layout. Establishing an organising principle for the location of public space, routes and urban blocks does this. The main structure of a site design is often created by the use of a hierarchy – a central space to which others are related, or a dominant path which links other paths and a sequence of urban events (e.g. gateways or landmark buildings). These are the elements of the urban armature to which the site must be directly or indirectly connected. This structure of routes and urban blocks, which must relate both to the proposed use of the site and to the surrounding context, provides a framework for the individual buildings whose internal circulation becomes an extension of the external spaces.

The case studies in Unit 8 illustrate how a site plan

or an urban design brief can be developed. Although the case studies are described in a simple linear way, it is most often the case that the design process is an iterative one.

Summary

This unit has made the following points:

- The process of formulating an urban design brief or masterplan (site planning) involves reconciling the needs of the client and the urban design requirements of the site.
- The process of site planning does not usurp the role of the architect, but considers the manner in which buildings address the public realm and the proposed pattern of urban form.
- A detailed site analysis needs to be carried out as a continuation of the area analysis.
- Urban designers need to be aware of issues affecting the control-led environment within buildings as well as issues affecting the arrangements of buildings.
- A first attempt at establishing a layout can be made from this analysis and a consideration of an organising principle for the site; however, it should be remembered that the design process necessarily involves a cycle of review and refinement.

Unit 8 Case studies

David Seex and Bill Erickson

Introduction

In this unit a series of case studies are used to illustrate the ways in which an urban designer might take the analysis forward to develop a specific urban design proposal. Each case study is examined in the same way, and will be described in the following sequence:

- a brief description of the background and context with a summary analysis;
- the urban design objectives of the proposer (designer and/or developer);
- the design strategy adopted and its relationship to the urban armature;
- The design of the urban tissue or fabric: blocks and streets, buildings, density and scale;
- a comment on any noteworthy features or economic issues.

Cambourne

Background and design objectives

The Cambourne new village design brief results from an outline planning permission in 1994 and represents levels 16 and 17 of the hierarchy of design guidance (Carmona 1998: table 3.7). It is intended to provide for and create a 'sustainable community' 10 km from Cambridge in eastern England, and to make a contribution towards the demand for new housing in England which is associated with growth in household formation and which cannot all be met on 'brownfield'

sites. Rather than simply build a 'village' of housing that would effectively become a detached suburb of Cambridge, the developers intend to provide a mix of uses, including residential, employment, and service/public land uses all within walking distance of each other and designed to facilitate public transport to other higher-order communities. Another aim of the proposed development is to respect the traditional English settlement pattern and village form and character, and hence to produce buildings that will contribute to this character and conserve 'community life'. Conservation of the landscape, of natural habitats and biodiversity, and of energy were all identified as priorities in the initial brief.

Design strategy

The initial design approach was an investigation of local small urban settlements and their generic forms, as well as a site investigation that paid particular attention to nature conservation. As a new (rather than 'organic growth') settlement, it was important that the new village could be constructed in discrete phases that could operate independently initially and thus a polycentric form was preferred. This led to *linear* and *clustered* types of urban form being examined in more detail (Figure 8.1) and the form finally chosen envisages three residential quarters, each with a 'village centre' (Figure 8.2). There are in effect six parts:

1–3 three residential districts each with their own 'centre';

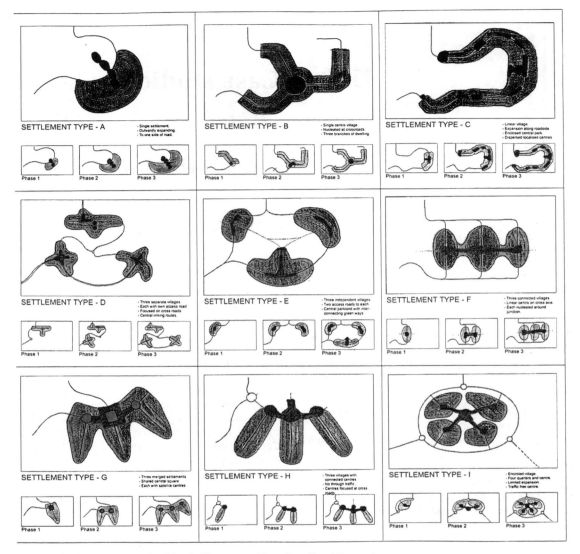

Figure 8.1 Cambourne: study of local village types (Terry Farrell and Partners).

4   a 'spine' which comprises most of the features of the armature;

5   a business district connected to the spine and to the local main road network;

6   a 'green' network of planted and open land providing recreational space and ensuring that the urban forms relate closely to the landscape.

This structure enables the settlement to be phased in that each element can be built as a complete unit.

The *structure* is centred upon a strong *armature* (the spine) which embraces movement, public space, and public/community/service land uses:

- buildings are gathered along the spine road which links the four districts to each other and to the local road network;
- there is a hierarchy of roads that branch from the spine road;
- the density of development is related to the road hierarchy: as you move down the hierarchy and

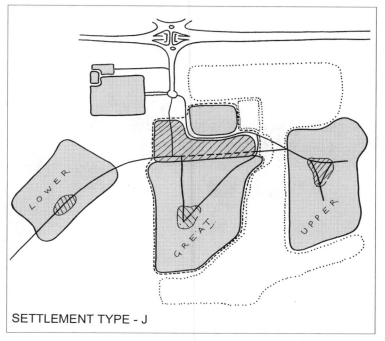

SETTLEMENT TYPE - J

Figure 8.2 Cambourne: generic form for new settlement (Terry Farrell and Partners).

away from the centres, the density of the development decreases;

• each district has its own centre based around a village green so the structure is to some degree fractal.

Figure 8.3 illustrates this structure, with higher densities towards the village centres and an armature that is developed along the spine road.

Formal *public space* is created along the armature between buildings with public functions (e.g. small square in front of shops) and the street itself is given a high degree of enclosure in order to create a sense of

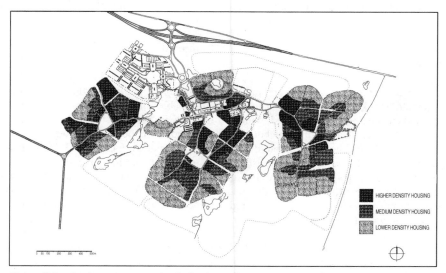

Figure 8.3 Cambourne: masterplan indicating residential densities (Terry Farrell and Partners).

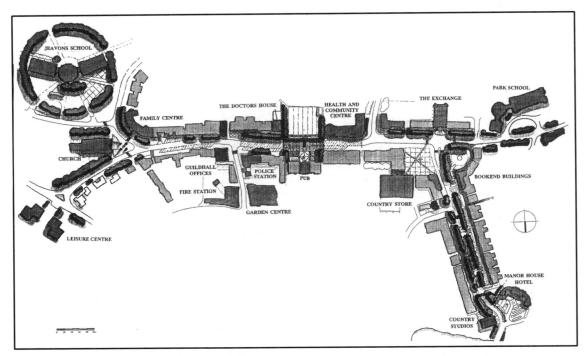

Figure 8.4   Cambourne: the settlement centre forming the core of the armature (Terry Farrell and Partners).

place (Figure 8.4; in order to relate to Figure 8.3, note that this drawing shows north to the bottom). Each residential district has open green space, providing some less formal public space, at its centre (Figure 8.5). There is a clear hierarchy of public spaces, ranging from the formal and enclosed to the less formal, softer and more intimate spaces, which gives the settlement a 'nested' scale.

Design guidance

The form and character of the public spaces and public buildings that create the key part of the armature (effectively the village centre) are indicated with a high degree of detail (Figure 8.6a). Within the housing districts guidance is given on the *form* of buildings, with emphasis placed on the formation of distinct public space including streets (Figure 8.6b). A similar approach is adopted for the office/business district, where guidance proposes buildings are gathered around public spaces and a focal point. However, while guidance is given on form, character is not detailed, leaving freedom in this area to the individual building designer (Figure 8.6c,d). Thus with the exception of the more important armature, guidance is given

on the form of buildings – since this affects issues fundamental to the design strategy such as the nature of public space and energy consumption – but not on character or style. The resultant urban form is likely to be highly legible: key public buildings are used as landmarks along the principle routes and there is a strong hierarchy of paths and of the built development.

Comment

This project is a good example of a design-led development brief, but it nevertheless raises questions about sustainable urban development, and whether new housing in general should be provided through new settlements or located in or adjacent to existing ones. The projected population of 3400 is unlikely to support an effective public transport service and this alone might suggest that this is not the right scale of new settlement. While the design structure follows urban principles, the proposed density range of 5.6 to 13 dwellings per acre (average 10 dwellings per acre) is much more suburban in nature and may make it difficult to ensure the degree of enclosure desired for the main elements of the public realm. Furthermore, car parking is provided for by meeting the current

Figure 8.5 Cambourne: the village green at the centre of the village with local focal buildings (a) the cricket club; (b) the village shop; (c) and (d) the village pub (Terry Farrell and Partners).

standards of the South Cambridgeshire District Council, which may militate against the sustainability objectives of the brief. Clearly there is scope for sustainable development in both existing urban centres and rural locations, and the balance between these is open to debate. To the extent that there do need to be such developments on 'green field sites', this is a good example: it seeks to be 'sustainable' in transport terms and has a positive strategy towards impact upon the natural environment. It is a new rural village based on sound urban design principles.

Crown Street, Glasgow

Background

The Crown Street neighbourhood forms a central part of the Gorbals district of Glasgow, an industrial suburb that grew rapidly between 1860 and the late 1880s. By the mid-1950s the Victorian housing had degenerated to slum conditions, and an almost ruthless but optimistic scheme to sweep away everything associated with this past and bring about a new green

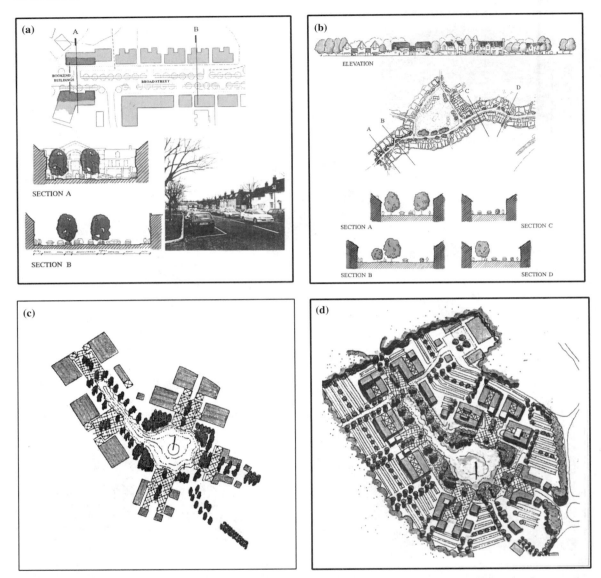

Figure 8.6 Cambourne: (a) builtform of high street; (b) builtform of village spine roads; (c) form of office park; (d) open space network of office park (Terry Farrell and Partners).

city of high-rise living was approved by Glasgow City Council. Five projects of tower blocks and deck-access flats, primarily by noted contemporary architects including Robert Matthew and Basil Spence, had been constructed by 1970. Twelve linked deck-access blocks (originally known by the anodyne title of 'Hutchesontown E') were constructed around the area's main street, Crown Street, in 1968. However, by the early 1980s these flats had become unletable and a programme of demolition began in 1987.

Today only a few of the better tower blocks of the post-war Gorbals remain. In 1990, the City Council established a dedicated team to oversee the redevelopment of what they had renamed the Crown Street area. In addition to managing the development of a new community, the team was faced with the following tasks:

- making the Gorbals a place where people actually desired to live;

- developing a new image for the Gorbals as a popular balanced community;
- assisting in bringing new energy and growth into the Gorbals economy;
- integrating the new development into the social and physical fabric of the existing community;
- providing solutions that will stand the test of time.

The intention was to create what is now termed an 'urban village' centred on a revitalised Crown Street. A national urban design competition was held, and, from four finalists, London architects CZWG were chosen to draw up a masterplan. CZWG's masterplan was provisionally adopted in late 1990 and subjected to extensive negotiation with interested parties including the highway authority (which was not at that time the city council). A revised scheme, based upon but differing in a number of details from the 1990 plan, was adopted in 1994 and is now under construction. The following case study commentary is based upon the 1990 masterplan (Figure 8.7).

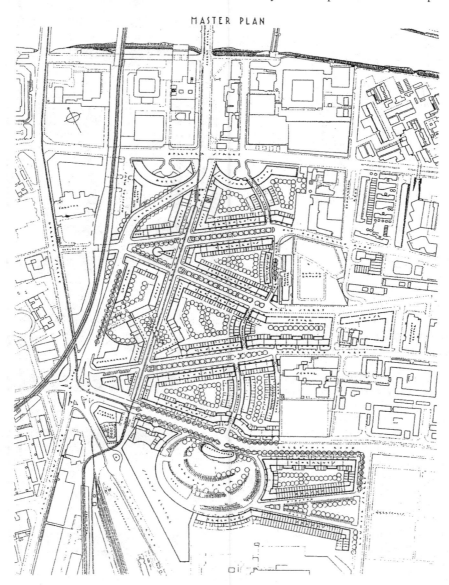

Figure 8.7   Crown Street: the 1990 masterplan showing urban blocks and ground-floor uses (CZWG Architects).

Design objectives

CZWG developed the above five priorities of the project team into a series of urban design objectives which sought to relate those aims to built form. These design objectives were as follows:

- to recreate a neighbourhood with its own clear identity;
- to tie the new district into the surrounding areas;
- to base development upon the traditional Glasgow urban types (streets, blocks and tenements) adapted to the values of today;
- to respect the 'hard edged' character of grids with occasional street terminating vistas found in central Glasgow;
- to add to the character of the city as a whole;
- to integrate existing historic or otherwise significant structures into the new development;
- to create a 'very liveable city' with a mix of 'shared institutions, work, schools, shopping and play' integrated within a residential matrix;
- to reduce the impact of the private car.

These design objectives are articulated in the masterplan through a design strategy based upon urban links, street and block typologies and detailed design guidance (representing levels 17 and 18 in the hierarchy of design guidance identified in Carmona 1998: table 3.7).

Design strategy

The design team adopted a series of strategies based on various components such as streets and urban blocks.

Streets   Traditionally the main traffic thoroughfares of the city were the widest, reducing in width down to the common residential street built to the minimum bye-law standard. The great boulevards were often lined with the grandest terraces; they were seldom shopping streets. Shopping and other local transactions took place on the mid-sized streets, with ordinary residential streets tending to be the narrowest. CZWG propose that present-day conditions require this hierarchy to be reversed (Figure 8.8). Residential streets are proposed as wide boulevards with avenues of trees and space for parking. Shopping streets retain their position in the middle of the hierarchy, and are designed to accommodate more intensive levels of transaction. To this end they include public transport, wide pedestrian zones with space for cafés and other outdoor trading, and room for service vehicles (Figure 8.9).

(a)

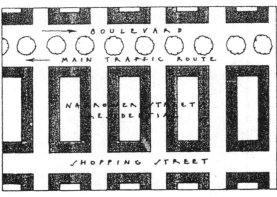

(b)

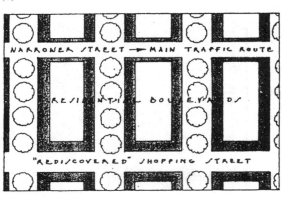

(c)

(d)

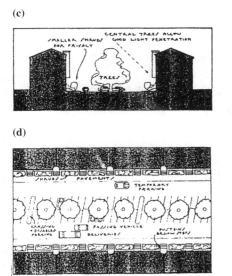

Figure 8.8   Crown Street: the (a) traditional and (b) revised street hierarchies and a typical (c) section and (d) plan of a residential boulevard (CZWG Architects).

Figure 8.9   Crown Street: (a) three-dimensional view and (b) typical section of a shopping street (CZWG Architects).

Public space   To make the city a liveable place, 'the strenuousness of the public realm must be countered by a secure and peaceful private space' (CZWG Masterplan Report 1990). Just as there is a hierarchy of streets, so there is a hierarchy of public space: the high street with its pedestrian-only spaces, public parks, and residential boulevards form distinct components of the public realm, complementing the clearly defined private gardens.

Urban blocks   The design has drawn upon the traditional Glasgow block form of (usually four-storey) tenement buildings arranged around a small courtyard in regular rectangular blocks. In this project the block is seen as a 'doughnut', a continuous ring of building dividing the public street from a large private space in the centre. This space forms a communal private garden with access through the building only, similar to those found in many nineteenth-century developments in west London. A variation of this model provides for the ground-floor or lowest dwellings to have their own private gardens between the building and the communal garden (Figure 8.13). Although the resulting blocks are much larger than those traditionally found in Glasgow, they still create traditional streets with continuous built frontages, and the design guidelines ensure articulation of, for example, street corners.

Links and movements The overall layout of the streets and urban blocks is determined by the need to link the communities of the Gorbals together. The new residential boulevards run east–west, connecting adjacent districts. One principle realigned north–south street crosses and links them as well as three new urban spaces (Figure 8.10a). This street becomes the new shopping street, and a new tram line is proposed, connecting the area to the city centre in the north and the suburbs to the south. Traffic movement is simplified and junctions are collected into one point forming an identifiable nodal place. The modified junction releases space around an historic church that is cur-

rently surrounded by busy, fast roads; this becomes a focus of one of the new spaces. The major north–south through route is moved slightly west to bring it adjacent to an existing railway line (Figure 8.10b) and thus further from the new neighbourhood, bringing the additional benefit of creating better development sites. Pedestrian circulation is concentrated on the new north–south shopping street (Crown Street) and the residential boulevards. Buildings are located to terminate vistas within and from without the project, and to create visual links between the project and the wider city. The longest views are aligned with the principal shopping street (Figure 8.11a).

The armature

The scheme envisages the creation of a vivid urban armature, its principal component being the new north–south shopping street, Crown Street. This is a realignment of the pre-existing Crown Street such that it passes between two retained tower blocks and its

(a)

(b)

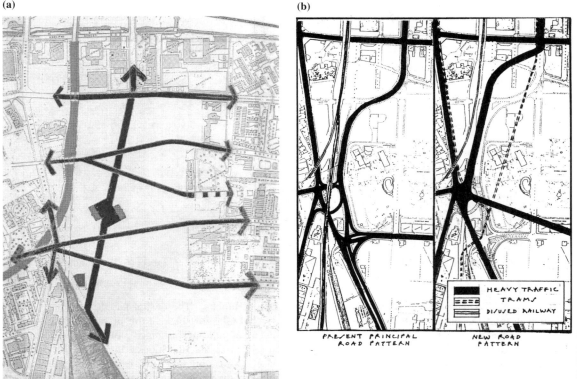

Figure 8.10 Crown Street: (a) the new east–west links and realigned shopping street, and (b) the revised and simplified principle road network (CZWG Architects).

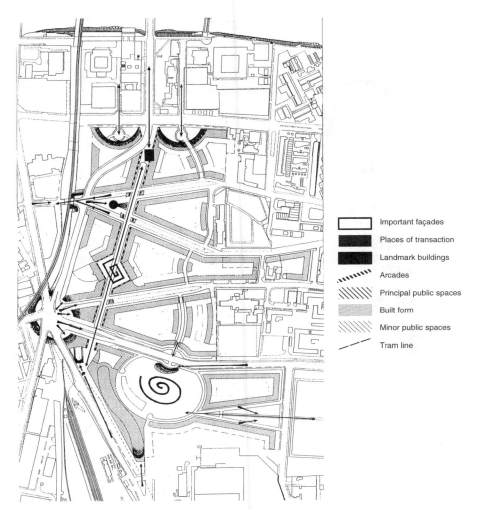

Figure 8.11a Crown Street: the visual structure, showing views, vistas, enclosed spaces and important frontages (CZWG Architects).

southern end terminates at an existing historic church. With fast through traffic concentrated on the adjacent main road, Crown Street is freed for pedestrians, public transport (trams) and local traffic. The street is punctuated by three pedestrian-friendly public spaces which are each associated with dominant buildings and public uses. At the southern end, the (ruined) historic church forms the edge to a new square which is also framed by a library, sports centre and public house. The central space is a more formal square, aligned to accentuate the two existing housing towers retained from the post-war redevelopment. Towards the northern end of the street a clock tower is envisaged, taking its cue from similar towers in the city centre. This forms a distinctive local landmark and creates an entrance feature when entering

the area from the city. Along the street are ranged a number of commercial and retail activities, especially at ground-floor level. Arcades extend the public realm and provide shelter for pedestrians. Crown Street accommodates the majority of public activities, and creates a spine that links all the other elements of the scheme. This has the effect of concentrating life and activity along this armature (Figure 8.11b).

Design guidance

Detailed design guidelines are provided in the form of a code which deals with, in particular, minimum and maximum building height and depth, building lines,

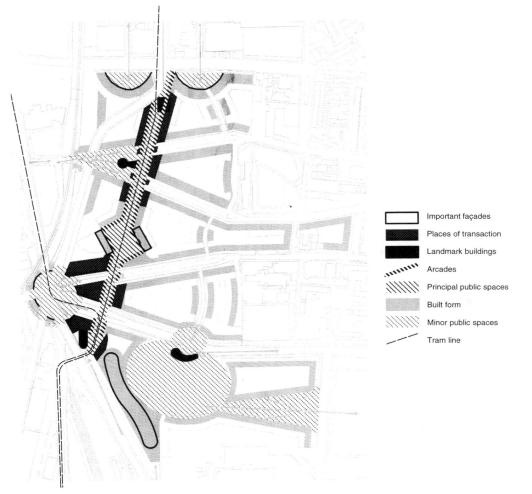

Important façades

Places of transaction

Landmark buildings

Arcades

Principal public spaces

Built form

Minor public spaces

Tram line

Figure 8.11b   Crown Street: the visual structure, showing the urban armature (CZWG Architects and Bill Erickson).

and articulation of elevations and corners. Schematic plans and sections are provided for different types of urban block (Figure 8.12). Traditionally, buildings in Glasgow are built primarily of one material, often local sandstone; thus buildings and often whole streets have one predominant colour. There are very few stone buildings left in the Gorbals, so CZWG propose that bricks are utilised in two limited colour palettes.

Comment

This is a rigorous and comprehensive masterplan document which deals with both large-scale strategic issues and detailed guidance on built form and uses. It is an interesting example of a masterplan that extends

its remit to also provide urban design briefing for urban blocks or development parcels. However, it was perhaps in some ways too ambitious, or maybe simply ahead of its time – with not even the coordinating organisation of the Crown Street Regeneration Project able to deliver the more complicated elements. Upon implementation those of its design strengths which relied upon radical interventions, such as the realignment of Crown Street and the major through road and associated junction improvements, have had to be abandoned. Both the main north–south through road and Crown Street have retained their 1960s routes and accordingly some of the urban blocks and public spaces have been adjusted in size and location. Crown Street has lost its central formal square and terminating historic church, which remains marooned in a

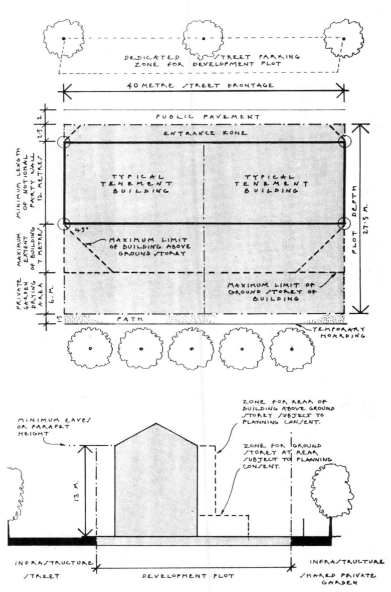

Figure 8.12 Crown Street: typical example of design guidance, showing plot sizes, building lines and heights, and private space (CZWG Architects).

traffic island. It has also lost some of its urban sense of enclosure, with a considerable length of frontage now occupied by a low supermarket building and car park for the retained housing tower (Figure 8.13). However, the original design objectives have been largely met: there is a new district with a distinct centre and its own identity, new building types and residential boulevards respect and evolve from the Glasgow tradition, there are good links to adjacent neighbourhoods, and, critically, there is a concentration on mixed uses within a quality public realm. CZWG suggest that a high-quality built environment demands more stringent control than is provided by the British planning system, and in this case the existence of the Crown Street Regeneration Project provided a mechanism that has helped to achieve such detail control. The institutional arrangements in the Gorbals also enabled the architects to establish development

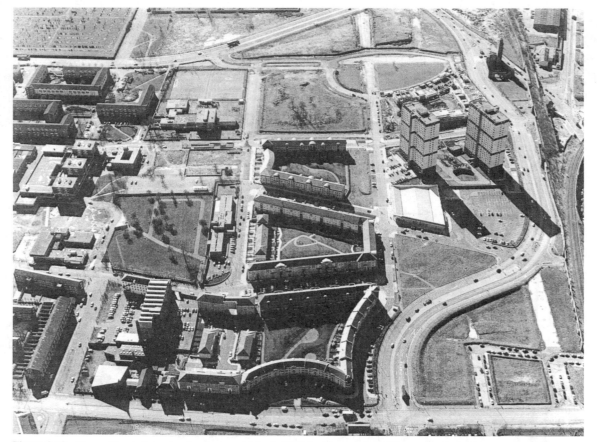

Figure 8.13   Crown Street: the redevelopment as at March 1998, looking south and illustrating the revisions to the 1990 masterplan. Crown Street has lost its entrance clock tower and does not pass between the tower blocks to terminate at the church tower (top right). The residential boulevards and large urban blocks with small individual private gardens and communal private space can be seen to the east (left) of Crown Street (Guthrie Photography, Glasgow).

parcels smaller than whole urban blocks while ensuring continuity of the design ethos and straightforward establishment of the private communal gardens. Other masterplans of this nature may need to incorporate proposals for the organisation of such detail control over design and implementation.

North Street, Clapham

Background

This site in inner south London was occupied by a part one-storey, part two-storey factory building dating from the early years of the twentieth century. It had been empty for several years before being acquired by a developer who saw it as a site suitable for residential development. However, the local plan-

ning authority, anxious to retain as much employment within the immediate area as possible, had designated the site for industrial or commercial use in the local plan. The developer commissioned an urban design study in order to achieve an amount and form of development that met his commercial objectives and secured a detailed planning permission, while also satisfying the objectives of the local planning authority. This type of site planning or masterplan represents level 18 in the hierarchy described by Carmona (1998: table 3.7) as it provides a 'three-dimensional vision of future form (allowing some architectural freedom within limits of defined form)' which maximises certainty for a developer while retaining a degree of architectural flexibility. It is thus ideally suited to a developer client who will have specific prerequisites in terms of floorspace and viability, and who will demand the degree of certainty that can be provided. In this case the site and the design (with planning permission) was subsequently sold on to another developer whose own architects made changes to the details of the project which nevertheless retained its underlying urban design principles.

Creating an urban design proposal or masterplan requires a site/area analysis and an early decision as to the most appropriate urban design approach to adopt, in order to make an initial decision on the organisation of buildings and spaces. In this case historical and morphological analysis traced the development of the area, which comprises many narrow-fronted terraced houses interspersed with a small number of larger plots. At the end of the nineteenth century the North Street frontage of this site comprised narrow three-storey houses with shops occupying the ground floors, while the Fitzwilliam Road frontage comprised grander houses with large gardens. The industrial development came about following road widening in the 1890s, which gave access to these large gardens. The present 1930's factory is seen as a long single-storey elevation closing a vista beyond an attractive Victorian school building when viewed northwards from Clapham Common, Old Town and North Street, which together create the local armature. The analysis identified the inappropriateness of the factory building in townscape terms as well as in terms of land use and morphology. North Street, which forms the end of the armature of Clapham Old Town, is lined with two- and three-storey buildings with commercial uses at ground floor; the single-storey blank wall of the factory creating a damaging break in this continuity (Figure 8.14).

Design objectives

The analysis suggested that a morphological approach should form the basis of initial design decisions. Design objectives flowed from this decision:

- to recreate a built and active frontage to North Street in order to reinforce the local armature;
- to introduce more appropriate land uses and to increase permeability;
- to create an appropriately scaled built frontage to the Fitzwilliam Road frontage; and
- to form an appropriate visual termination to the vista from the south.

The developer brought his own objectives to the brief:

- the commercial requirement to create 16 to 20 new residential units; and
- a desire to build utilising the architectural language of the area.

The design objectives are set out schematically in Figure 8.15 which shows the recreation of the rhythm of tall narrow houses, commercial/active frontages to North Street and Fitzwilliam Road, a new semi-public space with access from both main streets, and housing tucked into the sheltered rear of the site.

Design strategy

The design strategy (Figure 8.15) adopted the morphological approach indicated by the design objectives. The factory was clearly an unfortunate intervention that preceded planning control, and the opportunity was taken to repair the urban grain and townscape in this prominent location. Although a large site, it was possible to recreate the traditional urban form and grain by rebuilding the two- and three-storey frontage as a series of individual units, each with a 6 m frontage (which could be combined to create larger commercial units), thus providing a traditional vertical rhythm while maintaining commercial viability.

At this stage an alternative scheme which explored the potential of amalgamating the site with the adjoining cottages at Rectory Gardens was drafted in outline

Figure 8.14   North Street, Clapham: site context (David Seex and Andrew White).

(a)

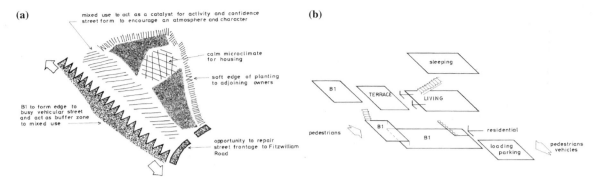

(b)

Figure 8.15   North Street, Clapham: design strategy. (a) Concept diagram; (b) how the mixed-use units work (David Seex and Andrew White).

(Figure 8.16). The cottages are all in one ownership and are in poor condition, with many unoccupied. Amalgamating the factory and cottage sites and the demolition of one cottage could both improve permeability and create the opportunity to provide several of the cottages with some private open space. The developer actively pursued this option but was ultimately unable to acquire the cottage site. This does, however, illustrate the importance of giving consideration to site boundaries when preparing urban design schemes.

The change in level across the site from pavement level to site level was utilised to achieve a floor to ceiling height suitable for today's commercial users and which met the local planning authority's requirement that the units could accommodate industrial equipment where needed. The two-storey commercial section fronting North Street becomes a buffer zone to protect residential buildings from the noise and bustle of North Street. These aspects of the design solution are illustrated in Figure 8.17. The potential back–front conflict created by utilising the full depth of the site was resolved by creating a new street, which also improves permeability and provides the new semi-public space. The proximity of the existing dwellings to the north and east of the site meant that planning standards had to be treated flexibly and with ingenuity. Sketch perspectives illustrate the form and massing of the proposed buildings and give some indication of architectural style (Figure 8.18). In fact, the detail design was worked up as this was a commissioned urban design proposal – a site planning exercise.

Comment

Neither a single-use commercial development as initially favoured by the local planning authority, nor an entirely residential scheme as preferred by the developer could have created the public space, sense of place or sympathetic urban forms of this proposal. Built to the current density standards of the local planning authority, neither would have been dense enough or high enough to repair the townscape. By combining the two uses and creatively interpreting the planning standards, the designer has managed to bring to the site the maximum number of houses and also add commercial space such that the client has got more from the site than originally hoped for (albeit in a different form). This additional financial return should enable a high quality of architecture and detailing of the public realm to be achieved as benefits over and above those of the urban form. Unfortunately, lengthy delays in securing the planning approvals led to this small developer selling the site on and some of these benefits may now be more difficult to achieve.

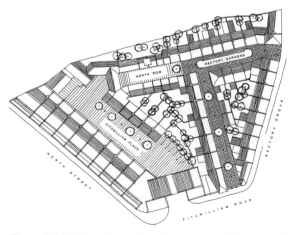

Figure 8.16   North Street, Clapham: design solution – roof plan (David Seex and Andrew White).

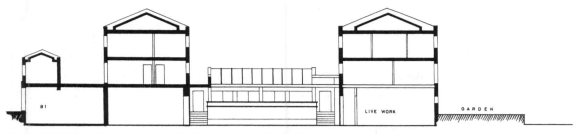

Figure 8.17   Fitzwilliam Place – sectional elevation (Andrew White).

Kowloon Station

Background

Kowloon Station is part of a new rail link that will connect Hong Kong Central to the new airport at Chep Lap Lok. The station development forms the core of a dense new city district to be developed on reclaimed land and has been masterplanned by Terry Farrell and Partners.

The brief required a complex mix of uses – office, retail, hotel and residential accommodation, and public space – to be developed in phases by different developers.

Design strategy

The design strategy is to create a central concourse or square that links the two main movement systems (rail

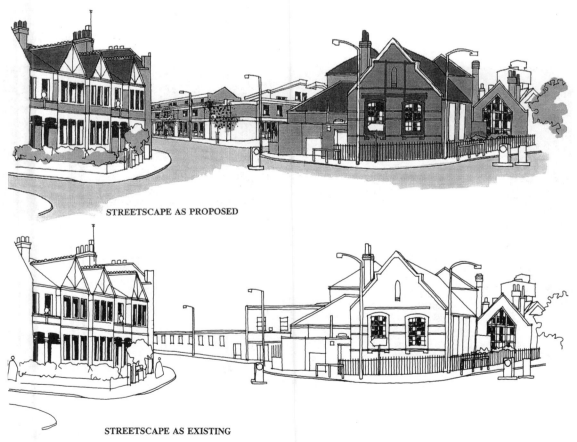

Figure 8.18   North Street, Clapham: design solution – streetscape (David Seex and Andrew White).

and pedestrian) to each other and to the principle buildings, with this square itself linked to the rest of the city through pedestrian bridges (Figure 8.19). This square and its connected public spaces and routes can be considered to be the armature of the project. The Station Square forms the core of the scheme, which is layered horizontally but designed to be constructed as a series of nine separate vertical parcels in phases. The need for these phases (which, because of the scale of the project, will be completed over an extended period) to integrate fully in terms of both pedestrian movement and land use at a number of horizontal levels results in design guidance that is almost architectural in its detail. The urban space concept takes as its starting point the internal malls, which are common on Hong Kong, and these are reinterpreted as linked squares and public spaces. These spaces are integrated with the pedestrian routes for the associated developments and each given a different identity.

Comment

The Station Square forms a pedestrian concourse at a series of higher levels and is connected to a number of smaller spaces by pedestrian routes. It is an interesting example of a three-dimensional armature which has, however, proved difficult to link to the wider armature of the city because of the large-scale roads surrounding the site. It is possible to read this project as 'big architecture'; however, the mixed-use nature of the project and the use of urban design principles means that we can consider this as an urban design rather than an architectural composition.

Clerkenwell

Our last case study will use two of the generative techniques: *axes* are set up by creating links, and the development is hung around new public *space*, i.e. use of the street and the square – the two most fundamental elements of urban form.

Background

The analysis outlined in Unit 6 shows us that the area is divided by major paths into quarters which not only have different morphologies but also different land

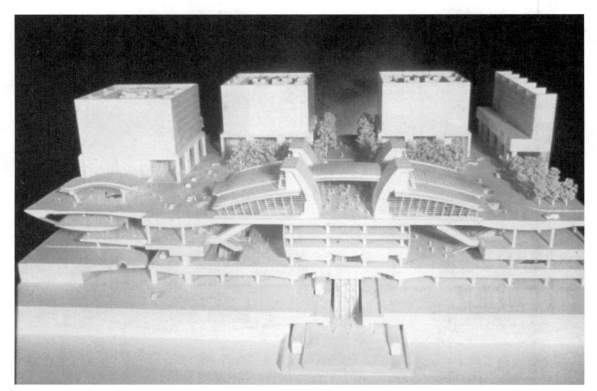

Figure 8.19   Kowloon Station: model (Terry Farrell and Partners; photographer Nigel Young).

uses. The brewery site restricts permeability to the east of St John Street yet it is the key to linking the 'grid' area to St John Street. The grid suggests a possible layout of streets and blocks as well as ideas for building typologies for the site. There is a potential visual and/or physical link to Clerkenwell Green. The buildings fronting Compton Street have residential upper floors and this will constrain land use and building height at the northern end of the site.

Design strategy

The strategy drawing and concept sketch (Figure 8.20) illustrate the broad principles of development in a purely diagrammatic way. There is a strong pedestrian link to Clerkenwell Green, and the small square reinforces this link visually, while perhaps demanding a landmark of some form. These elements together form the link to the urban armature of St John Street, the 'bud' referred to in Unit 3. The grid provides the basis of the urban structure that can enhance permeability throughout the area. An appropriate mix of uses would enable the site to seamlessly link the residential area to the north with the commercial area to the south, and this should have been specified at this stage.

The urban space and building use rationale drawings (Figures 8.21 and 8.22) show how the diagrammatic concept is translated into an arrangement of buildings and spaces. The locations of the buildings are shown, as are their footprints, in a very generalised way. At this stage the designer has a broad idea of their uses and so the width and depth of the proposed buildings can be illustrated diagrammatically. The visual and physical connection to Clerkenwell Green is established and the new open space located at its eastern end in order to emphasise the importance of both elements. These will form the link from the 'grid' to St John Street which forms part of the urban armature of Clerkenwell, and are thus illustrated in more detail on the space rationale and scheme drawings than the new north–south route is. The building on the north side of the square is shown with a prominent corner element to signify its role as a landmark. The building-use rationale drawing elaborates on this by identifying the fronts and backs of buildings and relating these to the public and private space. The scheme plan drawing (Figure 8.23) shows realistic building footprints and the formal qualities of the public realm, while the axonometric drawing (Figure 8.24) also indicates the form and massing of the proposed buildings.

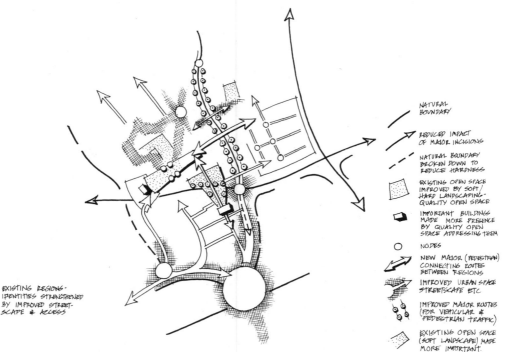

Figure 8.20 Clerkenwell: strategy (Martin Evans).

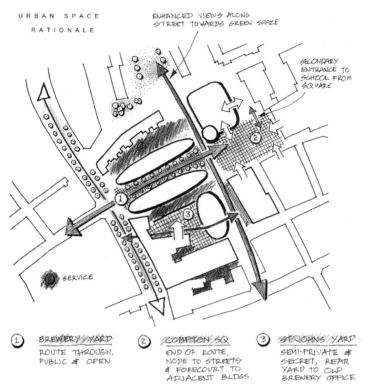

URBAN SPACE
RATIONALE

ENHANCED VIEWS ALONG
STREET TOWARDS GREEN SPACE

SECONDARY
ENTRANCE TO
SCHOOL FROM
SQUARE

SERVICE

KEY

QUALITY HARD-
LAND-SCAPING
RELATED TO
ADJACENT BLDGS.

GREENED UP ROUTES
TO BE PEDESTRIAN
FRIENDLY &
GENERALLY SOFTER

SOFT-LANDSCAPED
AREAS ACKNOWLED.
BY NEW ROUTES
& BUILDINGS.

OPEN SPACES SHOULD HAVE
USES/FUNCTIONS & RELATE
TO ADJACENT BUILDINGS

① BREWERY YARD
ROUTE THROUGH,
PUBLIC & OPEN

② COMPTON SQ.
END OF ROUTE,
NODE TO STREETS
& FORECOURT TO
ADJACENT BLDGS.

③ ST JOHNS YARD
SEMI-PRIVATE &
SECRET, REAR
YARD TO OLD
BREWERY OFFICE

CONCEPT SKETCH –
GRID-IRON NETWORK
RIENFORCED

Figure 8.21   Clerkenwell: urban space rationale (Martin Evans).

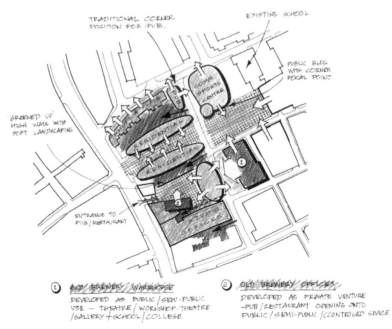

TRADITIONAL CORNER
POSITION FOR PUB.

EXISTING SCHOOL

PUBLIC BLDG
WITH CORNER
FOCAL POINT

GREENED UP
HIGH WALL WITH
SOFT LANDSCAPING

ENTRANCE TO
PUB/RESTAURANT

KEY

GOOD QUALITY EXSTG.
BUILDING WORTH
KEEPING & PUT TO
NEW USE

SITES FOR NEW BLD.
TO FORM EDGES TO
STREETS, SQUARES
& SPACES

FRONTAGE TO BLDGS

SERVICE ROUTES/ZONES
(REAR OF BUILDINGS)

NEW OPEN SPACES
PUBLIC & PRIVATE

SECOND LEAGUE
RENOVATED BUILDINGS

ENCOURAGE BUILDING USES
THAT ARE BASED ON LOCAL
DEMAND & ARE COMPLEMENTARY
TO EXISTING BUSINESSES
& ECONOMY

REFURBISH & USE EXSTG.
QUALITY BLDGS GIVING
NEW USES ASSOCIATED
WITH AREA

① OLD BREWERY WAREHOUSE
DEVELOPED AS PUBLIC/SEMI-PUBLIC
USE – THEATRE/WORKSHOP-THEATRE
/GALLERY + SCHOOL/COLLEGE

② OLD BREWERY OFFICES
DEVELOPED AS PRIVATE VENTURE
–PUB/RESTAURANT OPENING ONTO
PUBLIC/SEMI-PUBLIC/CONTROLLED SPACE

Figure 8.22   Clerkenwell: building use rationale (Martin Evans).

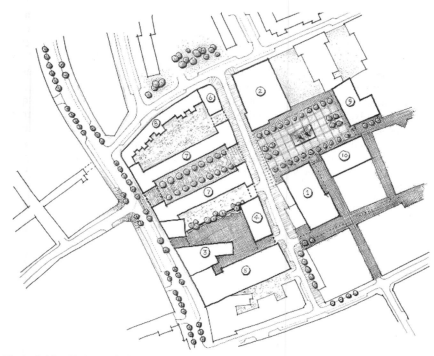

THE SCHEME

SITE PLAN

① CONVERT BREWERY WAREHOUSE INTO "SCHOOL OF PHOTOGRAPHY & FILM" WITH PUBLIC GALLERIES & LETTABLE STUDIO SPACE. THIS UTILISED THE LARGE SPACES

② COMMUNITY/SPORTS CENTRE BENEFITING ADJACENT SCHOOL & LOCAL COMMUNITIES

③ PRIVATELY OWNED PUB AND RESTAURANT "ST. JOHN OF JERUSALEM" OPENING ONTO SEMI-PUBLIC-PRIVATE SPACE

④ OFFICE & STUDIO SPACE ABOVE SHOPS

⑤ OFFICE & STUDIO SPACE

⑥ PUBLIC HOUSE

⑦ TOWN HOUSES EITHER SIDE OF "BREWERY YARD"

⑧ EXISTING SHOPS WITH FLATS ABOVE TO SERVE LOCAL COMMUNITY

⑨ EXISTING 1960's BLOCK RENOVATED AS STUDIO SPACE (PERHAPS RELATED TO THE SCHOOL) WITH SMALL SHOPS & CAFE ON GROUND FLOOR OPENING ONTO SQUARE

⑩ EXISTING STUDIO/OFFICE BUILDING WITH 'FACE LIFT' TO ADDRESS SQUARE

GENERALLY THE ROADS ARE COBBLED TO LOSE KERBS & AWKWARD HARD-LANDSCAPING

Figure 8.23   Clerkenwell: the scheme (Martin Evans).

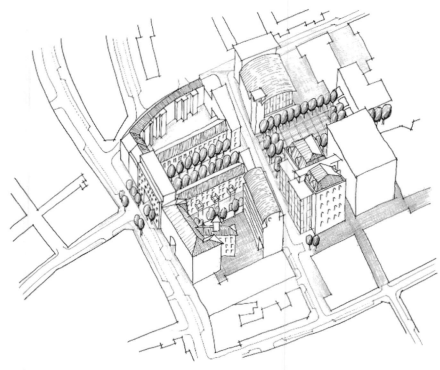

THE SCHEME

AXONOMETRIC

RESIDENTIAL BUILDINGS ON BREWERY YARD ARE 3-4 STOREYS WITH LIVING ACCOMMODATION ON 1ST FLOOR

OFFICE/STUDIO BUILDING OPPOSITE SCHOOL OF PHOTOGRAPHY IS HIGHER TO BUILD UP HIERARCHY TO THE SCHOOL

FLATS AT THE WEST END OF BREWERY YARD ARE HIGH TO CONTINUE GRAIN OF ST JOHNS STREET

THE COMMUNITY/SPORTS CENTRE IS GIVEN CORNER ELEMENT WITH CLOCK TOWER TO GIVE IMPORTANCE TO SQ.

MAJOR SPACES ARE 'GREENED' UP TO CONTINUE FLOW OF NEW FORMED ROUTES - INCLUDING ENTRANCE TO BREWERY YARD OFF ST. JOHNS STREET.

Figure 8.24   Clerkenwell: the axonometric scheme (Martin Evans).

Comment

Together the rationale drawings form the urban design brief for the site. They give a clear indication of urban structure and built form as well as recommending land uses. However, the brief is not prescriptive and does not actually design any of the buildings. There are two areas where this brief does not fully resolve the issues, perhaps because it is a student project and possibly because it has not had client or local planning authority input and thus does not fully recognise commercial realities. There are back–front conflicts where the new public space in front of the old brewery offices over-looks the rear of the new residential block to the north. This problem has been identified, but the solution of a high wall screened by landscaping is not satisfactory. It provides inadequate active frontage to the open space while also overshadowing the southerly aspect of the residences. The second unresolved issue is the amount of new public space. In addition to the square mentioned above, there is a major new square to the north-east which alone is as large as Clerkenwell Green. There is neither such a shortage of open space in the wider area, nor enough development proposed on this site, to justify the amount of open space proposed.

BLOCK IV THE PROJECT IN PRACTICE

Unit 9 Urban design and development economics

Chris Marsh

Introduction

On the face of it, good design should equate with better returns and profit in the property investment and development process. It would appear reasonable to assume that a well-designed building in an attractive urban design context would attract an occupier of higher standing (known as covenant), prepared to pay a higher rent. That in turn would underpin the developers profit and thus make the building more desirable to the long-term investor in property who seeks low risk and a secure income stream.

Conversely, it would seem equally obvious that a poorly designed building in a bland and characterless urban context, would not be selected by a quality tenant and that this would adversely affect the building's value and the attention of investors. Indeed, it would appear logical at the outset that good design leads to viable, profitable property developments and that bad design will not occur because such schemes would never achieve a satisfactory return. In other words, new development activity meeting occupier requirements and well-designed buildings in attractive surroundings should be complementary characteristics in a successful property market.

Unfortunately, in reality, the built environment cannot be analysed in such a simplistic manner. Existing buildings and their surroundings do vary hugely in their design qualities and while it would be nonsense to suggest that a poorly designed building was the result of a deliberate act, the relationship between design quality and financial viability in new and existing developments is clearly complicated.

This unit examines this relationship in the following ways:

- by explaining the attitudes and perspectives of property investors and developers;
- by focusing on the property investment and development process, from which successful and less successful development projects emerge, while others fail to be implemented;
- by considering the role and status of 'good design' in this process and its effect on development outcomes; and
- by using case study material to demonstrate the relationship at work.

The underlying theme of the unit is that although historically the property industry rarely recognised the merits of good design and well-planned environments, just as the particular functional requirements of occupiers were largely ignored, attitudes have changed. Indeed, one beneficial result of the recession in the property market in the early 1990s, the worst for over twenty years, has been that occupiers have had much greater choice of buildings at far lower rents. Functional and aesthetic qualities have thus become more important determinants of tenant choice, and as a result, developers and investors have become much more discriminating and increasingly acknowledge good design in a building and an attractive environment as marketable characteristics.

This does not of course imply consensus in defining what is 'good design' and what is an 'attractive environment'. Neither does it prevent broad agreement on what are useful basic building design principles, identified by English Partnerships, the government-backed regeneration agency, as follows:

- a building should be appropriate to its place and harmonious in its composition;
- buildings should not ignore their neighbours;
- buildings must be built to last according to their use;
- buildings do not end at their perimeter; the public realm and landscape treatment are just as important for their success;
- building design must consider the needs of the users and especially the needs of persons with disabilities;
- buildings should be safe, environmentally friendly and energy efficient;
- respect for tradition should not rule out innovation and bold statements;
- building design and construction should avoid short-term savings that would obscure the benefits of good design and fitness for purpose; and
- the style of buildings and refurbishments should complement the assets and facilities they house (English Partnerships 1996).

Such building design principles, together with broader urban design objectives, are laudable but fail to explain why many buildings which obviously fall short of these qualities remain occupied and presumably therefore viable. To gain greater insight, it is important to understand the attitudes and perspectives of the various actors involved in the property industry.

The structure of the property market

The property 'industry' is unique in that it is made up of three distinct but closely related groups who approach property from different perspectives: occupiers, investors and developers.

Occupiers

While the majority of residential properties in the UK are owner-occupied, the majority of commercial premises are rented. To occupiers of the latter, therefore, property is one of many factors of production and their requirement for space will be determined by the level of production of goods or services being planned. Occupier demand is clearly linked to the broader economic cycle. An obvious example is that demand for retail property will always respond first to economic uplift and an increase in consumer spending and vice versa during recessions. The occupier market, levels of rent and vacancy rates are a direct consequence of the state of the economy. However, occupier requirements will also evolve over time for a variety of other financial, functional and technological reasons – changes that will often produce quite different buildings and urban design impacts.

Investors

To investors such as pension funds and insurance companies – the so-called institutional investors – who traditionally have been the principal owner landlords of commercial property, property is one element in a portfolio of investments. At any one time, the attractiveness of property in terms of the likelihood of rental and/or capital growth, the two determinants of investor interest, have to be compared with the prospects for alternative investments such as equities and gilts. The investors' attitude to property will therefore be much influenced by the state of the financial markets but also by the level of risk that they are prepared to accept. Investors are generally cautious, especially those who suffered during the recession, but the recovery that began in 1997 has prompted renewed investor activity in the sector (at least for the moment). However, the more general pattern over the last twenty years has been a steady shift by fund managers away from property. Twenty years ago, property on average made up approximately 20% of a typical portfolio. Today, average exposure is about 6%. This change is being driven by demographics, in particular the increasing number of elderly people. Their pension income requires funds to be more liquid, a characteristic that property does not always have, especially during economic downturns. Together these factors have encouraged institutional investors to be more discriminating when acquiring property and generally they will concentrate on prime property only – prime referring to buildings in the 'best' location, and housing the 'best' tenant occupier. Quality and flexibility of design will also be a determinant of prime property, which will be further affected by the characteristics of the building's surroundings. Good urban design is one of many factors that will have a direct impact on value, not least in attracting the attention of funds and tenants.

In addition to institutional investors, there are many other investors and investment vehicles which focus to some degree on property as an asset. Most important are property investment companies, who are responsible to their shareholders, and who acquire and manage property with a view to maximising the rental

Argent and Pru back design push
Estates Gazette, 2/11/96

Argent – developer of the £300 million
Brindleyplace in Birmingham – and Prudential, the
investment fund, have thrown their weight behind a
drive to produce top quality design in urban development.

Speaking at the launch of a joint RICS/DoE
document, Quality of Urban Design, Brindleyplace
director Alan Chatham said that urban designers
and masterplanners should be appointed on large
schemes 'from day one'. Masterplans were crucial
to create a sense of place and also helped to gain the
attention of funders and potential tenants, said
Chatham. 'This assisted us in clinching a 11,148 m²
(120,000 ft²) per-let to BT in the early days of the
scheme – otherwise, all we had to show them was a
muddy site'.

and capital value of their portfolio. This will often
involve 'active management'. For example, a run-
down shopping centre may have the potential to be
physically up-graded which then attracts better occupiers who achieve a higher turnover. This in turn is
reflected in rental growth, which increases the value of
the centre as an investment. In this situation, *good
building and urban design* will be a central contributory factor in generating value.

It is also important to recognise that many investment funds are global in their pursuit of rental and capital growth. Foreign investors are often attracted to UK
property for example, where the structure of long
leases provides particular certainty. This influx of
foreign funds, stemming perhaps from a more open-
minded investment culture, has also had an important
effect on attitudes towards mixed-use development, a
central plank of current urban design thinking, and this
will be addressed specifically later in this unit.

Developers

The third group in the industry are the property developers and construction companies, the producers of
buildings who are driven by their assessment of likely
profits, when comparing the value of completed buildings with the costs of construction. That calculation is
obviously very vulnerable to change; for example,
what level of rent will actually be achieved on completion of a building that might take two years to finish.
For many development companies beginning projects

in the late 1980s at the height of the market, only to
find that the market had collapsed by the early 1990s,
failure to predict market fluctuations was terminal.
From the developer's perspective, the ideal scenario is
obvious:

- In a strong market with rents and values rising,
identify a development opportunity and gain an
appropriate planning permission (quality in urban
design often being one important requirement of the
local planning authority).
- Identify an occupier with a top credit rating, i.e. a
highly regarded and financially well-founded
tenant, and pre-let the completed building to that
tenant. The building is therefore let before construction starts.
- Sell the completed development to an institutional
or other investor before construction starts – known
as forward funding.

While this approach is not risk-free (costs may
increase unexpectedly, for instance), risks are clearly
minimised. Unfortunately, pre-let, forward-funded
schemes are the exception rather than the rule, and so
the developer will invariably have to shoulder much of
the risk associated with development. In the boom of
the 1980s, many did accept that risk and went ahead
and built speculatively. In contrast, during the trau-
matic market conditions of the 1990s, almost every
scheme that went ahead was pre-let. The key is clearly
timing in what is a three-stage development cycle, as
summarised in Figure 9.1.

- In stage 1 (approximately 08.00 on the 'clock'), the
market begins to improve after the last recession
and the high level of vacant space starts to decline

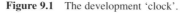

Figure 9.1 The development 'clock'.

as occupiers expand their activities. Levels of vacancy, however, will prevent rents from rising (supply still exceeds demand) and this will deter new development.

- In stage 2 (approaching 12.00), as the economy expands and vacant space declines, potential occupiers are unable to find appropriate property in a market characterised by shortages. Rents will rise and new development starts will be prompted. In the period up to completion, rents rise sharply, maximising profits to the developer and perhaps facilitating an early sale to an investor. In the meantime, many other schemes commence.
- In stage 3, the market, together with the economy, has peaked and started to decline. Potential occupiers cut back production and therefore space demands and rents fall. New development started in the later part of stage 2 continues to come on-stream and increases the level of vacancy, while other schemes are scaled down or abandoned. Economic and market recession ensues.

At the time of writing (autumn 2000), the commercial property market is between 11.00 and 1.00, approaching or just past a peak, although on this clock, time is not a constant and may vary in different locations.

Although occupiers, developers and investors approach property from different perspectives, there is clearly a close interrelationship between them. Indeed, the three functions can overlap. For example, the major corporate occupier with extensive property assets may manage that portfolio not only in terms of efficient production of goods or services but also in terms of property development potential. The development company which traditionally looked to sell on completed and let schemes as soon as possible in order to finance the next scheme, may retain completed buildings in order to benefit from rental and capital growth. Similarly, some major investors have acquired development companies too in order to carry out both functions. The property cycle, while a response to broader economic conditions, is largely an assessment of future prospects by these players although others will also influence outcomes, most obviously banks as lenders to the property industry.

Prime and secondary markets

The property market is made up of a multiplicity of property types, each with its own characteristics and each subject to its own market cycle. Indeed, although different property sectors (residential, retail, business space, leisure, etc.) broadly follow a similar cycle, the timing of those cycles may vary and this can produce interesting effects. For example, in the mid-1990s in London, when much of the commercial office market was still in recession and vacancy rates were high, the residential market was already recovering. This prompted a spate of office conversions to residential use, a market reaction that has helped increase the resident population of central urban areas and encouraged a greater mix of uses.

Clearly, some properties will be more attractive than others, and investors rank a building's attraction by classifying it as prime, secondary or tertiary. Prime property is considered the 'best' from the investors' perspective and thus the most sought after and highly valued. Prime property will have particular qualities:

- It is located in the best possible position to serve its function. For example, prime retail property in Oxford Street, London, clusters around the major department stores and underground stations where pedestrian flow is concentrated. Shops in those positions will achieve the highest rents.
- The structure of the building and the facilities provided in and around it will best meet the occupiers' requirements. What the tenants' requirements are will of course change over time. For example, many office buildings constructed in the 1960s and early 1970s were based on a floorplate that was 40 feet (12 m) deep, divided by a central corridor, which allowed small offices on either side, each of which received sufficient natural light. In the 1980s and 1990s, many office users, especially in sectors such as banking and financial services, required very much larger floorplates, uninterrupted by partitions, and where high technology and climate control facilities were built into the structure. Obviously, what was regarded as a prime office building in 1970 may today be viewed as secondary or even tertiary.
- Design qualities are also a fundamental consideration, not only in terms of functional efficiency but also in terms of building image, both of which will influence occupier and thus investor interest. Increasingly, occupiers of buildings are concerned that their corporate image is reflected in their building's image. For example, in the economic and property boom of the 1980s, some companies, especially in financial and legal services, projected their business success to existing and potential clients as well as the public at large, by occupying extravagant and expensive properties – so-called 'glitz' buildings. During the recession of the early 1990s and subsequently, in a more moderate econ-

omic climate, the glitz building lost favour, corporate occupiers preferring a stylish but more prudent building image, which conveyed to their customers value for money for services provided. Design and value clearly correlated.

The concept of prime and secondary property is complicated further as follows:

- Apparently identical buildings will always vary slightly in investment terms with regard to location, structure or covenant. Neighbouring shops, for example, will not necessarily have the same prospects and value, quality of design being one explanation.
- Prime locations may evolve, occasionally significantly. The major town centre retail redevelopment for instance, a common occurrence in many towns in post-war Britain and abroad, may change consumers' shopping habits. Indeed, the prime attractors in the high street – department stores and the major multiples – may relocate into the new centre and totally change the pattern of prime property as a result. Again, design is a contributory force.
- Ultimately, however, it is the role of building refurbishment and urban design in regenerating a declining location that underlines their relationship with property value. The run-down 1950s industrial estate with a high level of vacancy provides an obvious example, where active management on the part of the acquiring fund identifies an opportunity, implements a programme of building and environmental improvements, and changes the estate's appearance and image to an eco-friendly business park. Such upgrades have obvious financial as well as aesthetic and community rewards.

Prime properties are a small minority of total stock and are rarely traded. The vast majority of buildings lack at least one of the qualities outlined above to some degree and are thus secondary or worse, and are downvalued accordingly. They are nevertheless 'owned' and so it is self-evident that a second tier of investors also exists, some of whom specialise in such property. Clearly, however, lower order property means greater risk to the investor and greater risk means lower rents and capital values. Poor urban design will of course also increase risk.

It is now appropriate to consider the process of appraising the financial viability of development schemes in order to understand the sensitivity of the calculations involved to numerous influences, including the quality of urban design.

A suitable case for treatment
Estates Gazette, 20/8/87

The office market in Middlesborough is dying, if not dead, say agents in the heart of Teeside. They go on to predict a knock-on effect on the retail market if nothing is done to arrest the office sector's decline.

The key problems are a lack of parking and badly designed office blocks built in the 1960s and 1970s. The withdrawal of the now defunct Cleveland County Council, which employed a large number of workers, and bad urban design has made matters worse.

Development appraisal and financial viability

Greater attention to matters of urban design can help to make new development more acceptable to local communities and can therefore ease the development process.

(John Gummer, then Secretary of State for the Environment, launching the RIBA Urban Design Exhibition, October 1996)

There is no doubt that urban design issues have risen up the planning and development agenda in recent years and far greater attention is now being paid to such issues in adopted local plans. Predictably, property developers are only slowly appreciating urban design questions, which prompted Robert Jones, then

---

Planners rebuff L&G store plan
Estates Gazette, 24/5/97

City of Westminster planners slammed Legal and General's proposed scheme for 225–235 Oxford Street, London W1 on practically every point.

'The replacement building is wholly unacceptable in urban design terms,' the planners' report said. 'The proposed building is a poor quality design which has been conceived with little regard to the characteristics of the site and its surroundings.'

The report pointed out that the site is in an architecturally varied area. 'This richness and variety has been ignored by the architects in favour of an unimaginative and homogenous design.'

Environment Minister for Planning, to complain that developers were still putting forward proposals 'without any effort to accommodate urban design issues'. Not surprisingly, this is generating conflicts on occasions.

More enlightened members of the development industry have, however, had different experiences. For example, amongst the schemes presented at the RIBA Urban Design Exhibition in October 1996: was a project by the Hanover Property Trust of Lewins Mead in Bristol, which identified development opportunities in the area where it owns three large office blocks. According to Hanover's Peter Farnfield (1996): 'This urban design approach has been different . . . It is a valid process to secure proposals that carry local support and brings a level of democracy into planning that has been lost in recent years.' The proposals were of course also financially viable and, ultimately, determining that viability in the light of urban design considerations and many other requirements is the critical task.

The most commonly used method for appraising the viability of development proposals is the *residual method of valuation*. The method itself is simple and is available in pre-programmed formats such as Superdeveloper or can be presented in a basic spreadsheet. The problems with appraisals do not concern the method but the values attached to the variables in that method, and it is here that minor variations can have dramatic effects. Whether the proposals involve development, redevelopment and/or refurbishment, the residual method has three functions:

1 to determine the value of the land and therefore how much the developer can afford to bid in attempting to acquire the land from the landowner, bearing in mind that this is likely to be a competitive process and the landowner will normally accept the highest offer;
2 to calculate the overall value of the completed scheme and the level of profit the proposal will produce for the developer;
3 to assess the likely level of costs that will be incurred by the developer during construction in order to identify a cost ceiling which must not be exceeded if the development is to remain profitable.

These considerations can be linked together in a simple equation:

Value of the completed development − Costs of development and developer's profit = Residual land value.

Clearly, the value of land – the 'residue' – is deter-

mined by what can be developed on the site, the strength of demand for that space, the availability of alternative space elsewhere and thus the value and cost of the development. It is already obvious that the potential for error is considerable. Take development costs, for example. These may include costs for demolition, construction, infrastructure, landscaping, professional fees (for architects, engineers, surveyors, etc.), finance (the cost of borrowing), letting and sales fees, and legal requirements. These costs have to be estimated in advance of a building period which may be some years and therefore small inaccuracies in just some cost areas can easily upset the residual calculation. Obviously, great care must be taken in using residual valuations and while similar market transactions on other comparable developments in the area will provide some checks and balances, it is important to be aware that development projects almost always have characteristics that are unique to them and this will affect value.

The residual valuation calculation

The elements

In order to appreciate the elements of the residual calculation and how urban design may affect the variables, let us consider an example. The objective is to determine the site value (i.e. the maximum price the developer might bid in order to acquire the site). The site has planning permission for a mixed-use development comprising 500 m^2 of standard shop units on the ground floor and 2500 m^2 of offices on five upper floors. Based on local market evidence and professional advice, the following assumptions have been incorporated in the calculation:

- Construction could begin in 6 months' time and take 18 months to complete.
- Building costs have been estimated by the quantity surveyor to be £450 per m^2 for the shops and £750 per m^2 for the offices.
- Current rent values on comparable schemes in the area are £150 per m^2 for standard shops and £200 per m^2 for commercial offices.
- A 6 month period has been built into the calculation for letting the shops and offices.
- The scheme will be financed through short-term bank lending at an interest rate of 10% per annum.
- The developer will sell on the completed scheme to an institutional investor.

The calculation might appear as shown in Table 9.1.

Table 9.1 Worked example: development appraisal calculation

Value of the proposal		
Income		
Shops: 500 m² less 10% 5 450 m² @ £150 m²		£67,500
Offices: 2500 m² less 10% 5 2250 m² @ £200 m²		£450,000
Total income		£517,500
Yield @ say 7%		14.2857
Capital value		**£7,392,850**
Costs of the proposal		
Construction costs		
Shops: 500 m² gross @ £450 m²	£225,000	
Offices: 2500 m² gross @ £750 m²	£1,875,000	
	£2,100,000	
Ancillary costs		
Infrastructure, services, etc., say	200,000	
	£2,300,000	
Professional fees		
Architect, quantity surveyor *et al.* @ say 12.5%	£287,500	
	£2,587,000	
Contingencies		
@ say 3% of total costs	£77,610	
	£2,664,610	
Short-term finance @ say 10% p.a.		
On total building costs, ancillaries, fees and contingencies for say half the building period	£199,845	
	£2,864,455	
On total costs incurred on completion to full letting (letting delay of 6 months)	£143,222	
	£3,007,677	
Letting and sales fees		
Letting fees @ say 15% of income	£77,625	
Advertising and marketing, say	£30,000	
Sale to investor fee @ say 2% of sale price	£147,857	
Total development cost	**£3,263,159**	
Return for risk and profit		
@ say 15% of capital value	£1,108,927	
Total expected costs on completion	£4,372,086	£4,372,086
SITE VALUE (in 2.5 years time)		£3,020,764
Present value of £1 in 2.5 years @ 10%		0.7888
		£2,382,778
Less acquisition costs @ 2.5%		£59,569
SITE VALUE TODAY		**£2,323,209**

Explanations for the elements in the calculation can now be considered, together with comments on their sensitivity to external influences including urban design.

Income

Income represents the rent paid by the potential shop and office tenants on an annual basis per square metre of space. (The property industry struggled for many years to convert from imperial measurement to metric, and rents are invariably quoted on both a per square foot *and* a per square metre basis in agent's particulars.) Rental income is presented as net income, i.e. after responsibilities for repairs, maintenance, insurance, etc., have been taken into account.

Rents are calculated by determining net usable space, which is the space actually occupied for the activity in question. So, for example, where an office building is divided into numerous units for separate tenants, then more space is lost to foyers, stairwells and corridors and the management costs incurred by the landlord will be much higher. Small-space users will pay a higher rent than large-space users but the gross to net deduction will increase and, overall, rental income from a multi-let building is likely to be lower than from a single tenant building. This has predictable effects. *Prime* office areas tend to be dominated by large-space single tenants who take on virtually all the building responsibilities. The landlord has very little responsibility and therefore such buildings have traditionally been strongly favoured by investors. Buildings in secondary and tertiary office areas will be increasingly multi-let and have a higher turnover of tenants and thus a higher vacancy rate. All these factors will affect income.

Ultimately, however, while the investor will prioritise a secure rental income stream, it is the potential for rental growth that will be particularly attractive. On both counts, quality in the urban context will attract better tenants and increase the likelihood of rental growth. Indeed, urban environmental quality can generate significant returns. The transformation of the Covent Garden area of Central London, for example, driven by active programmes of environmental improvements, had a massive impact on rental growth and thus investor attitudes.

Investment yield

The investment yield (7% in the worked example) represents the means of converting the rental income into a capital value. In other words, how much would an investor in property be prepared to pay for the building in question (its capital value) in order to receive an annual income of £517,500 rent? The answer will clearly depend on how much risk is attached to that investment, and the yield is a measure of that risk. Determining the yield is a critical part of the appraisal process and will depend on an assessment of the following factors:

- the state of the economy and the general level of interest rates and other investment yields;
- the type and in particular the location of the property, and hence its rental growth potential (the famous retail agent's adage that there are only three rules to letting/selling a shop – *location, location and location* – comes to mind);
- the security of the income regarding the tenant's continued ability to pay rent;
- the condition and life expectancy of the building;
- the extent of management and other maintenance costs;
- the quality and popularity of the area and its general environmental image.

Assessing yield is obviously very difficult and, of course, is not fixed as many of the above factors will change over time. However, the basic 'rule' is clear:

> The greater the risk, the higher the yield, the lower the capital value.
> The lower the risk, the lower the yield, the higher the capital value.

The relationship in terms of the appraisal calculation can be summarised as follows:

Capital value = Annual rental income $\times$ 100/I
where I is the yield interest rate.

So, in the worked example, using a yield of 7% provides a multiplier of 14.2857. Had the proposal been considered slightly more risky and a yield of say 8% had been appropriate, then the multiplier would have fallen to 12.5 and the proposal valued at £6,468,750 (compared to £7,392,850). Determining and justifying the yield is therefore highly sensitive and fractional changes will significantly affect the calculation.

Urban design can be an important contributory factor in establishing yield. Indeed, it is not difficult to appreciate how better urban design, perhaps as part of a regeneration strategy for example, can change the image of an area, attract inward investment and generate added value as yields improve. Nevertheless, accurately applying the correct yield is far from easy.

Fortunately, the UK property market (unlike many other markets abroad) is reasonably transparent. Most transactions are recorded in accessible databases and often published, albeit in aggregated form. So, for example, *Healey and Baker's Quarterly* property review includes indices showing average rental growth and average prime yields on a regional basis (Table 9.2).

While this information is helpful in monitoring trends, it must be emphasised that averages here are likely to mask wide local variations and that local expertise will always be a vital ingredient in determining appropriate variables.

Costs

The third major element in the calculation is cost and, as the worked example demonstrates, costs arise under a number of headings. Actual construction costs are the most important and these will be estimated by the quantity surveyor on the basis of the gross internal area of the building, i.e. the area measured to the inside of the external walls. Like rents, costs are estimated on current values and are not normally projected; again, typical costs are easily available in published form such as Spons. In addition, ancillary costs must also be identified and these are tending to increase. Traditionally, ancillaries would have been limited to on-site infrastructure such as roads and services but, increasingly, government and local planning authorities are requiring developments to pay for off-site infrastructure that is a direct consequence of the

Table 9.2 Summary data

	East Anglia	East Midlands	North	North West	Scot-land	South East	South West	Wales	West Mid-lands	Yorks & Humbs	Great Britain
Prime rental growth to December 1997											
Retail											
Since June 1977	9.87%	9.37%	8.48%	9.17%	8.09%	8.27%	9.20%	8.59%	9.25%	9.28%	8.62%
10 Years	6.86%	5.35%	3.73%	5.69%	5.25%	3.60%	2.50%	2.53%	5.44%	3.30%	4.02%
5 Years	3.66%	2.79%	3.22%	5.55%	6.71%	5.74%	2.15%	4.12%	6.56%	5.78%	5.25%
1 Year	5.91%	3.46%	8.45%	18.68%	18.89%	16.97%	8.16%	19.02%	16.73%	9.69%	15.00%
1 Quarter	1.87%	0.00%	2.03%	3.45%	4.91%	4.18%	3.61%	8.53%	5.87%	0.80%	3.86%
Office											
Since June 1977	8.40%	9.13%	7.56%	8.91%	8.60%	7.12%	8.75%	7.25%	9.88%	7.57%	7.49%
10 Years	4.71%	7.18%	6.38%	8.79%	7.56%	1.21%	6.12%	7.22%	10.76%	7.81%	2.71%
5 Years	−2.33%	−0.55%	1.01%	1.76%	1.85%	4.73%	−1.70%	0.73%	1.10%	0.98%	3.25%
1 Year	2.56%	0.00%	6.72%	7.10%	5.56%	16.63%	3.08%	0.00%	2.74%	2.94%	12.27%
1 Quarter	0.00%	0.00%	0.70%	0.29%	0.00%	5.57%	−3.08%	0.00%	1.53%	2.94%	4.11%
Industrial											
Since June 1977	5.99%	7.07%	6.88%	6.77%	6.27%	7.05%	7.84%	6.73%	8.00%	6.57%	6.85%
10 Years	5.17%	6.66%	9.56%	8.17%	7.93%	5.51%	5.51%	8.12%	8.85%	7.98%	6.57%
5 Years	−0.61%	2.36%	2.93%	4.38%	1.89%	−0.28%	−0.27%	2.77%	4.00%	2.85%	1.09%
1 Year	19.75%	7.92%	18.18%	9.78%	6.67%	9.99%	7.84%	17.81%	12.85%	16.19%	11.09%
1 Quarter	4.30%	0.00%	2.97%	0.50%	2.75%	2.40%	2.80%	0.00%	0.00%	1.67%	1.92%
Average prime yields to December 1997											
Retail											
March 1997	4.92%	5.08%	5.31%	5.46%	4.92%	5.63%	5.10%	5.50%	5.35%	5.38%	5.43%
June 1997	4.83%	4.92%	5.19%	5.29%	4.58%	5.47%	5.10%	5.33%	5.35%	5.25%	5.29%
September 1997	4.50%	4.75%	5.00%	5.21%	4.42%	5.33%	4.85%	5.17%	5.25%	5.00%	5.13%
December 1997	4.42%	4.58%	4.81%	5.08%	4.42%	5.28%	4.80%	5.00%	5.05%	4.88%	5.04%
Office											
March 1997	7.67%	7.33%	8.63%	7.75%	7.67%	7.09%	7.60%	8.25%	7.80%	7.56%	7.48%
June 1997	7.67%	7.25%	8.56%	7.75%	7.67%	7.03%	7.40%	8.25%	7.75%	7.56%	7.43%
September 1997	7.67%	7.33%	8.56%	7.75%	7.33%	6.92%	7.45%	8.25%	7.75%	7.56%	7.38%
December 1997	7.67%	7.33%	8.50%	7.79%	7.17%	6.72%	7.45%	8.25%	7.75%	7.56%	7.28%
Industrial											
March 1997	8.17%	7.25%	8.50%	7.67%	8.08%	7.63%	7.70%	8.67%	7.40%	7.88%	7.79%
June 1997	8.08%	7.25%	8.50%	7.67%	7.92%	7.60%	7.70%	8.67%	7.55%	7.88%	7.78%
September 1997	8.17%	7.25%	8.50%	7.71%	7.92%	7.60%	7.70%	8.67%	7.55%	7.88%	7.79%
December 1997	8.17%	7.00%	8.44%	7.67%	7.83%	7.58%	7.70%	8.67%	7.45%	7.88%	7.75%

scheme in question – so-called planning gains. So, for example, a major residential development may well generate a requirement for road and public transport improvements, education, health and recreational facilities, all of which in the past would have been paid for by the taxpayer. The new approach is far more equitable but has the obvious effect of increasing costs and therefore decreasing land value.

Professional fees will also be an important cost and are usually based on a percentage of the construction costs, negotiated between 5% and 15% depending on the complexity of the project. It is also prudent to include a contingency sum to cover unforeseen costs that may arise, especially if the project involves refur-

bishing existing structures. Although the cost of borrowing is relatively small when compared to total costs, it will vary depending on the status of the development and the developer. The highly prized development may be forward funded by the acquiring investment institution as previously noted, in which case, actual borrowing is minimal, but in the majority of cases, developers will finance schemes by short-term borrowing from the clearing and merchant banks. The rate at which they can borrow will vary depending on their track record but is usually 2–3% above base rate. In the worked example, borrowing is divided into that required to fund construction and that required to cover the letting delay following completion. The main difference is that construction funding is not all required at the outset. In fact, a significant proportion of costs arise towards the end of the building period when the shell is being fitted out. To reflect this, it is normal appraisal practice to assume borrowing on total construction costs for half the building period. Finally, letting and sales fees have been added in on standard percentage terms, giving a total development cost of £3,263,159.

While lengthy, development costs are perhaps the most predictable element in the calculation, especially if developing new buildings on a green-field site; on previously built sites, which might be contaminated, and especially if refurbishing existing (perhaps listed) buildings, estimating costs is much more difficult and the calculation must include larger contingencies.

Return for risk and profit

Property development is founded on an assessment of risk and the appraisal will build in an anticipated level of profit to reflect the degree of risk. The greater the risk, the greater the level of profit included, in part as an additional contingency sum. This allowance is expressed as a percentage of development costs or as a percentage of the capital value. Since the objective of the calculation is to determine land value and that is one element of cost, it is easier to include profit as a percentage of the capital value (usually 15–20%, although higher or lower figures may be appropriate). The alternative is to apply a slightly higher percentage (say 20–25%) to all costs, including land.

The relationship between the two approaches can be simply explained. If the development being considered is worth £100,000 on completion and the developer requires a 20% of value profit, then the profit will be £20,000 and the remaining £80,000 will represent all costs including land. If the alternative approach is used, then a figure of 25% would be applied to £80,000, the resulting profit being the same, £20,000.

Residual site value

The site value in the worked example therefore represents what the site is worth on completion of the scheme, on the basis of the variables built into capital value, development costs and profit. The site value today, i.e. what the developer can afford to bid for the site, requires two further adjustments:

1 an allowance for the land acquisition costs expressed as a percentage; and,

2 the borrowing costs necessary to finance the land acquisition. These are calculated by determining the amount of interest that would accrue throughout the full development period by using a discount or 'present value' table. With a 10% interest rate and a development period of 2.5 years, a multiplier of 0.7888 is applied.

The bid value is therefore £2,323,209 but it is abundantly clear that very slight variations in the values included will produce widely differing results. The quality of urban design is one of many factors that can influence value, and in some cases, dramatically – most obviously in areas subject to regeneration initiatives.

Mixed use, urban design and the property market

The important role played by mixed use in reinvigorating urban areas, especially central areas, is promoted in central and local government planning guidance, not only because of its contribution to more sustainable development principles, but also as a contributory element in creating better urban design. While a mixture of uses in older areas and in older individual buildings is common, the property industry has deliberately avoided mixed uses in new developments for many years. The rationale was that occupiers did not want floorspace in mixed-use buildings and that institutional investors would not fund such developments. Where mixed uses were unavoidable, vertical separation of uses between buildings rather than horizontal divisions within buildings would be preferred. At an area level, the town planning system has also promoted relatively strict land-use zoning until recently. Together, the planning and property market processes have combined to produce uniformity of use in many areas, perhaps most conspicuously in central business districts, bustling during working hours and deserted at other times. While planners have now recognised the advantages of mixed use, the legacy of single-use buildings and areas and the inherently conservative attitudes of the property world, combine to provide a significant constraint on better urban design.

However, there are signs that investor attitudes towards mixed-use buildings are changing to some extent and contributory factors include the following:

1 *The effects of the recession*: the length and depth of the recession in the property market in the early 1990s forced many investors to review their approach, especially those with portfolios including secondary property which was hard to let. High

vacancy rates and poor returns from unsaleable buildings prompted some owners to convert space to other uses and while this was generally another single use (e.g. offices converted to residential use) it has nevertheless encouraged more mixed-use areas.

2 *Property sector cycles*: the 1990s has also been characterised by variations in the property sector cycles. For example, while the business space and office markets in the mid-1990s remained subdued, the residential and hotel markets were rising sharply. For some investors, this has encouraged the view that returns are more consistent and secure from a mixed portfolio.

While the benefits of mixed use in urban design terms are clear (and considered elsewhere in this book), property market views remain critical if such developments are to be implemented, and here there are two schools of thought: those who argue that current interest in mixed-use developments is a short-term fashion, and those who believe that the property industry is in the early stages of a more fundamental change of attitude.

The short-term fashion school of thought points to the continued preference for prime single-use developments from most investors; there are shortages of prime stock which are producing rental growth and which, in turn, will prompt redevelopment or refurbishment of existing stock. With the development 'clock' or at about noon, this line of thinking, dependent as it is on a strong demand for commercial property, seems somewhat optimistic. The longer term 'fundamentalists', while remaining a minority, point to the large number of mixed-used schemes implemented in the last three years, and while some of these schemes were pursued to facilitate disposal, there are signs of a more general recognition of the benefits of mixed use and this is encouraging.

Mixed use: the Clerkenwell case study

The more positive market signs do not imply that mixed-use schemes, especially on any scale in urban areas, will be straightforward. The student-led Clerkenwell brewery site project, referred to earlier in this book (see Figure 8.23), illustrates the complexities of developing mixed-use schemes, even in up and coming areas.

The brewery site had planning permission for a large office development to cover the entire site in the 1980s. When permission was granted, the City and Central London were trying hard to maintain their status as the main office centre. Suburban authorities were also trying to cash in on the office boom and this may explain why this site, somewhat away from the City itself, received an office consent.

In contrast, today the market has a new leader in this area, with housing schemes largely taking over from offices, particularly in areas such as Clerkenwell and Islington, and developers are responding strongly to the buoyant market conditions. Local authorities are also reacting and encouraging mixed-use developments in an attempt to achieve a better balance of uses in revitalised districts. While their approach may not be purely market-driven, developers are realising that purchasers and lessees are looking for additional service facilities.

In response to these conditions, the proposals are a combination of new build and refurbishment, the details of which are summarised in Table 9.3. The scheme in total provides 35,815 m^2 of floorspace and therefore represents a very considerable development, 58% of which is residential in various forms. Somewhat contentiously, the proposal sought to 'exchange' the Unitary Development Plan requirement for 20% of affordable housing, for a swimming pool and sports centre. The existing obsolete swimming pool site would be made over to the developer and represent additional potential profit.

Commentary

The scheme put forward is obviously complex in development terms but reflects the scale and nature of the area. Bearing in mind that the urban design students who prepared this project had little or no background in development appraisal calculation, the summary spreadsheet shown in Table 9.4 represents a very good effort at assessing the viability of the

Table 9.3 Schedule of accommodation

	m^2
Residential	
Loft apartments	3600
Town houses	4800
Flats (new build)	5700
Flats above shops	2880
Public house/restaurant	2250
Offices	4040
School of Photography	3588
Sports centre	3200
Livework spaces	2938
Shops	900
Infrastructure: hard landscaping/roads	4400

Table 9.4 The Clerkenwell brewery site development appraisal: a student-led project

Property	Sale/rent	Floor area (m²)	Cost per m² (£)	Construction cost + profit (£)	Building value (£)	Yield (%)	Residual land value (£)	Profit (£)
Residential:								
Loft apartments	Sale	7640	630	8,663,760	11,460,000	–	2,796,240	1,443,960
Town houses	Sale	4800	750	6,480,000	8,400,000	–	1,980,000	1,080,000
1/2 bedroom flats	Sale	5700	580	5,950,800	7,695,000	–	1,744,200	991,800
Flats over shops	Sale	2880	630	3,265,920	4,320,000	–	1,054,080	544,320
Residential totals		21,020		24,330,898	31,875,000		7,544,102	4,060,080
Offices	Rent	4320	1050	7,756,560	9,234,000	6.75	1,477,440	952,560
Public house/restaurant	Sale	750	750	3,037,500	4,500,000	10	1,462,500	506,250
School of Photography	Sale	3587	650	4,197,374	4,484,475	12	2,048,090	1,139,390
	Rent	2938	499	2,638,911	4,407,000			
External works		10,125		781,850				
Totals		32,615[a]		42,743,093	54,500,375		11,757,282	6,658,270 (2)
Sports Centre		3200	1300	6,240,000				
Amended totals		35,815[a]		48,983,093	54,500,375		5,517,282>	>Or 418,270

[a] Excluding external works.
[b] Former swimming pool site could yield an additional £2 million profit

proposal. Based on considerable local market evidence gathered by the group on the ground, the scheme is imaginative and intricate.

Table 9.4 has been amended slightly in order to highlight the main issues identified by the appraisal, which can be summarised as follows:

1 The residential and office elements are clearly financially well founded and yield healthy profits and land values, although the office yield of 6.75% may be rather optimistic in a fringe location, in which case that element is somewhat over-valued.

2 The public house/restaurant element appears to make reasonable returns while the School of Photography, based on a rent of £150 per square metre (psm) is certainly viable too.

3 On the face of it, therefore, the proposal is valued at £54,500,375, with total costs and profits estimated at £42,743,093. This leaves a residual land value of £11,757,282. In fact, this figure is slightly exaggerated in that the student group applied a 20% on cost profit element but did not include the land cost. As a result, profit was underestimated by approximately £1.5–2.0 million and land value over estimated by the same figure. Nevertheless, the commercial elements of the proposal do 'stack up', albeit with a little adjustment to the calculation – a process which is of course constantly checked throughout the development period as actual costs and values become clear.

4 The problem with the development proposal is obviously not the commercial elements but the sports centre. Although the proposal is based on the existing swimming pool site being available for commercial development and it has been assumed that this may yield a further £2 million in profit, the new sports centre is being made over to the local authority as a community facility at no cost. While this is laudable, it makes little commercial sense. The costs of construction are estimated at over £6 million and that assumes that the land in question has no value, which is clearly not the case. The effect on the appraisal calculation is dramatic and noted in the bottom right cells of Table 9.4. Either £6 million is deducted from the developer's profit, almost wiping out any return, or the land value is reduced by the same figure. On the assumption that the landowner would not wish to accept a much reduced land value, the developer must consider other options, which might include the following:

- looking for some return on the sports centre from the local authority in order to offset the development costs;

- running the sports centre fully or partly as a commercial proposition;
- reducing the size of the centre or simply making the land available to the authority but not the building;
- reconsidering whether to include affordable housing instead, which although not highly profitable would yield a modest return.

In effect, the appraisal calculation in Table 9.4 has 'tested' this particular mix and scale of uses and the proposal will need to be refined in the light of the results, which is precisely what happens in reality.

EDAW scoops Manchester brief
Estate Gazette, 9/11/96

Manchester's prime shopping core, ravaged by the June bombing, will swing northwards under an ambitious £500m plan to create an extra 49,237 m² of shopping, leisure and open spaces in the city centre.

Victory in the International Urban Design competition went to a consortium headed by London-based EDAW and including architects Benoy and Simpson and surveyors Hillier Parker.

Conclusion

Although the property investment and development industry is conservative, it is also responsive to consumer demand and on occasions when consumer requirements change, the industry evolves. Just as mixed-use developments are still in their infancy and ignored by some investors, the same would have been said of leisure developments five years ago and yet today leisure investment is booming. A recognition of the 'value' of urban design by the property industry is also in its early stages, but the signs are promising.

- Joint professional approaches are emerging and awareness is increasing.
- The need for a 'quality' property product is appreciated and increasingly demanded by more discriminating occupiers.
- The legacy of the last recession has forced developers and investors to recognise that bland characterless buildings and environments are more vulnerable to market fluctuations than interesting, vibrant, characterful locations, all of which is encouraging.

Given time, the property development and investment process will help deliver better quality buildings and urban design, but not without professional help.

Unit 10 Evaluation and user perspectives

Clara Greed and Marion Roberts

Introduction

This book seeks to provide guidance on 'doing urban design' in a variety of locations, as opposed to considering the issues that surround urban design as a field of study. The purpose of this unit is to suggest to readers various ways in which urban design proposals might be evaluated from a user perspective and to explore in greater depth variations in cultural attitudes to urban design proposals. To illustrate this, and to alert the reader to these dimensions, we will revisit Clerkenwell. The account will be interspersed with examples from the wider national and international context of urban design. The purpose of this unit is to raise awareness and encourage the reader to think laterally about how the social agenda might be borne in mind within the urban design process, rather than to offer prescriptive standards or rules. At least, it is hoped that this approach will encourage lateral thinking, reduce potential blind spots, and open the reader to a more comprehensive view of urban design.

A framework for evaluation

At the start of this book it was suggested that students set themselves design objectives for each set of proposals they wish to make. The most obvious source of evaluation is provided by those objectives, and readers are advised to return to them throughout the course of the design process.

In the world outside the academe, when proposals are implemented, others make judgements on those proposals. Different interest groups are represented in the design process, as is demonstrated in Units 9, 11 and 12 of this book. Often, those who will inhabit the area, either as employers or workers, or as residents, cannot be consulted directly because the site is empty. Similarly it can often be difficult to consult the wider community within which a development is placed. For example, a transport interchange and its hinterland may be used by literally thousands of people who pass through it every day, some of whom may also use its immediate surroundings in terms of the shops, bars and other facilities which may be located there. To consult these potential 'consumers', although possible, raises considerable difficulties.

Designers therefore have to take on a wider responsibility towards their fellow citizens in the defence of civic virtues. These may be difficult to think out from first principles, but Punter (1990) provides a distillation of the work of nine authors which he suggests are the 'ten commandments of urban design'. Table 10.1 sets out a series of evaluative measures which are based on Punter's own table, including some additions. Consideration of each of these headings will enable readers to evaluate their own projects and to refine and improve their designs. The priority that is given to each quality will vary, depending on the project brief, the nature of the task and the student's own intentions.

Clerkenwell

The proposals for Clerkenwell will be evaluated with regard to the qualities listed in Table 10.1. The proposals have already been evaluated against their own

Table 10.1 Evaluative measures of urban design

Quality	Brief description
Place making	Appropriate spaces and activities
Relationship to historical context	Dialogue between history and context
Vitality	Mixture of uses, public–private interaction
Public access	Quality of public access, movement systems, access for disabled
Scale	Relationship of parts to surroundings, to each other, to human activities and to senses
Articulation	Legibility, hierarchy of routes (where appropriate)
Adaptability	Ability to respond to change
Stimulation	Sensory delight
Safety	Surveillance, protection
Community process	Social justice, empowerment (where possible), social mix
Efficiency	Costs, re-use of resources, phasing

design objectives and against the criteria for development economics (see Units 8 and 9). In this unit, more consideration will be given to other criteria which may be given higher priority by other interested parties. The purpose of this is to demonstrate that, in practice, urban design is a complex process which, in common with town planning, involves balancing competing interests. The Clerkenwell scheme has been chosen because readers will be able to familiarise themselves easily with the proposals and hence to understand the detailed comments more readily.

Place making

Place making was a key design objective and the proposals respond to this criteria well, creating a definitive urban form with coherent streets and spaces. The types of uses that are proposed relate to Clerkenwell's evolution, e.g. the new types of residential use such as loft apartments and town houses. The School of Photography is a rather specific proposal and may not be taken up in practice, but echoes Clerkenwell's craft origins. The other uses are all appropriate to Clerkenwell's position as a rapidly gentrifying district in an inner London borough, which despite some of its glamorous occupants, is actually home to some of London's more deprived inhabitants. For example, 20% of the borough's population were born outside the borough, 20% are over 60 years of age, 40% are car-owners, and 13% have some form of physical disability or long-term illness. In contrast (using similar

but not identical social indicators), 5% of the total UK population are classified as belonging to an 'ethnic minority', 67% of the population have driving licences, and slightly less than the Islington sample are over 60 years of age, while the disability figure in Islington is higher than national averages.

The proposals make an appropriate compromise between the needs of the poorer existing residents and richer incomers. The provision of converted flats above existing shops and a sports centre to the north of the site relates well to the existing council housing estate. The loft apartments, offices and restaurant relate well to the recent gentrification which is gradually changing the area. Students may often wonder how to incorporate social objectives into a proposal, and the Clerkenwell scheme provides an example in the way in which it retains an existing run-down Victorian terrace of shops and a pub and enhances facilities with the proposal of a sports centre.

Relationship to historical context

The relationship to Clerkenwell's historical context has been carefully considered and formed part of the key objectives. The re-use of existing buildings and the careful attention to the morphology and the townscape of the surrounding area have all been carefully and sensitively addressed. Readers should bear in mind that 'relationship to surroundings' is not just a form of words but in a real sense means studying the context and using conscious strategies to address it.

Vitality

Vitality was a key design objective. The proposal provides a good mix of public and private uses and of different uses. The potential clash between the users of the pub yard and the inhabitants of the loft apartments has been resolved by suggesting that the yard is closed at night. The proposal to include facilities that would have night-time as well as daytime uses, such as the sports centre, offices, further education and the pub/restaurant would ensure that the objective of providing activities that 'peak' at different times of the day would be achieved.

Public access

Public access formed one of the key design objectives of the proposals and has been carefully thought through. The opening up of a new route from the south to the housing estate in the north provides helpful public access for local people. The establishment of two east–west pedestrian links also helps to 'mesh' together former enclaves. The key objective of providing greater permeability through the site has been achieved. More, however, could be said about these routes in terms of safety (see below). The proposal has also thought about vehicular movement and servicing. By making the new north–south road both for vehicles and pedestrians, the servicing requirements have been met and vehicular movement through the site has been restricted.

There are no sudden changes of level proposed, so those with walking difficulties would have few difficulties moving around the site. The public buildings are accessible by car, which again would help many disabled users. The town houses in Brewery Yard would pose some problems for some disabled users, as they are inaccessible by car. The hard landscaping of Compton Square could be of positive benefit for wheelchair users, providing them with an accessible, car-free open space.

Scale

Scale also formed one of the design objectives and in this particular design task, formed part of the dialogue with history. The scale of the development and its spaces is also appropriate in that it is not 'cataclysmic' in Jane Jacobs' terms, i.e. it is not proposing a wholesale demolition and rebuilding at a much larger scale. The proposals are for building shapes and public spaces of a size that forms a convincing enhancement to the surrounding 'grain', yet at the same time can accommodate contemporary uses.

Articulation

A hierarchy of fronts and backs has been established throughout the site. This provides a greater sense of articulation in that the major route, St John Street, has been given further definition and importance, through the completion of a continuous building façade, traffic calming and street enhancements, and the proposal for a higher building above the gateway to the pedestrian route. Although one of the aims was to continue the 'back alley' quality of Clerkenwell, the proposal makes suggestions to enhance the legibility of the scheme by marking corner buildings. The continuation of the grid by making a new north–south route also enhances the legibility of the area.

Adaptability

The proposal is for a set of buildings and spaces that could gradually enhance and accommodate change. Two of the proposals are for specific uses: a sports centre and a school of photography. In practice, a brief would be made in consultation with a developer and a local authority, such that proposed uses could be 'floated' at an early stage to assess their viability. However, both blocks are of sufficient size and shape to accommodate other uses. For example, the block designated as a sports centre could accommodate a community facility such as a library with flats above, or a day centre with flats above. Similarly, the Victorian warehouse which is proposed as a school of photography could just as easily be used for gallery space or studio space on the ground floor with flats above. Alcock et al. (1985) propose a criteria of 'robustness', i.e. the provision of a building envelope which can be readily converted to other uses. This is a useful concept to observe although it may not be applicable to all building envelopes on every site. Imagining how uses could change in the future and checking whether such change could be accommodated is a useful part of the iteration process in urban design.

Stimulation

The proposals allow for the enjoyment of some sensory pleasures. The pedestrian route through Brewery Yard to Compton Square passes through a gateway, opens out into the small intimate scale of Brewery Yard with its shady trees, is pinched and then opens out again into the Square itself. The contrast between the small 'green' space of Brewery Yard and the open hard landscaped area of Compton Square would be enjoyable and could form an effective end-sequence to a route from Clerkenwell Green. There is opportunity for further sensory expression with the provision of a water feature. Similarly the daytime route through the intimacy of St John's Yard, which would form an enclave secluded from the daytime bustle of St John's Street, would also be pleasurable. The new north–south route could be quiet, but the opening of the new square off it would produce a memorable feature on the route.

The brief does not go into the details of materials beyond mentioning the 'warehouse' style, but there are opportunities for visual richness in the detailing of new buildings using features present in the existing nineteenth-century warehouses (see Unit 6). These might be a repertoire of brick colours, concrete dressings and elaborate window details. The designation of the corner sports centre as a landmark building and the suggestion that it has an imaginative roof shape also provide the opportunity for a landmark building in an eye-catching contemporary style.

Safety

Safety is the aspect of the proposals that gives most cause for concern. Daytime use is well-catered for, with a mix of well-surveilled pedestrian and vehicular routes. At night, it is possible to imagine that the scheme would become more threatening. The most 'dangerous' route, through St John's Yard, would be closed. However, walking along the route to Compton Square would mean passing through the quiet pedestrianised space of Brewery Yard before reaching Compton Square. The proposal is that this should be well-lit, as the squares in some cities in mainland Europe are, with lighted bollards and floodlit buildings. Although this could give some sensory pleasure in terms of its contrast to the darkness of Brewery Yard, it is at the expense of feelings of safety. It is probable that pedestrians would walk around Compton Street at night to access the public buildings in Compton Square, rather than along the pedestrian route.

Community process

As this is a student project, the process of implementing a design brief does not arise. In the case of this site it is also not clear who is going to live in the area, and therefore one cannot 'participate' with a group who does not yet exist. However, one can make an educated guess as to the likely types of people who would live here based upon trends in surrounding development. It would be possible, in the course of developing the brief in practice, to interact with the residents on the neighbouring housing estate, with the businesses to the east of the site and with the residents of houses in the neighbouring conservation area. In this way, not only would the neighbours of the proposals be consulted, but groups representative of the types of people likely to occupy the buildings on the site would also be able to provide information of use to a local authority and a developer.

Efficiency

The costing of the proposals is discussed in depth in Unit 9. Again, as it is a student project, phasing has not been considered. It is possible that it could be phased quite readily. As with the concept of robustness, checking the proposals to see whether they could be constructed in discrete parcels could be usefully incorporated by students into their design process.

Summary

The above checklist of headings provides a useful tool for urban designers to refine their design proposals. The precise issues to be considered under each of the headings will vary, but the list is sufficiently flexible to allow for a comprehensive appraisal.

Issues in a user perspective

The consideration of a user perspective on urban design raises a number of dilemmas. This section considers some of them briefly, in order to raise students' awareness of the need for further observation and of the necessity of making some kind of response.

Awareness of social difference

Urban designers need to be aware of the social divisions, spatial enclaves and social conflicts within their chosen study area or site. Statistics for social differences, such as tenure, ethnicity, employment and age, are generally only freely available on the level of a ward within a local authority area. Since most study areas, even in densely occupied inner-city wards, tend to be much smaller, urban designers tend to find themselves using the background statistics as a guide and making on-site interpretations and observations. Obviously, in this process, it is necessary to be acutely aware of one's own origins and biases.

Social differences and changes in character within a local authority do not necessarily come in 'big blobs'; indeed, they may be on a minute, hair's-breadth scale (Figure 10.1). Even in areas of ostensibly the 'same' type of London terraced town housing, 'locals' may easily being able to 'read' and recognise the social nuances and changes signalled by the types of cars parked outside houses, and by the nature of the curtains, front-door and overall 'feel' of the street façade – as well as the numbers of skips, and the types of builders used. A trip to the estate agent for a look at house prices will immediately confirm these visual clues. The sensitive urban designer would be careful to 'map' these social boundaries and nuances, and take them into account in defining meaningful 'environmental

Figure 10.1   Some evidence of a little local diversity.

areas', particularly in respect of the likely financial implications of design intervention and conservation policy.

Design policies must be careful to enable a healthy mix of shop façades and facilities, without implying that some types of ethnic minority businesses are 'lesser' than 'normal' (Anglo-Saxon) ones. If Halal butchers are located in the same row as Pakistani newsagents and upmarket 'continental' (i.e. European) restaurants this creates a visually diverse mix. But there may also be a place, as has been found in North American cities, for 'China Town' or 'Little Italy' type areas, and this diversity should not be designed out but accommodated. If projects are carried out in unfamiliar territories then more subtle social divisions may be difficult to 'read'. Here gaining information from local planning officials, other professionals and residents is often extremely helpful. The problem is compounded if the project is in a country where a foreign language is spoken as sources of written information, such as newspapers and magazines, become much more difficult to obtain or understand.

Gentrification versus local identity

A visual survey of types of local shops, places of religious worship, types of public and community buildings, and 'street life' will readily indicate which types of people are in occupation in a particular district, particularly in terms of ethnicity and religion, but also potentially in terms of age, family type and class. For example, many regeneration areas have a high proportion of single-parent families and low-income households, which is likely to lead to a demand for 'cheap shops' and communal facilities. Urban design policies that seek to 'upgrade' an area and sweep away the 'cultural chaos' and 'bad taste' are inappropriate in such situations, and conceptually and aesthetically are politically incorrect in these days of postmodern diversity.

There have been many examples over the years of areas having been 'done up', gentrified and given conservation area status, with the result that the poorer original inhabitants are simply pushed out into an adjacent area or simply made homeless. The dilemma for urban designers is obvious. Many design interventions will require private finance and as Unit 9 has shown, new developments need to be viable. Upgrading shops and facilities inevitably means a hike in rents, which in turn may mean that the types of shops and uses that make an area interesting and lively, such as corner shops and artists' studios, are driven out.

Some design solutions are achievable. First, as Bentley (1996) points out, there is the possibility of using cross-subsidies. These are the deployment of high profit earning uses (e.g. offices) on one part of a site, to subsidise a use that may earn no profit (e.g. social housing). In many parts of the country, including the London boroughs, local planning policies require developers of certain sites, predominately housing, to provide a certain measure of social housing. Debate rages as to whether this requirement has to be on-site or off-site. From the point of view of a successful scheme in urban design terms, it is highly desirable for this housing to be on-site in order to promote diversity and encourage a range of services to be attracted to the locality. In order to achieve this 'fine-grained' approach to social difference, it is suggested that the following aspects are investigated:

- changing social structure;
- cultural enclaves and life-styles;
- property market and house prices;
- existing community contacts and local organisations;
- what is happening in the area generally.

Privately controlled public space

One issue that frequently recurs in the discussion of urban design schemes is that of the ownership and control of public space. There is an increasing tendency for public space to fall into private ownership, as in say shopping centres, the courtyards in an office complex, or the circulation and parking areas of leisure centres. Other public spaces may become more closely managed, as is happening now with many town centre management schemes. The issue of control and its implications, such as the expulsion of 'undesirables' from such areas, is something that designers need to be aware of. In terms of student projects, it is important to think about how the public and semi-public spaces proposed in a design brief might be owned and managed. Could they be subject to autocratic control? If there are privately managed semi-public spaces, it is also worthwhile considering what impact they would have on the rest of the movement systems when they are enclosed. Would the pedestrian be forced to walk through a serv-

ice area? Can they be sealed off with little overall effect on the quality of other routes and spaces?

Consultation

In 'doing urban design', it is vital that there is a strong 'bottom-up' component of input from both existing local residents and users of the area (Greed and Roberts 1998). There has been a tradition of 'planning for people' in many of the London boroughs, yet many failed social and architectural experiments. Within Islington there have been several high-profile planning 'battles', some of which still continue, particularly in respect of the development of the King's Cross site (as discussed at length in Askew 1996), and concerning the development of the Arsenal football ground. Participatory approaches such as 'Planning for Real' originated within the voluntary sector, and were promoted, for example by 'Planning Aid for London'. Many participatory activities have centred around the King's Cross site within the borough.

Significantly, in recent years Islington Planning Department has taken on board some of the approaches pioneered by community and pressure groups, not least the emphasis on the long term, and on more meaningful participation, rather than the 'hit and run' questionnaire approach of the past. Meaningful urban design must be done '*with* the people' as well as '*for* the people', as discussed in Greed and Roberts (1998). Urban design consultation may also be tied in with participation in other policy areas, such as education in Islington (Fullick 1997), and 'citizen jury' initiatives (Hall 1997). Consistent consultation with people on a range of subjects, over several years, using a range of representative focus groups, is more successful than sudden approaches. If there is no one to consult, as in the case of new developments, then adjustments to design practice might be made using research and observations from likely types of future residents and users groups, particularly as certain complaints, such as lack of security and accessibility issues tend to come up again and again on new residential developments. Alternatively, in a student project, a list of stakeholders in an area could be drawn up and their probable interests and concerns conjectured and examined.

Accessibility: pedestrianisation

Many are wary of 'pedestrianisation' policies which do not take into account the experiences of pedestrians themselves. As discussed in *Introducing Urban*

Design (Shaftoe 1998), the use of the Radburn system of separating cars and pedestrian routes and other segregatory measures within residential areas may increase road safety but may also decrease personal safety. Proposals for alleyways and for setting car parking in tucked away locations behind buildings, as shown in the case study proposals, require careful consideration in terms of safety. Similarly the creation of 'threatening dark caverns' by the pedestrianisation of existing main shopping streets, has been found to deter many pedestrians from using these streets, and has encouraged their use by 'youths'. Careful design detailing is required to maintain security without deterring public use. Simply letting the traffic back in during the evenings can actually increase the sense of safety and the level of natural surveillance. Increased street lighting, and leaving these lights on all night, is another popular option (unless you are one of those who has a street light shining through your bedroom window) and has already been adopted in many parts of inner London. In contrast, many provincial cities still turn the street lights off after midnight, and residents' groups in some gentrified rural areas in Somerset, for example, have campaigned for 'street-light-free' and 'pavement-less' villages, in order to keep incipient urbanisation at bay.

Accessibility: conflicts between movement systems

If, according to the jargon associated with public participation, 'planning is for people' presumably 'urban design is for people' too, which includes pedestrians, cyclists and drivers, moving through the same urban spaces. In 'doing urban design' one needs to acknowledge the importance of the qualitative and cultural aspects of 'movement' and the designer would wish to contribute towards reducing, or at least rationalising, pedestrian–vehicular conflict. In many inner city locations there are higher than average numbers of cyclists (and motorcyclists), many of whom are engaged in despatch riding. Some women, particularly those with small children, often feel threatened by young males cycling aggressively on the footpath. Proper provision needs to be made for cyclists which endangers neither them nor pedestrians. As a pedestrian, one is likely to find simply 'walking around' quite a difficult achievement, because existing pavements are littered with boards, black plastic rubbish bags, builders' skips, plus a variety of recycling bins, bollards, lumps and bumps, litter, padlocked akimbo bicycles, and illegally parked cars (Figure 10.2). And should one assume that the new pavements and roads

Figure 10.2 Conflict between movement systems: pavement parking (Clara Greed).

in any new schemes will be any different? Parking in many congested areas is expensive and so the temptation to encroach upon pedestrian space is strong. In developing detailed urban design strategies much greater functional and aesthetic attention needs to be given to the zone between the road and the building front, i.e. the pavement. Possibly 'nodal points', where the pavement widens, might be used to collect together so many of the ancillary uses (not least waste collection and recycling).

Access: disability

Movement is so much more than being about cars or even just able-bodied pedestrians. Attention must particularly be given to the needs of the disabled and those who are pushing baby buggies, suitcases with wheels (all those lost tourists), and delivery carts. Much literature and advice on disabled access already exists in other sources (and see Appendix 4). Indeed in the case of Islington and many other councils there are already agreed standards on ramps, doorways, disabled access and egress, parking bays, etc. published by the planning departments (this matter is also discussed in the appendix of Greed and Roberts 1998).

Summary

In conclusion to this section, it must be restated that one cannot give absolute 'standards' as to how to apply the principles discussed because everywhere is different. It is important to be aware of these wider dimensions, and to take care with the detail of the implementation of the scheme. Also, ongoing maintenance and supervision should be an integral part of the design strategy.

Key points to note are as follows:

- social differences need to be observed and accommodated;
- potential conflicts between different user groups should be anticipated;
- do not assume everybody is able-bodied;
- management, safety and the control of public and semi-public spaces are critical issues.

International comparisons

Introduction

This section steps back from the details of Clerkenwell and considers 'urban design' from an international per-

spective. The discussion of Clerkenwell has focused on British culture and the problems of inner-city London. In other countries, different traditions and problems give rise to different design solutions and this last section gives some consideration to two particular aspects of this: high-rise buildings and climatic considerations. Only a brief discussion is possible here, but the issues raised are indicative of the wider global diversity and complexity inherent in designing abroad, and readers may wish to pursue the themes raised in respect of the country of greatest interest to them.

The continuing high-rise movement

While Britain has had an unhappy relationship with high-rise, other countries, particularly in South East Asia and North America, continue to build very high, and a particular form of 'high-rise urban design' has evolved, appropriate to both New World and Tiger economies. The case study example of Farrell and Partners' Kowloon Station provides an example of this (see Unit 8). Many British architects, such as Richard Rogers, Norman Foster and Terry Farrell, are still getting commissions to build high-rises overseas. In February 1996, Petronas Towers in Kuala Lumpur became the tallest building in the world at 452 m, consisting of 1.6 million m^2 of floorspace, incorporating offices, shops, apartments and a mosque, within an equally crowded, intensively developed inner-city area.

While English opinion has swung against high-rise as a suitable form for housing, it should be remembered that across much of mainland Europe and in the major cities in Scotland the apartment block is the predominant form of urban housing. For example much of Barcelona consists of a continuous grid of apartment blocks with shops and cafés at ground level (Barcelona 1996; Greed and Roberts 1998). Far from seeing these as 'non-conforming uses', or as 'over-crowded', great pride and emphasis are put upon this arrangement, so much so that plans to extend the city along regained coastland are based upon continuing the grid to previously undeveloped areas of the city. The only concession to modern demands has been the decision to include underground car parking in some of these blocks. In investigating urban design in different countries it is most important not to judge others' cities by English garden suburb standards. Appendix 3 provides examples of how differing densities of people may be accommodated in varying types of housing forms and also gives some international comparisons.

Notable high-rise structures (The Concrete Society 1997)	
TV Tower, Delhi, 1988	235 m
Eiffel Tower, Paris, 1889	300 m
Empire State Building, New York, 1931	381 m
Sears Tower, Chicago, 1974	443 m
Menara TV Tower, Kuala Lumpur, 1996	420 m
Petronas Towers, Kuala Lumpur, 1996 (tallest building)	452 m
TV Tower, Moscow, 1967*	540 m
CN TV Tower, Toronto, 1976 (tallest mast structure)	553 m
London comparisons	
Canary Wharf	243 m
NatWest Tower	182 m
BT Tower	176 m
Nelson's Column	56 m

At time of writing, partially destroyed by fire.

Climatic factors

Not wishing to fall into the bottomless pit of 'geographical determinism' (i.e. local geography shaping the form of development), it is nevertheless significant that hotter countries do tend to favour higher density development (although admittedly there are many other factors beyond climate alone which determine building type, including financial and tenure considerations). In southern Europe, there has been an historical preference for buildings and dense street layouts that create shade (in the side streets at least). Traditional Islamic architecture has been concerned with creating cooling breezes and with internal courtyard design, resulting in 'nothing but blank walls' confronting the uninitiated; these give no indication of the richness of the urban form within, which is hidden from view.

Scandinavian countries have also been instigators of high-rise in the immediate post-war period but for different reasons. Because of the extreme, dark, cold winters, there is greater emphasis upon spacing out buildings in order to attract as much sunlight as possible, upon glass walling to get the maximum daylight in the building (Küller 1998) (a climatic necessity which subsequently became transplanted as part of the 'modern' style of architecture), and upon the advantages of communal heating systems in apartment blocks (many retain a separate traditional wooden 'summerhouse' in the countryside). Interestingly, in such countries it appears that the city planning departments seek to achieve sustainable development, 'women and planning' objectives, public transport that runs on time, and interesting urban form – in spite of sub-zero temperatures and vast amounts of snow (Skjerve 1993).

However, there are disadvantages in subarctic cities in having too much space and too wide roads, because of snow clearance and biting winds. Nevertheless, many Canadian cities include large areas of suburban, low-density housing. Many municipalities require all new residential developments to include an additional wide zone between the sidewalk and front lawns where ploughs can deposit the snow in winter. In fact, studies of subarctic and Arctic cities suggest that most are designed with little consideration of extreme climatic factors – the classic 'soviet' street grid plan with large squares being the very worst in creating wind tunnels, freezing the inhabitants in a world in which queuing for hours for basic necessities and public transport is far from a thing of the past.

The logical solution, as found in many Canadian towns, is to create extensive underground shopping malls. In Toronto it is possible to walk underground through connecting malls and subways for around 3 km, and if one lived in one of the central high-rise apartment blocks that have lifts/elevators which go down to the malls beneath, one would not necessarily need to go outside until spring arrived (Figure 10.3). In such cities the appearance of the city will differ greatly from summer to winter. Indeed, cities such as St Petersburg, Russia appear to have been designed to be 'seen' predominantly in the summer. Likewise much vegetation and landscaping in Scandinavian cities only comes into its own in summertime, and Midsummer is a sacred festival time celebrated as a major urban event. Such cities vary so much seasonally that each of them is effectively two cities, a summer city and a winter city.

In conclusion, this brief consideration of differing international traditions emphasises the importance of considering social and cultural factors in urban design. Contrasting design solutions may be reached according to differing cultural and social preferences. It has been impossible in this brief account to even point towards solutions. Instead we have tried to alert readers to the possibilities of difference.

Summary

This unit has emphasised the following points:

Figure 10.3 Entrance to a Scandinavian shopping mall: not much to be seen from the outside, but inside is a world of underground and indoor town centres (Clara Greed).

- the use of an evaluative framework for assessing design proposals: such a framework can be employed in the iterative design process, enabling the designer to check proposals against criteria;
- the necessity for urban designers to be aware of social difference and the potential effect that their proposals might have in the social composition of an area;
- noting that management and safety in public and semi-public spaces are critical issues;
- an awareness that urban designers may have to make a judgement on the conflicting requirements between stakeholder groups in any one locality;
- the need for sensitivity to social and cultural difference on an international scale, which might be manifested in custom, culture, climate or other factors relating to built form and urban structure.

Unit 11 The context for urban design in practice

Tony Lloyd-Jones

This unit provides a brief guide to who urban designers can expect to work for in practice, how they may determine and take account of the needs of different interest groups or 'stakeholders', and how urban design proposals can be implemented.

Organisations

Urban design can take place in a variety of development contexts – public, private, community and mixed development contexts. Typical clients or employers include the following:

The public sector

- Local authorities – in planning policy and project development or development control
- Central government – environmental and urban policy development

In the public sector, an urban designer will be working in (or as a consultant for) a local planning authority. They might be helping to produce development briefs for particularly important sites or providing urban design input into larger planning or conservation studies. They might have to devise masterplans or urban design frameworks, strategies or guidelines for conservation areas, city neighbourhoods or wider urban districts, or design guidelines for particular sectors such as housing or shopping centres.

In the UK, we can expect an increasing demand for urban design policies to be incorporated into local plans and to relate to demands for sustainable planning through integrated local transport policies, higher density housing, and mixed-use development. Local area regeneration initiatives also demand an urban design perspective (see Lloyd-Jones 1998: 34–5).

The intermediate sector

- Regeneration/development agencies and partnerships
- Large public or quasi-public landowners, such as health authorities
- Housing associations
- Community development trusts, tenants' co-ops and associations

Increasingly the skills of the urban designer are called upon by other public or quasi-public development agencies and public–private partnerships, e.g. central and local regeneration agencies and development area authorities, housing associations and large public landowners such as health authorities. Since such bodies are directly investing in development, there is a stress on masterplanning – providing the framework for the physical development of larger parcels of urban land, in terms of the layout, land uses, built form and phasing of development.

The private sector

- Mass house-builders
- Large private developers
- Transport infrastructure, power and water companies with large land-holdings
- Large retail and commercial organisations

For private sector clients, large institutional landowners, house-builders, corporations and other commercial organisations, urban design is called for at the feasibility and masterplanning stages in much the same way as for public development and regeneration agencies and partnerships. Investors tend to favour larger scale projects, many of which (e.g. housing schemes, industry, science, retail or office parks) require a masterplanning approach.

Private clients are often faced by planning constraints, whether relating to townscape and conservation issues, or other issues such as land use, layout, density or intensity of development, which potentially may prevent or slow the progress of a proposed site development. In such instances, planning consultants are often used and contextual or urban design studies commissioned to inform the brief for the architects' designs which follow.

Clients and users

The client, in most instances where an urban designer is employed, is likely to be one of the larger public or private organisations described above. They are the bodies responsible for funding a new development or for devising and implementing new planning policies affecting a particular site, area or urban type.

Users, on the other hand, will in most cases be numerous and diverse. Normally, as individuals or small-scale local organisations, they will wield considerably less decision-making power than the client organisation. We are talking here about the residents, businesses, employees, customers, tourists or other visitors on a particular site or using a particular street, set of streets and public spaces, neighbourhood or a larger area of a city.

In many instances, although not directly responsible for the financing or financial management of the development process, users participate in the briefing stage of the design process. Participation ranges from weaker forms of consultation, such as the procedures adopted by local authorities (and more publicly minded developers) to consult local residents and businesses over planning proposals (questionnaires, letters or announcements inviting comment, public meetings or formal inquiries) to the direct involvement of user groups in the briefing process. Examples of the latter might be tenants' organisations advising designers on housing layouts for housing association developments or on housing estate improvements for local authorities, or community organisations or small business associations involved as partners in urban area regeneration strategies.

There are two aspects to this process of user involvement. The first is pragmatic: users are best placed to provide detailed knowledge on how a place works, the problems they face on a day-to-day basis and the issues that concern them. The second aspect is a concern with local democracy: users ought to have a say in proposed changes to their environment. Those who argue that users should have the greatest say in how their environment is altered are calling for some kind of 'user empowerment'.

User empowerment

Empowerment of user organisations is achieved by their having control over the briefing process and sometimes over the whole development process. In urban regeneration, this occurs where the funding organisation (the local authority, or development or regeneration agency) hands over financial control of a project budget as a grant to a community organisation formally constituted as a non-profit-making trust or charity. Housing co-operatives are often set up in this way.

More commonly, development agencies make funds available to business and non-business organisations for the initial feasibility stages of projects that will lead to local area improvements – social, economic and environmental. In such cases, the user becomes the client and will employ their own business, financial or design consultants.

Local empowerment tends to be on a small, local scale and therefore is unlikely to require the services of an urban designer. Urban design skills, however, are likely to be useful where an initiative involves a series of linked local sites or where realising the development potential of a site or building requires a good understanding of the urban context. The urban designer is more likely to encounter the user-client as a partner with more powerful public and business bodies in regeneration partnerships or if asked to set up a framework for consultation with or participation of local users as part of the briefing process. Urban designers are often knowledgeable in techniques that can be used to facilitate participation. 'Action planning' and other tools that can be used to do this are mentioned below.

Clients' and users' requirements

How does an understanding of the needs of clients and users translate into a usable brief for the urban designer? What are the factors likely to be of concern in urban analysis or in developing criteria by which urban design proposals can be measured? In urban design terms, major user concerns are likely to include the following:

- quantitative aspects of space: relative areas of public, communal and private space, building footprints and total floor areas for different uses;
- overall layout: the shape of spaces and their relationship to one another, the physical relationship of private to public space in terms of security, outlook, or being overlooked;
- access and circulation of people and vehicles;
- the physical quality of the external spaces and environment, landscape and communal spaces;
- external appearance, aesthetics and the image/sense of place.

Where distinct from the users, the client will have use requirements that may be the same or similar, but often with different priorities. Clients will usually be more concerned with issues of cost than users, where the latter are not footing the bill for any new development.

Local authority and planning requirements

The urban designer's client may be concerned with developing a site but, as we have seen, the client is just as likely to be a local authority that is concerned with broader public issues. In any event, the urban designer will need to reconcile any proposed intervention with the requirements of the local authorities as set out in relevant planning policies and development control regulations.

A local authority acts as arbiter of the larger public interest, more specifically the interests of those who can vote or are liable for taxes within the boundaries of the administrative area that the authority covers. In setting out its requirements, a local authority will be seeking to reconcile these broader interests with the interests of local users. If not directly funding a development, in line with the users it will be less constrained by financial constraints in setting out these requirements. However, there will also normally be pressures, depending on the balance of local political power and public opinion, in favour of commercial development to bring new investment, people and jobs into an area (and tax revenue to the authority). Thus, depending on the political complexion of its local authority and where an area lies on the spectrum between relatively wealthy conservation areas and run down, poor areas in need of regeneration, urban design guidelines will need to take account of the needs of commercial development.

There is a broad, but not complete, area of overlap between urban design studies carried out for local authorities and the requirements of planning policy and regulations which act as another set of determinants of the design process. In the UK, planning policy is usually embodied in the local development plan (or unitary development plan). The sort of issues that students should be aware of in a theoretical urban design (or architectural) project include the following:

- Land use: previous and established uses, adjoining uses, mixed uses.
- Related land-use policy on employment, housing (including requirements for social housing), shopping centres and frontages, recreational and green spaces, provision of social facilities, etc.
- Intensity of development: plot or floor area ratios which set out the maximum allowable floorspace to net site area.
- Residential density: standards relating to the number of people, dwelling units or habitable room per hectare (and instances where these may be relaxed).
- Building lines in relation to the street, building setbacks and minimum distances for overlooking/ privacy, daylighting and sunlighting requirements (less used these days).
- Car parking and servicing requirements (parking levels are increasingly set at maximum as well as minimum levels for reasons of controlling the level of traffic and urban air pollution).
- Means of escape and building access where this affects the broad site configuration.
- Special urban design policies relating to the character of built form in urban areas, limits on building heights and on buildings obscuring important views, etc.

UK planning constraints are less prescriptive than they used to be, with much greater emphasis on the interpretation of written policy by local officers. Local planning policy is strongly influenced by written government guidelines set down in national and regional policy guidelines. The number of physical standards has been considerably reduced but, unfortunately, the tendency is for development control officers to rely more heavily on those that remain. The result is that planning constraints on development are often more rigid than intended.

Additionally, contradictions occur between developing planning policy and existing regulations. For example, residential density standards and car parking standards in many development plans, if rigidly adhered to, lead to suburban housing layouts that may be at odds with the existing urban form and the need to build more sustainable, higher density urban housing. Similarly, existing land-use zoning regulations may constrain more sustainable mixed-use development. In this type of situation, urban design studies can reveal the policy contradictions and limitations of existing regulations. This may result in revisions to the local plan or in the production of development briefs for particular important development sites, or guidelines for development areas that can supplement or stand in place of the local plan provisions. Additionally, urban design guidelines and frameworks focus on spatial issues that may be missed in the written policy of local development plans. These issues are dealt with in more detail in Unit 10.

Implementing urban design

Unit 5 describes a methodology for developing urban design proposals. While this is fine for student projects, in practice it provides only half the picture since the proposals also have to be implemented. This is a matter of obtaining the necessary support – both political and financial – and ensuring that the longer term management strategy is in place.

In practice, these are issues that are dealt with continuously and involve inputs from the urban designer from the earliest stages. Where there are physical development proposals that will be financed by private investment, financial appraisals of urban design schemes need to be carried out at an early stage to test their feasibility. Even if the aim is to provide urban design guidelines for a local authority development brief, it is useful to carry out such calculations to test whether the constraints on development are realistic or not. It is similarly important to understand the financial implications of larger area framework plans.

Alongside the financial appraisal, the management implications need to be understood. If the development itself is to take place over an extended period, phasing will need to be considered and cash flow managed (see Unit 8). Will the occupiers of a development be tenants, freeholders or leaseholders? How will the shared open spaces be managed and maintained? In proposals for public realm development, what are the maintenance costs and management implications for the authority that has responsibility for the area concerned? This can become complicated where responsibilities are shared among a number of public bodies and where the management of private properties fronting onto public areas also has an important impact.

Public participation

To ensure that any urban design proposals reflect local interests and gain the necessary political support, it is necessary to involve the leading stakeholders from the earliest stages. (A stakeholder is anybody with an interest in a particular development or other intervention such as any planning framework or local authority brief that will affect future development.) In practice, an urban designer might be expected to employ action planning methods and other aids to public participation to ensure a people-centred approach with user involvement and support. This issue is referred to in Unit 10. For further details of techniques, readers should consult Cowan (1997), Wates (1996), Wates and the Urban Design Group (1998) and Wates (2000).

Summary

This unit may be summarised as follows:
- Urban design can take place in a variety of development contexts – public, private, community and in mixed development contexts – but urban designers are most likely to be commissioned by the larger public and private bodies.
- The public sector client is most likely to be a local planning authority but other public or semi-public development and regeneration agencies are increasingly important.
- Private sector clients, large institutional landowners, house-builders, corporations and other commercial organisations have a need for urban design at the feasibility and masterplanning stages and in planning negotiations.
- Although not directly responsible for the financing of the development process, other individuals and organisations will have a stake in the urban design process. Their participation in the briefing stage of the design process and empowerment of user organisations are desirable goals.
- To ensure that any urban design proposals reflect local interests and gain the necessary political support, it is necessary to involve the leading stakeholders from the earliest stages.
- The urban designer will need to reconcile any proposed intervention with the requirements of the local authorities as set out in relevant planning policies and development control regulations.
- Urban design proposals can only be implemented by obtaining the necessary support – both political and financial – and by ensuring that the longer term management strategy is in place.

Unit 12 Urban design in the planning system

Tim Townshend and Ali Madanipour

The aim of this unit is to introduce some of the main issues of 'design control', i.e. the ways in which the planning system attempts to deal with design issues. It focuses on the various planning documents that address design, including the following:

- central government advice to local authorities;
- design policies in statutory local plans;
- supplementary guidance produced by planning authorities.

There is also a brief introduction to some issues of design control in the United States and France, to provide the reader with some preliminary examples of different approaches to the topics covered.

The question of design control

Town planners often find themselves dealing with design issues in the process of development control. This interface between planners and designers has perennially brought about several questions:

- Are planners well equipped to intervene in design control?
- How much intervention is appropriate?
- Is it possible to intervene in a field perceived to be largely subjective?
- Who should intervene and who sets the standards?
- What is involved in a design control process?

Designers often complain about the restrictions of the planning system, arguing that it limits their freedom of expression and undermines their creativity; some even seeing planning control as an unnecessary obstacle in their work. However, even without the intervention of planners, designers are not always completely free: they are subject to a brief by a client and to the restrictions of the development industry and the property market, which means designs often change in the process of being implemented. Planners, on the other hand, argue that their concern is with the public accountability of development schemes, which lies at the heart of the planning system. Without it, they stress, a local community will be unable to have a say in the new developments in their area. However, the extent to which the planners can represent the needs and aspirations of a locality has been questioned.

There are, therefore, a number of arguments for and against design control (Table 12.1). As in many arenas, the question is to what extent these arguments should or should not be settled by state intervention.

What is involved in design control?

At a more detailed level, one of the main debates is about what design issues are and what is involved in design control. As stated above, many wrongly assume that design issues only involve aesthetics. One implication of this notion is that design is perceived as superficial, lacking the importance of, for example, economic considerations. Design issues are thus seen as subjective and therefore unimportant issues, subordinate to the more urgent issues of economic development and job creation.

It is true that one of a designer's major preoccupations is with appearances. Aesthetic matters are, however, open to discussion and negotiation, as every

Table 12.1 Arguments for and against design control

Arguments for design control	Arguments against design control
Prevents outrages	Stifles imaginative expression
Introduces a democratic element to design	Reduces freedom of individuals
Bridges professional and lay tastes in design	Makes a nonsense out of an architect's professional training
Improves standards in design	Rarely stops poor buildings
Decisions are accountable because they are made by elected councillors	Gives power to those without design training

designer who has worked with a client knows all too well. Also, in some cases an attempt is made to classify beauty objectively. Certain natural areas, for example, are publicly declared as Areas of Outstanding Natural Beauty. Here the aesthetic judgement cannot be seen as entirely subjective as it involves a large number of people. The organisation of space and its social and psychological significance, therefore, may be less subjective than the arena of aesthetics and as such, design control will inevitably be a more objective process. There are also some who argue that the aesthetics of built form are not entirely subjective, such as architects of the Classical tradition who believe there is an inherent superiority in an architecture derived from natural laws.

Planning documents and design

The planning system is essentially involved in regulating the development and use of land in the public interest. To do so, it relies on a number of documents. There is, however, a basic three-tier system. The top layer is advice from central government, which takes a number of forms, though Planning Policy Guidance (PPG) is particularly important. Below this, all local planning authorities produce statutory development plans which reflect government guidance within the local context, and underneath this layer they may produce supplementary planning guidance covering issues of particular local concern.

Central government guidance

PPG1: General Policy and Principles

(DOE 1997) sets out the government's policies on different aspects of planning. The government's approach to planning is explained under three headings:

- sustainable development
- mixed use
- design

All three include elements of urban design issues. Under sustainability, for example, the pattern of new development is to be shaped so that the need to travel is minimised. Under mixed use, compactness, accessibility and a mixture of uses are promoted to create vitality and diversity, particularly in town centre environments. Where it specifically refers to design, some more detailed considerations are outlined in the main document, as well as in Annex A. PPG1 promotes good design and considers the appearance of a proposed development and its relationship to its surroundings as material considerations in determining planning applications and appeals. These considerations will include building and urban design, the latter being defined as the complex relationships between all the elements of built and unbuilt space. Local authorities are asked to enhance the character of their areas and promote local distinctiveness. But they are warned against paying attention to too much detail, or trying to arbitrarily impose a particular architectural taste or style, which could stifle innovation, originality or initiative.

Some of these ideas are spelt out in Annex A. It advises local planning authorities to develop their policies on the basis of a careful assessment of the context of their local area and concentrate on guiding the following:

- overall scale
- density
- massing
- height
- landscape
- layout
- access

These aspects should be considered in relation to the surrounding buildings and locality. The use of supplementary design guidance (guides and briefs) is encouraged in conjunction with development plans. Applicants for planning permission are encouraged to provide written as well as visual material and to consult at an early stage with all those who may have a relevant and legitimate interest in the development proposal.

Other PPGs also impinge on design issues:

- *PPG3: Housing* (DoE 1993) stresses the importance of quality design and landscaping, attention to site characteristics and so on.
- *PPG12: Development Plans and Guidance* (DoE 1992) stresses the importance of sustainable policies.
- *PPG15: Conservation Area and Listed Buildings* (DoE 1994) sets out policies for developments in areas of historical or architectural importance.
- *Design Bulletin 32* (DoE and DoT 1992) and *Places, Streets and Movement*, a companion guide to *Design Bulletin 32* (DETR 1998).
- *By Design. Urban design in the planning system: towards better practice* (DETR 2000). This guide aims to be a companion to advice contained in the PPGs and intends to promote higher standards of urban design in the planning system.

Design Bulletin 32, subtitled *Residential Roads and Footpaths: Layout Considerations*, was first produced in 1977 and revised in 1992 (DoE and DoT 1992). It offers detailed advice on the design of street systems in residential areas, aiming to help strike a balance between planning, housing and highway considerations in the design of new residential developments and improvement schemes. It outlines the main considerations that need to be taken into account in the preparation of design briefs, discusses the overall layout of roads and footpaths, and pays attention to the detailed design of carriageways, junctions, turning spaces, footways, verges, footpaths and parking spaces. While *Design Bulletin 32* remains the technical guide, *Places, Streets and Movement*, a companion guide to *Design Bulletin 32, Residential Roads and Footpaths* was added in 1998 to encourage more imaginative interpretation of the guidance (DETR 1998).

Documents produced by or for local authorities

Statutory development plans

Development plans are documents prepared by local authorities to regulate the development and use of land. Development plans, and the planning system in general, are seen by the government as the most effective way of reconciling the demand for development and the protection of the environment. A plan-led system is meant to ensure rational and consistent decisions, greater certainty, and public involvement in shaping local policies, allowing the planning process to work faster, and reducing the number of misconceived planning applications and appeals (DoE 1997: 7).

Development plans to date have shown a very low emphasis on design, as found in a study that examined 73 samples of plans (Punter *et al.* 1994: 217), which noted an overall lack of general design strategies or strategic design considerations. Design issues appear to be treated as marginal, dispensable considerations, concentrating heavily on individual buildings rather than being integrated into the plan's overall strategy. Most plans avoid either detailed coverage or prescription, and fail to relate design policy to local context. Moreover, while all plans are meant to reflect government guidance and are scrutinised by regional offices of the DETR, plans are never criticised for their poor attention to design (Punter and Carmona 1997: 67).

Only slightly more than one in ten plans included in the above research contained a well-developed design policy throughout, as exemplified by plans for Leicester, Bristol, Westminster, Guildford, Sheffield, Richmond and Haringey (Punter and Carmona 1997). The Bristol draft plan, for example, included a series of examples, suggesting correct and incorrect approaches to design solutions (Figure 12.1; Bristol City Council 1992). It therefore set out guidelines or benchmarks against which new developments could be assessed. In this approach it was very much influenced by earlier US precedents (see, for example, San Francisco Department of City Planning 1989). However, some of the illustrations were subsequently removed from the draft plan on recommendation from the DoE inspector who conducted the public inquiry.

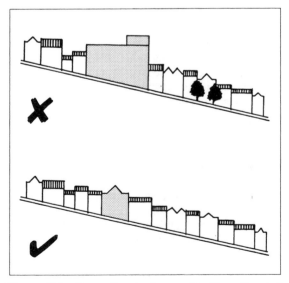

Figure 12.1 Responding to topography (from the draft Bristol local plan).

Design guides

Design guides are documents prepared by the local planning authorities as additional information and guidance regarding design matters. Design guides, as distinct from development plans, do not have statutory status and are classified as supplementary design guidance. Supplementary design guidance, however, can play a significant role in ensuring good design. This is especially so if it has been subjected to public consultation and formally adopted by the local planning authority (DoE 1997: 4, 12).

Where design guides have been prepared, they are often of a general nature to cover most eventualities. They may deal with large areas, or with specific topics, such as housing, shopfronts, security grilles and advertisements. Distinctive from these design guides, and ideally set within their framework, design briefs deal with specific sites and with more specific issues. Where design guides do not exist, design guidance may be limited to the general design principles within the local plan.

Example 1: Essex – a residential design guide   The first Essex *Design Guide for Residential Areas,* produced in 1973 (Essex County Council 1973), was a major document that influenced a generation of design guides across the UK. The guide has recently been rewritten and updated to include current concerns such as sustainability and the introduction of mixed uses (Essex County Council 1998), though the main concern of the guide remains what it refers to as the unacceptable 'suburbanisation' of the county.

The guides addresses both physical and visual design policies. Under physical design policies, the envelope and curtilage of the house, its services and standards of maintenance are discussed. Visual design policies concentrate on the principles of spatial organisation and design of buildings. In particular, the guide sees two major systems of spatial organisation to be at the opposite ends of a spectrum of spatial density (Figure 12.2). One is a rural system, where the land-scape contains buildings, and the other is an urban system, where buildings contain space (Essex County Council 1998). It argues that between these two systems is unsatisfactory suburbia where the buildings are too intense for the landscape to dominate, but are too loosely grouped, or are not commanding enough, to enclose space. The solution it promotes is one of new rural or new urban development.

Example 2: A city centre design guide   A well-known example of a city centre design guide was produced by a firm of consultants for Birmingham. The *City Centre Design Strategy* (Tibbalds, Colbourne, Karski & Williams 1990) was the first of a series of studies on the city, with the aim of presenting 'a robust, coherent, apolitical vision of how the physical environment of Birmingham's Central Area can be gradually improved over the next 30 years or so' (ibid: 1). It contains a mixture of generic models of good practice and more detailed visions for individual sites.

The first main concern of the strategy is to help people find their way around. This is a concern for legibility of the urban structure, and for increased accessibility within it. To achieve this the strategy outlines plans for the following:

- identifying transport nodes as gateways to the city centre;
- making movement around the city easier;
- marking places and spaces by landmarks (Figure 12.3);
- promoting livelihood in the city at night as well as by day.

The strategy recognises that landmarks not only assist in creating a legible city, but they also contribute to the *image* of the place which people form and take away as memory. The second main issue addressed by the strategy is consequently the development and protection of views. The specific aims are as follows:

- to only allow distinctive tall buildings, to create landmarks;

| Rural situation | Arcadia | Boulevard planning | Unsatisfactory suburbia | Urban situation | City scale |

Figure 12.2   Spectrum of visual density from the Essex Design Guide (Essex County Council).

(a)   **(b)**

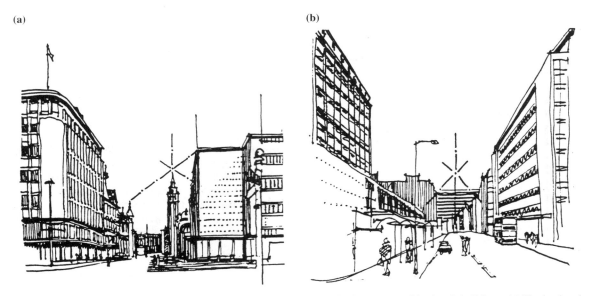

Figure 12.3   An illustration from Birmingham's design guide showing the importance of landmark buildings. (a) The landmark of Central Hall helps people to navigate. (b) The busiest railway station in the country is visually insignificant from approach routes.

- to protect existing views;
- to enhance views towards key landmark buildings;
- to reinforce the topography of the city, which was ignored by post-war development;
- to recreate streets and blocks obliterated by post-war redevelopment;
- to sweep away clutter;
- to soften the city and enhance open space.

It is hoped that the outcome will be a tightly knit urban fabric with carefully created and managed public spaces and landscapes.

Points of good practice to note from the Birmingham and Essex guides are as follows:

- there is a major over-arching theme to both documents;
- under the main theme of the guides there is a hierarchy of policies from the broad brush to the finely detailed;
- the policies are clear and concise and avoid the use of jargon;
- all policies are backed up with reasoned justifications;
- they are analytical rather than descriptive;
- they use a range of excellent illustrations;
- they were both the result of widespread consultation.

Preparing a design guide

Design guides can therefore be produced 'in-house' by a local authority as the Essex design guide was, or by consultants working for the local authority as in the case of Birmingham. As is evident from these examples, the preparation of a design guide draws upon two sources of information: the locality and design literature. Design guide authors should therefore undertake the methods and procedures that are advocated in this book. In addition, design literature offers an understanding of the qualities of the environment as well as normative ways of designing in the environment. Historic precedents from around the world have always played a prominent role in design literature. Also, international debates on design issues have been very influential in the cultivation of taste and development of new conventions, such as the debates taking place around the development, and adoption or rejection of modernist design. It is therefore through a combination of careful analysis of the locality's social and physical context and an awareness of the design literature that it becomes possible to prepare a design guide.

Village design statements

Village design statements (VDSs) are a recent innovation in the UK planning system and have a similar status to design guides (i.e. they are supplementary planning guidance), but deal specifically with rural settlements. They are a concept that the Countryside Commission in England has been working on since 1993 in reaction to the standardisation of developments, particularly housing, in rural settlements throughout the country (Countryside Commission 1993). VDSs are based on the concept that the residents of a village have a unique perspective on the character of the place in which they live and that this can be translated into a document to inform planning policy. The aim is that VDSs will be written primarily by the villagers themselves and used by the local authority to guide new development. In this way they perform a role similar to a design guide.

VDSs are an interesting development because of their direct engagement of the public in design issues and though intended originally for rural areas they are already being adapted for non-rural locations, such as Tynemouth, North Tyneside. The documents produced so far vary in their content since they are highly specific to their particular settlement, but the Cartmel in Cumbria VDS, for example, includes sections on the following:

- evolution of the village
- the landscape setting of the village
- form and space
- building materials and styles

The Cartmel document has been successfully used by South Lakeland District Council, which has adopted it as supplementary guidance, to refuse permission for a development which villagers felt would be detrimental and to uphold this refusal at appeal.

Design briefs

The design brief is another form of supplementary design guidance. The term 'design brief', however, has a variety of meanings and is used inconsistently. Different planning authorities use different terms – planning brief, development brief, principles of development, planning guidance, planning framework etc. – along with design brief. One of the common characteristics of the different definitions of briefs is that they all offer detailed development guidance for specific sites, distinguishing them from design guides which focus on areas or issues (Madanipour *et al.* 1993).

A design brief has been defined as incorporating 'the full range of requirements specified by the local planning authority for the development and design treatment of particular sites, with explicit emphasis on the appearance of the development' (Owen 1979: 1). The Royal Town Planning Institute's definition of the development brief is 'a summary statement of the author's policy position on development matters relating to the site and/or premises', and any other relevant material (RTPI 1990). This is largely in line with an earlier DoE (1976: 25) definition suggested in the context of housing development: 'A brief for a site is a detailed statement of what development the local authority would like on that particular site alone.' A brief is often prepared for sites that are economically, socially or architecturally sensitive; for local authority sites that are being released; and for many residential developments.

The RTPI (1990) acknowledges a variety of terms and forms, stating that 'briefs are non-statutory documents and there are no regulations specifying their role and format'. However, it also attempts to offer a clarifying framework for terminology in the preparation and use of briefs. The RTPI suggests the term 'development brief' as a general term which can cover these various areas of concern. It includes the following:

- planning briefs, which deal with planning, land use and transportation matters;
- developers' briefs, which address financial and land management aspects;
- design briefs, which cover townscape and other design aspects, and aesthetics.

In practice, however, as the RTPI notes, some or all of these matters are often combined in such documents.

Apart from design briefs prepared by the planning authority, briefs are also prepared by architects as the beginning stage of a project, covering the requirements of the client for a site or even putting ideas forward to the client. A design brief in this context is therefore 'information, both general and specific, assembled for the purpose', which clarifies the circumstances and requirements (Powell 1980: 374). It is 'the factual foundation of the project' (Cox and Hamilton 1991: 221). Conventionally, the architects have the task of producing a design which, in their judgement, satisfies the client's brief completely (Thompson 1990: 95). In this sense, the meaning of 'design brief' for architects and planners overlaps, though the two professions have different positions regarding the preparation and implementation of briefs. Whereas planners prepare briefs as frameworks for development, architects and developers work within this framework and a framework of their own.

There are two major component parts in a brief:

1. a descriptive part which contains information on the characteristics and the context of the site; and
2. a prescriptive (to varying degrees) part in which the

intentions of the planning authority for the site are spelled out.

The contents of a brief are largely determined by the nature of the site and the range of issues that the authority wishes to address in the brief. Both of these vary widely. Briefs can be very broad and short or very specialist and detailed. Some briefs cover almost everything from planning background to design content, which can include density, size of development, amount of open space, highway access, relationship to neighbouring properties, landscaping, and designing out crime. The building design content could stipulate the form, massing, scale, context, materials, and very occasionally the actual architectural style of the development. The brief could also contain some element of community gain it is hoped will be achieved, such as play areas, crèche facilities, community rooms, and access for the disabled.

Not all briefs are structured in exactly the same way, though most include the following:

- background and the purpose of the brief;
- location and description of the site;
- planning and design requirements, including vehicular/pedestrian access and circulation; parking and garaging requirements; public open space and landscaping;
- engineering and construction requirements;
- procedure of application;
- plans of the site.

Some briefs also categorise their requirements into essential and preferred.

Example 1: City Centre Brief – St Paul's Chambers Planning

The St Paul's Chambers brief (Sheffield City Council 1997) was produced to guide a regeneration project at the heart of Sheffield's city centre. It provides a vision for the building and its adjoining public spaces and sets out how this fitted into the city masterplan: The Heart of the City Project (Figure 12.4). The plan includes written information, such as background and contextual issues, plans for an adjacent public space, planning context, detailed information such as access for the disabled, and visual material in the form of appropriate plans and illustrations. Finally it includes those policies that are relevant from the Sheffield Unitary Development Plan. Design briefs are documents through which the intentions of the planning authority for the development of a site are expressed. The level of certainty with which the planners can express these intentions varies widely according to circumstances. In most cases, however, documenting these intentions provides a framework

Figure 12.4 City centre brief: St Paul's Chambers Planning Brief (Sheffield City Council 1997).

for negotiation with the potential developers. The outcome of such a negotiating process is again dependent on circumstances.

The success or failure of briefs cannot always be evaluated in terms of their resistance to change and their assertion of an original intention, and they should not be judged in this way. If, however, they are evaluated according to their success in initiating a dialogue, then they have a potentially promising capacity. Their success lies in the fact that this dialogue can create a sense of certainty for the applicants and the best possible use of resources for the local authority. To ensure success, briefs should strike a balance between the need for control and the need for flexibility. They should be prepared only after a wide process of consultation, both inside and outside the local authority, and in the context of an overall design vision. In this sense, design briefs are potentially an essential tier of policy in a planning process which attempts to manage change and development in the built environment. Design briefs, design guides and development plans can be seen as complementary devices in the planning process.

Design control in the United States and France

The USA

In the United States, the term 'design review' is used to refer to 'the public review of the design of private development proposals' (Scheer and Preiser 1994: 308), a practice which has been increasingly adopted by American local planning authorities. As a recent study showed, 87% of cities with populations over 10,000 have embarked upon some form of design review. This could range from informal, *ad hoc* advisory groups to formal boards making decisions through legally binding procedures. It shows a substantial growth of interest in design control in the last two decades, as only 12.5% of cities had design review procedures in place before 1970. However, design review is still disliked by designers, who complain about the lack of reviewers' qualifications. Furthermore, design review is very much within the control of local bureaucracy, as public participation was allowed in only 18% of the cities' design reviews, none of which had a significant impact on the outcome of the design review process (Scheer and Preiser 1994).

Despite signs of converging trends, the main difference between British and American planning and design control is that the former is discretionary, whereas the latter is based on legally binding written regulations. The main method of regulation, with most influence on the shape of the cities, is the zoning system of land-use control. A classic example is the Chicago Zoning Ordinance, which lists 22 types of use-district and 71 categories of floor:area ratio. The bulk of this Ordinance deals with prescribing dimensions, beyond which there is no other reference to design and aesthetic objectives.

An alternative way of controlling design has been by the following of a 'stylistic imperative', where the planning authority expects development to be in keeping with the surrounding architectural styles. Private landowners who subdivide their land may also call for stylistic harmony, asking individual developers to follow some design rules (Delafons 1992); an example of this would be Seaside in Florida (Figure 12.5).

France

In France, debates about the control of architectural design between planners and architects occur in the same way as they do in Britain. The demand for protecting the character of areas under heavy development pressure has again led to new forms of design control. The Plan d'Occupation des Sols (POS), or French land-use plan, is a legally binding document and if a proposal meets its requirements, it must be approved. Many of the plans, however, are not sufficiently sensitive to the character of the localities they deal with. Such was the case at Asnières sur Oise in 1987, as outlined below. To prevent the suburbanisation of the town, a new system of design control has been devised, which has been endorsed by the French minister of the environment and has been used in three other communes in the Ile de France (Samuels 1995).

Example: Asnières sur Oise Ansières is located 35 km north of Paris and was identified by developers as a desirable location for new residential development. The new houses, however, tended to be in the form of *pavillons*, detached single-family houses, whose suburban morphology contrasted with the existing character of the town and its traditional streets lined by continuous buildings.

The new POS in Asnières draws upon the Italian morphological approaches and British design guides (such as the Essex Design Guide) to analyse the local character and to specify the preferred forms that would maintain this character. Through direct observation, discussions with local experts, and desk research, the new POS analyses the morphology of the settlement at six different levels of resolution:

- districts
- streets
- blocks

Figure 12.5 Houses in Seaside, Florida, have to conform to strict design guidelines.

- plots
- building form
- elements of construction

At each level, a range of acceptable varieties are then put forward. At the district level, for example, a range of acceptable land uses and plot types are identified. Within each plot type (with its minimum dimensions, plot proportions, buildable area and plot coverage), there are typically three to five acceptable building types. The two elements of construction, roofs and walls, include details of acceptable types of chimneys, dormers, openings, doors and windows.

The range of choice at the lower level of resolution, i.e. the detailed elements of construction such as doors and windows, is far more restricted than at the higher levels; there is more choice of plot size and building arrangement, for example. This is in contrast to the housing developers' formula to achieve diversity in their developments, where details may vary within a limited range of building form and plot type. There are also commonalities to be observed within districts and between them. In each district, for example, there is a common range of possibilities for length of façades, type and degree of roof pitch, length of gable wall, and a range of permitted storeys and of proportion between building height and building depth. The common range of details for all districts covers gutters, chimneys, dormers, façade opening arrangements, types of doors, window frames and shutters, wall and roof materials, and even hedging shrubs (Samuels 1995).

The Asnières example can be seen as being positive in several ways:

- the process was democratic, the plan was regularly exposed to public input, and the decisions to protect Asnières' character can also, therefore, be seen as democratic;
- it shows non-professional applicants the range of possibilities open to them;
- when applied correctly, the outcome can be visually, functionally and financially successful.

Conclusion

Design control, as part of the process of urban planning, has been the subject of much controversy and debate. Some see it as a necessary tool in safeguarding the quality of the environment, while others see it as stifling and restrictive. We have seen, however, that it is not possible to dismiss it as dealing with a subjective issue, as design has a considerable impact on the shape and quality of places and, through them, on people's lives and minds. That is why we notice an increased sensitivity to design issues in Britain, as well as in other countries including the United States and France.

In dealing with design issues, planning documents may be most effective when they contribute towards an overall design vision – a vision that is linked to the formal plan policies, is supported by public consultation, and avoids excessive prescription, leaving room for innovation. Design documents, no matter how well produced, however, will not in themselves lead to better design, this is still very much dependent on the skill and commitment of those who use them. It is to be hoped that a wider adoption of good principles in urban design, throughout the planning system, will encourage a greater emphasis on urban design training. Such knowledge and skills would also have to be disseminated throughout the development industry, in order to achieve Kevin Lynch's ideals of 'good city form'.

Summary

Design in the built environment is concerned with the organisation of space, the way places are shaped and used, and not simply about aesthetics; design control is not only about controlling the appearance of buildings.

In the UK there are basically three tiers of planning documents dealing with design control:

- *Central government advice* – issued mainly through PPGs. This gives general principles which the government hopes will contribute towards good design, e.g. stressing the need for sustainable development.
- *Statutory local plans issued by every local authority*. These should reflect government advice on design control within the context of the local authority's area, though the extent to which they do this varies greatly.
- *Supplementary planning guidance* – produced by or for the local authority in a number of forms, from authority-wide design guides and strategies to topic- and site-specific design briefs.

BLOCK V INFORMATION

Appendix 1: Getting started

Tony Lloyd-Jones

Defining the context study area

Defining the boundary of the local context in which the detailed appraisal is carried out depends to a degree on the time and resources available. If the boundary is drawn too widely, the physical surveys will be too arduous or will be done superficially. In some cases, it might be appropriate to focus on the immediate site context and concentrate on the sort of information that can be obtained from inspecting the site and its immediate adjoining properties.

It is always useful, however, to carry out some of the map-based studies since they can provide clues to how a particular site development or other physical urban intervention might be designed which may not be apparent from a limited site survey.

Sometimes, the area for an urban design study is defined in the client's brief, for example where a local authority is interested in developing an urban design framework or guidelines for a given urban quarter, neighbourhood, conservation or economic regeneration area. Otherwise, the criteria for defining the study area include the following (Figure A1.1):

- natural barriers to movement or 'edges', e.g. railways, rivers and canals, fast roads or sharp changes in level;
- gateways: important points of entry into the area, e.g. railway stations, road junctions;
- survey areas: areas that can be covered on foot to carry out visual surveys in the time available – initially a radius of 250–300 m may be used;
- administrative boundaries: if broadly coincidental with the above, these can be useful in collecting statistical data and relating to local authority management functions – an administrative or statistical unit of 50–100 ha.

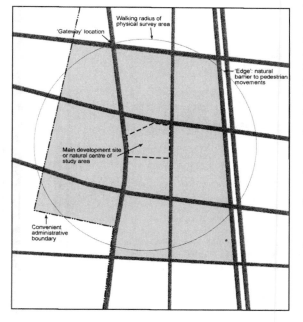

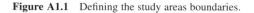
Study area using appropriate local parameters

Figure A1.1 Defining the study areas boundaries.

Base maps and drawing scales

In any urban design exercise, it is important to obtain

(a)

(b)

(c)

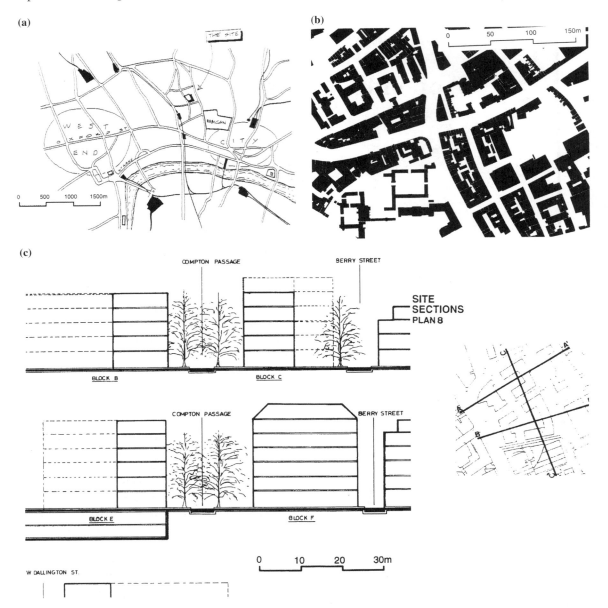

Figure A1.2 Examples of the use of different scale in drawings. (a) Central London map showing strategic site location (Carlos Chamorro, Abdulla El-Hilly, Martin Evans, Jane Fowles, Saci Gabour, Daniela Lucchese and Caroline Lwin) (originally drawn at a scale of approximately 1:20,000). (b) Figure ground drawing of Clerkenwell (Stella Bolonaki, Carlos Chamorro, Eugene Dreyer and Abdulla El-Hilly (originally drawn at a scale of approximately 1:2500). (c) Block plan and site sections (Carlos Chamorro) (originally drawn at a scale of 1:500).

accurate maps of the study area at various scales (Figure A1.2). These can be used as base plans to plot survey information and carry out analytical studies. Typically, the following scales are used.

1:10,000 scale and smaller: study site in a city context

Maps with a scale of 1:10,000 are used to plot the strategic location of the area in relation to the city as a whole, major transport routes, important city locations, districts and broad land-use areas or in relation to strategic development factors. This can be done quickly and easily as a simple desk exercise. Small-scale maps might also be used to map the catchment areas of particular attractions that are the focus of the urban design exercise.

1:5000 scale: study site in a district context

At a scale of 1:5000, built form can be discerned but not in any useful detail. Such maps are useful for land-use and transport studies at the district scale.

1:1000, 1:1250, 1:2000, 1:2500: study site in a local context

UK Ordnance Survey maps are available at 1:1250 and 1:2500 scales, although other scales can be obtained through simple reduction or enlargement. Base maps at this range of scales are most useful for carrying out context and area studies. Built form is shown in some detail but the larger patterns of streets and blocks are also evident.

1:500, 1:1000: site planning

Site planning exercises and more detailed examinations of urban types and the built form of urban block, street or space in plan and section is best carried out at the 1:500 scale, although it may sometimes be necessary to go down to the 1:1000 scale.

1:200: building layout and analysis

The 1:200 scale is the largest scale that is likely to be used in urban design. It can be used to carry out more detailed studies of building sections and façades and general building layouts. While urban design is not generally concerned with the detailed plan form of buildings, it is sometimes necessary to know how the internal circulation works in relation to street

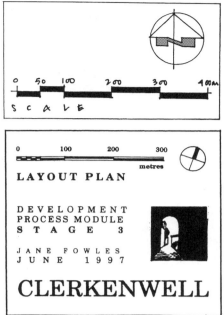

Figure A1.3 Examples of linear scales and north points in standard panels.

entrances and points of access, and how a larger building block is subdivided into smaller units, e.g. offices or flats.

On some of the more abstract and diagrammatic drawings (e.g. concept diagrams) the scale is not important, but map-based diagrams must show the scale to enable the person looking at them to get an idea of distance and area. Sometimes it is necessary to change the size of a drawing to fit it onto a standard sheet (A4 and A3 are useful as they can fit in reports) but they may no longer be to an exact scale. For this reason, it is always useful to include a linear scale, which can be used to measure off distances, as well as a north point to indicate orientation on map-based drawings (Figure A1.3). These can be provided alongside other essential information – such as what and where the project is, what the drawing shows and who has produced it – in a standard panel that is attached to each sheet.

Appendix 2: Urban types

Bill Erickson and David Seex

Urban grids

Grids have two constituent elements:

- a lattice of streets, and
- a series of blocks formed by buildings.

This seems obvious but the design criteria for each may differ and influence the outcome of the final design. The two will be related, e.g. larger, taller buildings may require wider streets. It is useful, however, to consider the two aspects separately.

Grid types

Regular grid

The most obvious grid is that where the blocks are regular and rectangular (Figure A2.1a). The streets form a tight network but while the grid may be regular, the buildings and plots may differ to a degree within the rigid layout.

Organic grid

Settlements that are less rigorously planned, such as traditional villages, have a more irregular and haphazard grid (Figure A2.1b). The example of a Greek island village illustrates this type. Here the layout is irregular and has evolved over many years, but the streets do join up to form a network and there are very few dead-end streets. Both streets and blocks are of differing sizes and meet at odd angles; however, on observation

it is evident that there is a degree of uniformity in the nature of the buildings.

Distorted grid

While regular grids are sometimes felt to be boring, organic grids are difficult to plan. A compromise is frequently arrived at by using a distorted grid, which creates more interesting streets but mostly in regular blocks (Figure A2.1c). In this example the streets curve and are of differing lengths; however, the blocks have a marked similarity, as do the buildings and plots.

Informal or highly distorted grid

The final example is where the streets are of various sizes and they curve to form organic shapes (Figure A2.1d). This could be called an informal pattern. The streets no longer form a network, and many of the streets do not join up at all. This forces people to make long journeys. However, on close examination it is evident that the roads have been placed in such a way that the building plots are all of a similar size and the buildings are more or less placed at a uniform distance. In some ways this can be thought of as a highly distorted grid.

Grid types and natural movement

The main function of the grid is as a space of movement. The roads provide access to the buildings that fill the blocks. The actual arrangement of the network of

(a)

(b)

(c)

(d)

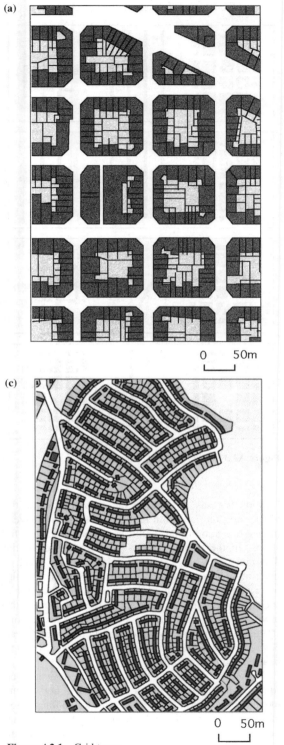

0   50m

0   50m

0   50m

0   50m

Figure A2.1   Grid types.

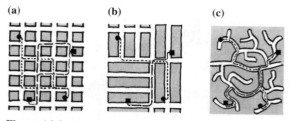

Figure A2.2 Grids and movement (a) a regular grid with a wide variety of possible routes; (b) a regular grid with fewer routes; (c) an irregular grid with few routes.

streets will affect the manner in which people move around the system. Consider the three examples in Figure A2.2. The first represents a regular grid, the second a grid with much larger blocks, and the third a more organic layout which could be thought of as a highly distorted grid.

In the first instance there is a wide variety of choices when making either of the journeys. In the second and third examples the choices are fewer and people are forced to use particular roads more than others. Any point in the system is a potential origin or destination, and at any one time a level of natural movement will be taking place between a variety of places. As people move about they are likely to take the most obvious or direct route and some streets will be used more frequently than others. The streets that will be used the most are those that are well connected into the system as a whole. This degree of connectivity is known as integration, and a technique to measure it using computer modelling has been developed at Space Syntax Laboratory, University College, London. Integration measures the average connectivity of any particular street to all other streets, not just those with which it has an intersection.

Figure A2.3 demonstrates how the measure of connectivity of streets changes with differing configurations of a simple grid. There are two ways to measure this. The first is to think of integration: a well-connected street will have a high level of integration and is shown in a darker colour, while a street with low integration is shown in a light colour. The second measure is proximity: here the distance one needs to travel from any particular point to all other points is averaged, and again well-connected spaces are shown in darker colours. Obviously spaces in the centre will be better off in this measure.

The first example shows a square grid and demonstrates how streets have a similar degree of integration while spaces in the centre have high proximity. This suggests that a location on any of the streets towards the centre would be well connected and a good

grid form   integration   connectivity

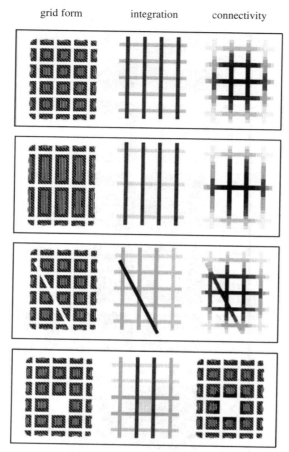

Figure A2.3 Grid types and connectivity.

location for, say, a shop. In the second example the blocks are long and thin and the cross streets have a higher integration and would be a better location for shops. In the third example the introduction of the diagonal street has a dramatic effect on the level of integration due to the fact that it crosses most of the other streets. Furthermore, because this one street has such a high level of integration, the average of the others is lowered and they become closer. This demonstrates how in some instances particular streets can have a privileged place in the network and are likely to be used more frequently.

In the final example a block is replaced by an open square. The square is like a street and is part of the movement network. It therefore adds to the integration of streets that pass through the square. Addresses that face the square will have better amenities and are highly integrated. This demonstrates how the locations that face the square become privileged and are likely to be higher value locations.

The properties of road networks are to a degree independent of the size of the blocks involved. This demonstrates that while on the one hand it is important to maintain highly permeable systems, inevitably some parts of the network will be more highly connected. These are the places where natural movement is likely to be highest and are the obvious locations for features that might be thought of as forming part of the armature rather than part of the fabric.

The size of blocks

Block size will be determined by the building types that occupy it (Figure A2.4). Where the buildings are detached, the size of the building in conjunction with any desired set-back will give a minimum plot size, and the block can then be subdivided accordingly. Some building types such as flats or offices may be well suited to square blocks, while others such as terraced or row houses are better suited to long thin blocks.

The open space inside a block may be associated with particular buildings within the block, e.g. in the form of a garden, or it may be shared between all the buildings in the block, e.g. as a car park. These outdoor spaces are essential to the functioning of the buildings as they provide light as well as usable space. The size of the block is a simple addition of the typical depth of the buildings plus the minimum size of the desired open space.

Blocks with private outdoor space

Gardens may belong to particular dwellings or be shared by a group of dwellings, but in any case, in addition to outdoor living space, they provide a physical separation between buildings which gives privacy. A minimum distance between buildings would be about 20 m, so if the buildings were two-storey houses each garden may be 8–10 m deep which would give a total block width of 40 m.

Blocks with public outdoor spaces

If the central space is to be used for servicing or parking the space needs to be large enough to allow access.

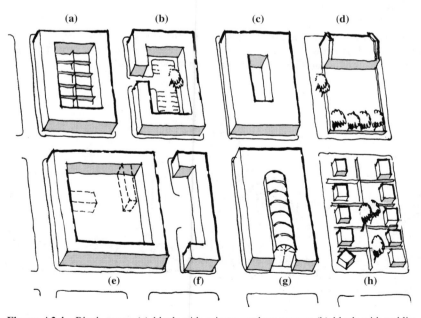

Figure A2.4 Block types: (a) block with private outdoor spaces; (b) block with public outdoor space; (c) thick building with courtyard; (d) detached dwelling; (e) large block with a large internal space; (f) thin block with rear access; (g) single-use block; (h) blocks with detached dwellings.

This will vary with circumstances but 20 m is a practical minimum.

Thicker buildings

Where building types suggest a thicker section, such as an office building, the internal space will shrink if the block size remains the same. In this case the space shrinks to a courtyard and while this may still provide light and air it will no longer provide privacy between neighbours. With uses such as offices this is not likely to be a problem.

Large blocks

If blocks are very large then the internal spaces will also be large and while this may provide a high level of amenity it will reduce the overall density. Over time this development pressure can lead to extending buildings into the internal space, which may be inappropriate. On the other hand, some building, such as schools, require large areas of open space.

Thin blocks

If the block layout is too thin it will provide room for buildings along one frontage only. This may not be ideal for uses such as housing where the privacy at the rear may be compromised. However, in other cases a thin block can be used to provide service access to the rear of buildings. This is particularly useful for rows of shops, for example.

Single-use blocks

Many modern buildings occupy entire blocks. They may include internal spaces that act like outdoor spaces, e.g. an atrium or a gallery. They can be sized in a similar manner by assessing the typical depth of the building and the size of the internal space. Single-use buildings are more adaptable and can fit into odd-shaped blocks.

Blocks with detached buildings

Many building types are associated with a good deal of outdoor space.

The street in section

Streets are three-dimensional spaces but one dimension is clearly dominant: the length. Streets are formed by rows of buildings which face onto the street, usually from both sides (Figure A2.5). The experience of being in a street will vary enormously, and several factors can be identified as contributing to this:

- *Movement.* Is the street a main road and full of traffic or does it just provide access to the buildings which line it?

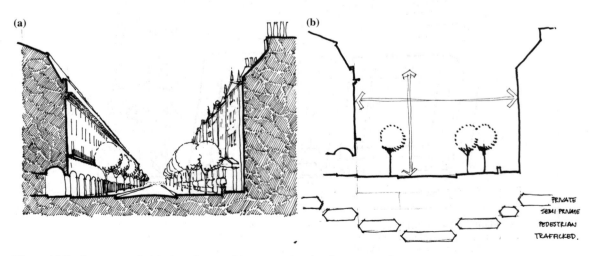

(a)   (b)

PRIVATE
SEMI PRIVATE
PEDESTRIAN
TRAFFICKED.

Figure A2.5   Street example (a) view of street; (b) street section showing aspect ratio.

- *Activity.* Is the street busy, is it a space of transaction and are the fronts active?
- *Containment.* Do the buildings form a strong edge or is one aware of spaces between and behind the buildings? Are the buildings high or low compared with the width of the street?
- *Built form.* The style and treatment of the building will influence the street. In particular, are the buildings similar and do they have common features? This will give unity to the street. On the other hand, if the buildings are diverse in size and style they will tend to dominate the space of the street more.
- *Perspective.* Some features can emphasise the length of streets, e.g. the constant repetition of objects such as trees, architectural features or consistent building lines. Features of the skyline can also be important.
- *Objects in the space.* Objects that fill the space of the street will add interest. Trees are especially important as they are often in rows, which emphasises the direction of the street, while at the same time obscuring the façades of buildings. Other objects may include street furniture such as lampposts, benches, signs, fences and of course people and vehicles.
- *Public/private interface.* A variety of spatial devices are used to separate the public space of the street from the private spaces inside. These may include private outdoor spaces, gardens, fences, etc. In some instances, the public space continues into the building line, such as in arcades or ground-floor shops.

The nature of streets is such that much of this information can best be described in section. Street sections are especially useful in comparative analyses.

Aspect ratio

The aspect ratio is the ratio of width to height. The width is usually to the building line and the height is from the ground to the top of the façade unless the roof is especially dominant (Figure A2.5b). Ratios are typically in the range of 1:3 to 1.5:1. In some areas they can be as high as 1:6, which is typical of canyon-like streets with skyscrapers, while low-density residential streets may be as low as 8:1. (Figure 2.6)

Carriageway

The carriageway is the area used by vehicles. A typical

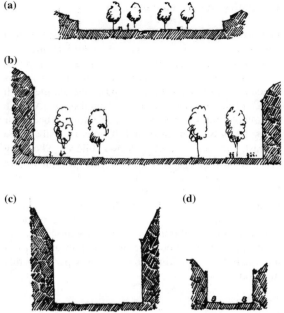

Figure A2.6   Range of street section: (a) suburban street; (b) Champs-Elysees; (c) Regent street; (d) Victorian row houses.

traffic lane will vary from about 2.5 m wide as a minimum in an access road to about 3.5 m for traffic moving at speed. A one-way service road needs to be at least 3.1 m wide to allow for fire tenders and refuse vehicles. A parking lane is about 2 m wide. This means that a typical carriageway with two lanes of traffic and roadside parking will need to be at least 10 m wide (Figure A2.7). This should be increased by at least 2 m if cycle lanes are included.

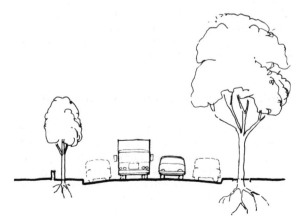

Figure A2.7   Traffic lanes.

Footpaths and pavement widths

Pedestrian spaces in streets often come last when it comes to competing for space. In addition, they are crammed with street furniture such as lamp-posts, trees, bus shelters and so on. A minimum of 2 m is needed to allow pedestrians to pass one another with ease and this is adequate in residential areas. A more reasonable minimum is 3 m, which allows wheelchair users to pass with ease and people to walk three abreast, such as an adult with two children. Shopping areas require 4–5 m and more if the pavements are used by people selling things or sitting at tables. Footpaths should be separated from traffic lanes. An ideal way is to place a row of trees between the pedestrian pavement and the carriageway as this provides a physical barrier and improves the microclimate. In any event, pedestrians should be at least 1 m away from moving traffic. A parking lane frequently performs this function.

Street trees

Trees can grow to be very large – some may grow larger than a house, for example. Given time and space, common species will grow to heights of 20–25 m, with a spread of up to 20 m. However, due to pollution and physical damage, growing conditions in streets are not ideal. In addition, trees in urban areas need to be pruned to prevent limbs falling in storms. This means that a more typical size for street trees is about 15 m high and 10 m wide. Trees also grow below ground and here too conditions are poor and congested, with little water because of the extent of hard paving. For this reason trees should have an area of soft paving at least a metre or two wide around their trunks to allow water and air to the soil. Obviously trees can occupy spaces above footpaths and carriageways but they need space to mature as they grow and a minimum of 3–5 m should be allowed for young trees.

Typical buildings and their requirements

Summaries of the space requirements of the principle building types and some of the standards applied to them by British and other European planning authorities are illustrated in Figures A2.8 to A2.11. Buildings provide protected space for defined activities by means of walls, a roof and internal subdivisions into rooms or 'cells'. We need to have an appreciation of how these cells relate to each other and to the outside

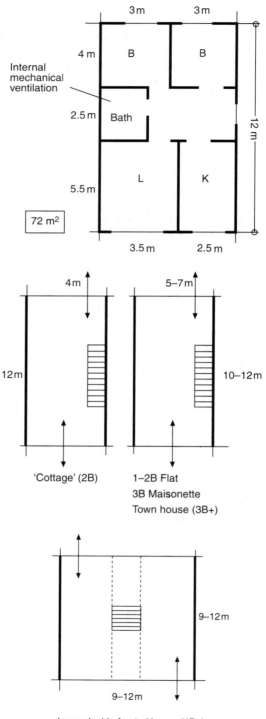

Figure A2.8 Urban house types.

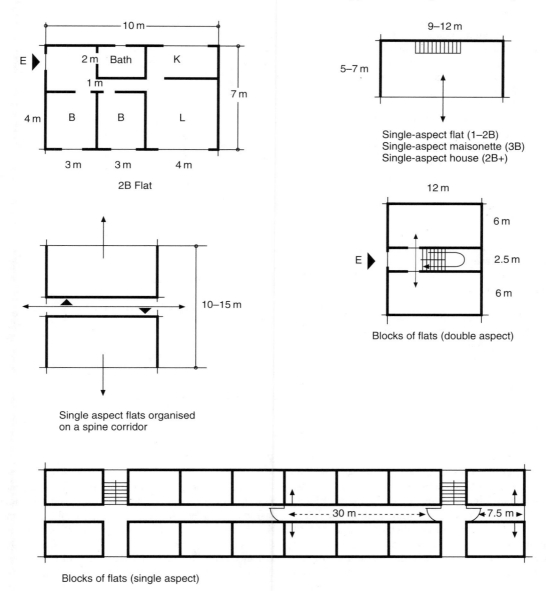

Figure A2.9 Types of flats.

world because they have an impact on, for example, where the external doors and windows of a building are and how close or distant they should be from other buildings or public spaces. Thus the designer must be aware of the constraints on the sizes and arrangements of rooms and buildings, e.g. the requirement for natural light or the maximum distance to a fire exit. Without this awareness we would be unable to produce a workable site layout or 'footprint' of buildings and spaces. The built envelope or structure of the building provides a controlled environment within the building. This control can be considered under two categories: control over the natural environment and control over human activity.

- *Environmental control*: this includes the provision of shelter from the elements (e.g. the walls and roof of the building), natural lighting (e.g. windows) and natural ventilation (e.g. windows).
- *Activity control*: this includes (i) physical access to and from the building (e.g. front doors, emergency exits), the different requirements for public, private and service access, horizontal and vertical movement within the building, and (ii) visual access including the requirement for clear visibility from the public realm of certain entrances and for views into or out of buildings.

Residential buildings

Dwellings are almost always shallow buildings – normally only two rooms deep – in order that all the 'habitable' rooms can receive natural light. The only common exception to this is the 'single aspect' dwelling one or one and a half rooms deep, which if grouped together back to back, as in a block of flats, will result in a building three or three and a half rooms deep. Dwellings normally have a clearly defined front for both physical and visual access (so that visitors can easily identify the approach) and a back (which would be accessed only from 'private' areas).

Office buildings

Office buildings normally need to accommodate a range of sizes of rooms for differing purposes, and will often be designed to allow for subdivision and subsequent re-subdivision in different configurations of cellular or open-plan spaces. An office building designed to be naturally lit and ventilated will be two and a half rooms deep (two office spaces plus a corridor) but these will be larger rooms than in a dwelling (Figure A2.10). A modern office building is normally designed around a structural grid of 1.5 or 1.8 m grid squares, and is made up of 'modules' based upon the grid.

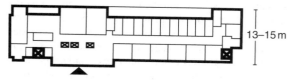

Figure A2.10   Dual-aspect office building.

Small stores <500 m²
Supermarkets 500–5000 m²
Retail warehouses/hypermarkets 5000–25,000 m²
Shopping centres 100,000 m²

Small retail:

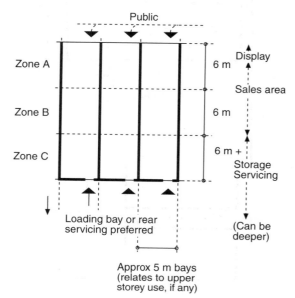

Figure A2.11   Dimensions for shops: storey heights 4 m, natural lighting, structural grid unit sizes.

Shops and stores

The size of shops varies enormously from the small lock-up to the superstore, but they all share the same design principles: the need for clear physical and visual access for shoppers, physical access for employees and a separate (vehicular) access point for deliveries (Figure A2.11). There should be short distances and direct connections between shop fronts, public transport and parking areas. Often shops have other uses above them (residential or small offices, for example) – a form of mixed-use development that good urban design principles would tend to encourage. This means that the building's structure, and hence the width of the shop's 'cells', may be determined by the space requirements of this other use.

Small industrial units

Design requirements for industrial uses include a substantial floor to ceiling height at ground-floor level, flexibility of internal layout, natural lighting and ventilation where possible, and access for service vehicles and visitors (differentiation of public and private space). These have structural implications, including a need for clear spans with no columns to interrupt the floorspace. It is becoming increasingly important for these buildings to be located in residential or mixed-use areas in order to minimise travel requirements, and to be flexibly designed to cater for a range of employment uses.

Appendix 3: Planning standards

Tony Lloyd-Jones

We include here some 'rough and ready' planning standards which can be used as initial guidelines for urban design exercises. These standards draw especially on Barton *et al.* (1995) for the UK context but also on a number of other non-UK sources. While the standards can be applied to any urban situation, they will be easier to achieve in richer rather than poorer parts of the world, and in richer rather than poorer cities.

Public facilities and their catchment areas

The following standards can be used to decide on the spacing of public and communal facilities and major employment centres in the design of new urban areas. Alternatively, they may be used for deciding which facilities are lacking in a particular locality and should be considered in an urban design framework or site development brief.

Table A3.1 shows possible planning standards for the distance of facilities away from homes. It is recommended that 80% of homes are located within the lower limit shown. The same table can be used to indicate the radius of the *primary catchment areas* of the facilities (their 'reach') and how such facilities should be spaced out (ideally, at a little less than double the distances shown).

In practice, the catchment areas of such facilities are usually much greater than this preferred radius and somewhere near to half the distance between the facility under consideration and the nearest equivalent facility in any given direction.

Financial viability of facilities

Urban designers cannot work only to preferred standards to meet public need; they must also consider the economic feasibility of providing such facilities. It is also important to remember that higher income groups are more likely to have access to a car, and lower income groups are more likely to use public transport or to walk.

Catchment and population density

The population density of catchment areas is critical. The more people that live within easy reach of a facility, the more custom there is to support it. A higher density urban authority will find it easier to finance closely spaced and accessible public facilities than a lower density suburban or rural area with similar income levels. The size of the population within a catchment area can be related to its density and to the radius, as indicated in Table A3.2.

Critical mass

Within the defined range or catchment area radius of a particular facility, the population needs to be of a certain minimum size – a *critical mass* – in order to support that facility. This depends on population density and explains why some facilities are only found in urban areas of a certain size. Table A3.3 shows catchment area population sizes for a range of facilities. These are rules-of-thumb which should

Table A3.1 Possible planning standards for distances of facilities away from homes

Facility	Preferred max. distance	Normal frequency of use	Time/mode of transport
Recreation			
Toddlers' play area	100–200 m	Daily	3 min walk
Allotments/communal gardens	200–400 m	Daily	3–6 min walk
Pub or bar	400–800 m	Daily, occasionally	6–12 min walk
Playground	400–600 m	Daily	6–9 min walk
Playing fields	800 m–1 km	Daily, weekly	12–15 min walk, 3–5 min bus/bike
Park	800 m–1 km	Daily, weekly	12–15 min walk, 3–5 min bus/bike
Leisure centre	1.5–2 km	Weekly, occasionally	5–6 min bus, 6–8 min bike
Major natural area	2–5 km[a]	Weekly, occasionally	6–15 min bus, 8–20 min bike
Cultural and entertainment facilities	5 km[a]	Weekly, occasionally	15 min bus
Education/community			
Primary school	400–600 m	Daily	6–9 min walk
Health centres	800 m–1 km	Weekly, occasionally	12–15 min walk, 5 min bus/bike
Secondary school	1–1.5 km	Daily	5–6 min bus 6–8 min bike
Technical college	2–5 km[a]	Daily, weekly	6–15 min bus 8–20 min bike
General hospital	5 km[a]	Occasionally	15 min bus
Shops:			
Local/convenience shops	400–800 m	Daily, weekly	6–12 min walk
District centre	1.5–2 km	Weekly	3–5 min bus, 5–8 min bike
Regional shopping centre or major commercial centre	5–10 km[a]	Weekly, occasionally	15 min bus, 15 min car
Public transport:			
Bus stop	300–400 m	Daily	4–6 min walk
Underground station	400 m–1 km	Daily	6–15 min walk, 5 min bus/bike
Railway station	600 m–1 km	Daily	9–15 min walk, 5 min bus/bike
Place of employment:			
Low income groups	2–3 km	Daily	30–45 min walk
	8–12 km		30–45 min bike
	10–15 km		30–45 min public transport
Other income groups	20–30 km	Daily	30–45 min car/train/express bus

Sources: Barton *et al.* (1995), Caminos and Goethert (1978), Garreau (1991).
[a] The 5 km distance is a preferred limit for 'compact' urban areas representing a city or city district of 225,000 at a gross density of 30 people per hectare, where the aim is to minimise the use of private vehicles.

be used with care, and in association with a consideration of income levels and local authority finances.

Local and non-local catchment areas

Many facilities also draw upon a wider catchment area within which customers make a longer, planned journey on a less frequent, regular or irregular basis. Many shopping and leisure facilities are used on a weekly or more occasional basis. As people are prepared to travel further for such trips by car or public transport, the catchment population may be very large and provide a critical mass of customers for quite specialised services or a greater choice of services (see Table A3.4).

Regional catchment areas

While a theatre may not be viable in a small town, a small city might support a single theatre, a large city a choice of theatres, and a large metropolis, such as London, a whole theatre district. Whereas many city dwellers might go to the theatre a number of times per year, those living outside the city may make a special trip on a less frequent basis, and the longer the journey time, the less frequent this is likely to be.

Table A3.2 Catchment area population sizes

Radius	Gross density (people/hectare)					
	30	40	50	60	75	100
100 m	90	130	160	190	230	310
200 m	380	500	630	750	940	1,250
300 m	850	1,100	1,400	1,700	2,100	2,800
400 m	1,500	2,000	2,500	3,000	3,700	5,000
500 m	2,300	3,140	3,930	4,710	5,890	7,860
600 m	3,400	4,500	5,600	6,800	8,500	11,300
700 m	4,600	6,100	7,700	9,200	11,500	15,400
800 m	6,000	8,000	10,000	12,000	15,000	20,000
900 m	8,000	10,000	13,000	15,000	19,000	25,000
1 km	9,500	12,500	16,000	19,000	23,000	31,000
1.5 km	21,000	28,000	35,000	42,000	53,000	71,000
2 km	37,000	50,000	63,000	75,000	940,000	125,000
5 km	235,000	314,000	393,000	471,000	589,000	785,000
10 km	943,000	1,257,000	1,571,000	1,885,000	2,357,000	3,143,000
20 km	3,771,000	5,028,000	6,285,000	7,542,000	9,428,000	12,571,000

Source: Adapted from Barton *et al.* (1995).

Table A3.3   Public facilities

	Population served
Local facilities:	
Primary school	2,500–4,000
Secondary school	7,000–15,000
Doctor's surgery	2,500–3,000
Pub or bar	5,000–7,000
Neighbourhood convenience store	2,000–5,000
Post office	5,000–10,000
Health centre (4 doctors)	9,000–12,000
Library	12,000–30,000
Church	9,000+
Community centre	7,000–15,000
Youth club	7,000–11,000
Sports centre	25,000–40,000
Regional facilities (indicative examples):	
University	100,000+
Museum	100,000+
Regional shopping centre	250,000+
Medical school	250,000–500,000
Opera	250,000–500,000

Source: Barton *et al* (1995), Garreau (1991), Alexander (1977).

Centres at the hub of a regional transport network therefore draw on a regional hinterland for certain services that are only provided in those accessible centres. The catchment for these services is organised as a series of concentric rings, with the inner rings where the population is most concentrated providing the greatest custom on the most frequent basis (Figure A3.1).

National and international catchment areas

Some facilities serve the whole country and will normally be found in the most accessible location. In the UK, this is most likely to be London or possibly one of the other major provincial cities.

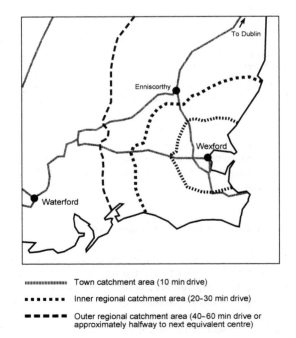

|||||||||||||| Town catchment area (10 min drive)

■ ■ ■ ■ ■ ■ Inner regional catchment area (20–30 min drive)

▬ ▬ ▬ ▬ Outer regional catchment area (40–60 min drive or approximately halfway to next equivalent centre)

Figure A3.1   Concentric catchment areas.

Table A3.4   Retail centres

Type of centre (and sales area)	Population served	Prime catchment radius (driving)	Site area
Local/neighbourhood shopping centre/supermarket (1,000–5,000 m^2)	3,000–10,000	5 min	1–2 ha
Superstore/district centre (5,000–20,000 m^2)	25,000–40,000	10 min	2–10 ha
Small city (sub-regional) shopping centre (up to 60 different retail shop types – 20,000–30,000 m^2)	100,000–150,000	15 min	10–15 ha
Regional shopping centre (70+ different retail shops – 50,000–100,000+ m^2)	250,000+	15 min	20 ha+

Source: Barton *et al.* (1995), Alexander (1977), Garreau (1991), Dawson (1983).

Urban designers are more likely to be planning for local facilities rather than those with a regional, national or global reach, but should be aware of the wider accessibility of the area under consideration and the potential for siting more specialised facilities. Siting new primary uses which draw people and income from outside a run-down neighbourhood can be a means of pump-priming regeneration.

Multipurpose centres, clustering of facilities

Increasing car ownership has meant greater mobility of the population and a tendency for facilities to become more spread out. However, people prefer to meet as many of their needs as possible in one centre or complex. In addition this concentration of facilities can create centres with considerable pedestrian activity and a sense of vitality which helps to make them more attractive.

Clustering of facilities is something that can be planned, as in a new in- or out-of-town shopping centre, or it can result from the more gradual accumulation of services in highly accessible areas, such as in town centres, along main roads, at major junctions or around public transport nodes.

Competition and spacing of facilities

Businesses will often locate close to where their competitors are already established and compete for a limited market because this is where people are and the success of the location has been demonstrated. Planners, on the other hand, may prefer to limit the number of different competing facilities of a particular kind to protect established businesses and encourage new businesses to locate in areas not currently well

served. Urban designers may need to address both points of view.

Transport and sustainability

Public transport links to employment centres

If new towns or communities or other facilities are proposed where there are no existing major public transport links, consideration has to be given to the feasibility of providing such links.

Density requirement for bus services

Bus services can be provided to quite small, local concentrations of services and employment, providing it is economical to pick up and deliver people to their homes in the surrounding catchment area. Residential population density is therefore the critical factor and studies have shown that a net residential density of 100 persons per hectare is necessary to support a good, frequent bus service. Less regular, more specialised services, e.g. for commuter, shoppers and school children, are feasible in lower density areas.

Railways and busways

Rail-based systems are many times more expensive to provide than bus-based public transport. A dedicated bus route (a reserved busway or guided bus system) is the most cost-efficient of all, with a capacity almost equivalent to a light rail system but at a fraction of the cost. Light rail systems have other advantages in densely populated areas but before proposing light rail or normal rail links to new employment centres, urban designers should be aware of the following:

- It is necessary for residential development which the new system is serving to be concentrated in high-density neighbourhoods within the catchment areas of stations and stops. Alternatively, or in addition, stations may be served by feeder buses. In this case the residential density may be lower but still needs to be sufficient to support the bus services.
- There needs to be a sufficiently large workforce housed in the new centre to generate sufficient use of the new transport link in order for it to be cost-effective. Just how large a development is required is shown in Table A3.5.

Density standards for development

Land utilisation and population density

The term 'density' is used loosely in relation to urban development, referring both to the density of buildings (i.e. as in a 'densely built-up area') and to the density of population (i.e. the number of people living within a given area). While the two often go together they are by no means synonymous and it is important to avoid confusion about this. It is possible for an area to be densely built-up but to have a low residential population density, where most of the buildings are in non-residential use. Population usually refers to the residential population but can sometimes specifically refer to the 'daytime population' of users of an area, including employees.

Avoiding misconceptions about density

In urban design, it is important to be clear about the way these terms are used. To make the difference clear, the term 'density' should usually refer only to population density and, unless otherwise stated, to residential population density. In referring to the density of built form, it is better to refer to measurable factors such as intensity of land use, or land or site utilisation.

Floorspace ratios

Intensity of land use relates to the amount of built floorspace on a given site. A *plot ratio*, *floorspace index* (FSI) or *floor:area ratio* (FAR) divides the total built floor area by the area of the site to give a common index. A plot ratio of 4:1 (400%) indicates that the amount of built floorspace is four times the area of the site. If the site is completely built over, it would be possible to accommodate this in a building four storeys high. If only half the site is built on, the building will need to be at least eight storeys high. Either of these situations may be perceived as 'densely built-up' but they have very different implications in terms of urban form.

Site utilisation

Site utilisation factors are sometimes used to limit the proportion of a site that can be built on, e.g. a site utilisation factor of 0.6 means that only 60% of the site may be built upon. By combining standards for plot ratios and site utilisation factors, planners can 'fine tune' the height and form of buildings in an area. Urban designers can go one step further and consider how the particular activities being accommodated on a site will impinge on the public realm.

Land utilisation

Land utilisation is a measure of how the land in an area is divided between public and private use. Since most land in public ownership is open space in the form of

Table A3.5 Public transport systems

Type of rapid transit system	Peak direction capacity pass/hour	Trips/day needed	Required no. of employees	Equivalent office floorspace in m2 @ 25 m²/employee according to proportion of workforce using public transport		
				100%	50%	12.5%*
Heavy rail system (underground/ suburban train)	50,000	30,000	15,000	375,000	750,000	1.5m
Light rail or tram	30,000	14,000	7,000	175,000	350,000	700,000
Busway	25,000	1,000	500	12,500	25,000	50,000

Source: Garreau, (1991: 467) Smith and Hensher (1997).
* Note: Garreau estimates that a new rail link could hope to entice just 12% of commuters to switch from using their cars. This is based on the very low residential densities and high car dependency found in American edge cities. New planned developments in Europe might be expected to achieve a much higher proportion of public transport use.

circulation for pedestrians and traffic, parks and other public open spaces, a high ratio of public to private will be associated with a high ratio of open space to built form.

Land utilisation considered in this way can give a measure of an area, both in terms of its built form characteristics and in terms of its identity and degree of public or private character. It can also help, in association with the standards given previously, in deciding how much land in large-scale new developments should be allocated to these broad land-use categories.

Net residential density

Net residential density normally refers to the ratio of residential population to the area of the site occupied by the residential development. This might include semi-private communal space in blocks of flats as well as outdoor spaces that relate to those dwellings and local access roads and footways on the site. It excludes major areas of open space and non-residential uses.

A 'gross site density' is often used in UK local plans, where half of any access road adjoining the residential site (or a 6 m strip, whichever is the smaller) is included in the measure of the site area. In practice, this does not make a significant difference to the measure of density, except on very small sites.

Residential capacity

Residential densities are sometimes also measured in number of dwellings or bed spaces per hectare, or, in local plans in the UK, the number of habitable rooms per hectare. Since sizes of households are subject to considerable variation over time and according to geographical location, there is no direct relationship between the number of rooms and bed spaces and the number of people actually occupying a dwelling unit.

Though usually referred to as density standards, these indices really give a measure of *residential capacity*, which is useful for planners in controlling the type of residential accommodation being provided. Table A3.6 relates residential density to capacity (assuming an average unit size), depending on the type of dwelling unit and the level of occupancy.

Gross density

Gross density figures are usually given for cities as a whole, and simply relate the total residential population to the total land area of the city. On average, *net residential densities are about one-third of gross densities for cities as a whole* (Newman and Kenworthy 1989). Neighbourhood gross densities refer to the figures for mainly residential neighbourhoods.

Density and 'town cramming'

Planners sometimes talk about *town cramming* in relation to high residential densities or capacities. There is often confusion between this and the overcrowded conditions that occurred in the past or in the slums of developing world cities today, usually in low-rise settlements with a very high degree of site coverage and very poor space standards (amount of living space per person).

However, there can be a genuine concern with an excess of demand for public space, facilities and infrastructure in an area. The provision of such facilities needs to be considered in any urban design proposal that will lead to a major increase in the population using an area, whether it is a residential or a daytime population. There is no automatic relation between high residential capacities and overcrowding or 'town cramming'. In particular, high-rise development does

Table A3.6   Relationship between housing type, density and occupation

Units/ha	Residential building type	Persons/ha		
		2P/U	4P/U	6P/U
10–20	Large plot detached family houses	20–40	40–80	60–80
25–30	Small plot detached family houses	50–60	100–120	150–180
40–50	Terrace housing (townhouses)	80–100	160–200	300
60–100	4 storey walk-up maisonettes	120–200	240–400	360–600
100–115	3–4 storey walk-up flats	200–230	400–460	600–690
150	4–5 storey walk-ups	300	600	900
150–200	5–10 storey high-rise	300–400	600–800	900–1,200
200–250	10–20 storey high-rise	400–500	800–1,000	1,200–1,500

Source: Adapted from Camino and Goethert (1978), Calthorpe (1993), Lynch and Hack (1994).

not automatically give rise to such problems. High-rise development can provide good space standards and a high-quality environment if properly designed, serviced and managed.

Other useful planning standards

Total area of playgrounds	0.5 ha/1000 people
Area for neighbourhood shopping including parking	0.25 ha/1000 people
Parking for car-accessed shopping centres	3–6 spaces/100 m^2 of sales area
Parking spaces/dwelling:	
Suburban	1.5–2
Elderly housing	0.3

Office space:	17.5–35 m^2 gross floor area/employee
Industrial districts:	
size	15–120 ha
plot ratio	up to 0.8
employee density	up to 200 employees/ha
Minimum pedestrian density for vitality (Alexander)	15 m^2 pedestrian area/person
Minimum pedestrian flow for vitality (Garreau)	1000 persons/ hour at midday
Minimum net population density for vitality (Jacobs)	600 persons/ha

Sources: Lynch and Hack (1984), Garreau (1991); Alexander (1997), Jacobs (1984).

Appendix 4: Disability

Clara Greed

The relationship between urban design and increasing accessibility for the disabled has already been discussed by Sandra Manley in Chapter 9 of *Introducing Urban Design* (Greed and Roberts 1998), with additional detailed material presented in Appendix II of that volume. Readers are advised to consult these sources for background material, which are fully referenced giving guidance towards other standard works in this field, such as by Imrie's (1996) *Disability and the City: International Perspectives*.

For more detailed specific design guidance and 'standards' it is recommended that readers consult the publications of the CAE (Centre for Accessible Environments), Nutmeg House, 60 Gainsford Street, London SE1 2NY (telephone 0171 357 8182; email cae@global.net.co.uk). CAE publications include design guides such as *Designing for Accessibility: An Introductory Guide* by Tessa Palfreyman and Stephen Thorpe. Also, the CAE produces Access Design Sheets, and No. 3 on External Surfaces is particularly relevant to townscape issues. The CAE also provides information on undertaking an access audit, an essential part of the design process. Specialist material on particular 'problems' includes a design guidance video on enabling access to historic buildings and those within conservation areas, entitled *Keeping Up with the Past: Making Historic Buildings Accessible for Everyone*. Talking directly to disabled people should also be seen as a key reference source.

Certain basic standards exist on features such as ramp design and disabled parking places, and these have been incorporated in earlier volumes in the *Exploring Town Planning* series (edited by C. Greed). Information on these standards is widely available at local planning authority level, and from organisations such as the Access Committee for England, and local voluntary disability groups. However, it is considered unwise to provide 'absolute standards' in this appendix on 'how to' design for disability. This is because many of the official standards are somewhat minimal and are often administered in isolation from wider urban design considerations. Also the situation is constantly changing because of the effects of recent legislation. In particular, the various sections of the 1995 Disability Discrimination Act are progressively coming into force, and these are substantially affecting access design requirements in respect of certain categories of building. The relevant British Standards, especially BS 5810, are also likely to be upgraded with time, as is the linked 'Approved Document M' – as explained in Appendix II of *Introducing Urban Design* (Greed and Roberts 1998).

It is recommended that readers consult CAE's journal, *Access by Design*, which is the only British journal dealing specifically with disability design in respect of the built environment. The mainstream professional journals occasionally include items and updates on disability design requirements, such as are to be found in the *Architects Journal*. It must be stressed that designing for disabled access should not be seen as a separate, stand-alone activity, characterised by the 'a ramp here and a ramp there' school of thought. Rather, all townscape features and urban design considerations should be developed while adopting a holistic, inclusive frame of mind, in which accessibility and mobility considerations are integral considerations in the design process.

This approach might mean at the micro level of

design ensuring that there are no unexpected projecting features impeding a person's progress along the pavement, and that street furniture such as seats, planter boxes and lighting columns are placed out away from the building to allow free passage. At the meso level it might mean ensuring that the overall design of a scheme enables direct routeways between building entrances, and that there are no dead-ends, 'interesting little townscape features' or confusing route choices to be made by the pedestrian. Issues of sound, light, colour and touch all need to be taken into account in the design process. Access ramp provision and 'special' paving should be integrated within the flow patterns and desire lines generated by the development, and not put (as often happens) around the back of a building. Although it is common to discuss 'accessibility', of course, people have to go 'out of' as well as 'into' buildings, so in designing for 'access', the question of 'egress' must also be considered (not least when considering the effect of gradients). At the macro, city-wide level of urban design, accessibility is likely to mean ensuring short distances between linked land uses (such as home and work). Therefore an emphasis upon mixed uses, with short walking (or wheelchairing) distances between essential facilities (shops, schools and public buildings) should be encouraged. In a nutshell, there is a need to plan for 'the city of everyday life' – everyone's life – so that people of all ages, types and levels of mobility can get around without difficulty.

Start from the perspective of aiming at an inclusive approach which includes disability considerations in the whole design process, rather than being obsessed with ramps alone.

Glossary

Words and phrases in the text *italicised* will be found as a related main entry that can also be consulted.

Action planning   Planning carried out in close consultation with the community (see Wates 1996).

Active management   A property investment term used to describe investments bought with a view to refurbishing and improvement, generating additional value and then (perhaps) being sold on at a profit.

Activity schedules   Observation of human movements, business, direction, conflicts, congestion points, trading, attraction to and avoidance of places.

Ancillary costs   Traditionally limited to on-site infrastructure such as roads and services but increasingly government and *local planning authorities* are requiring developments to pay for off-site infrastructure that is a direct consequence of the scheme in question – so-called *planning gain*.

Area appraisal   The examination and assessment of the study site in terms of urban design factors.

Area strategy   A means similar to a scenario within which to assess options for site development when there is no specific client brief.

Areas of Outstanding Natural Beauty (AONB)   Substantial areas of countryside designated by the Countryside Commission where the intention is to protect the area's natural beauty. There is specific legislation to do so and planning controls are often stringent on many matters such as use of materials, the extent to which buildings may be enlarged and the control of outdoor advertising.

Armature   Urban shape, scene, presence, profile, form and setting experienced through movement, comprising spaces (routes and public places), objects (buildings and monuments) and people (activities and traffic).

Article 4 directions   Powers given to a *local planning authority*, with the approval of the Secretary of State, to bring into their planning and *development control*, within Conservation Areas, certain operations that lie outside the requirements for formal planning permission.

Axis   A line, usually imaginary, from which a layout or plan is symmetrically arranged and measured.

Beaux arts   Term used to describe design solutions based on formal, classical principles as taught to architectural students in the Ecole de Beaux Arts in Paris in the nineteenth century.

Brownfield site   An area of vacant or derelict land, usually in an urban or suburban area, which is available for redevelopment and which has either been previously developed, i.e. for industry and is now redundant, or which is surrounded by other built-up or previously built-up areas.

Building line   Runs parallel to a public highway regardless of property boundaries and existing development. Usually laid down by the highway authority to designate the total road reservation, in order to ensure no further new development takes place on the road side of that line so that any compensation costs for further road widening or improvement of *sight lines* are kept to a minimum.

Building type   The categorisation of a structure according to the make-up and arrangement of its construction but not necessarily its use; although a highly specialist use such as a petrol filling station may be a determinant.

Built envelope   The cubic area of a building enclosed by its outer walls and roof.

Built form   The existing pattern of building site coverage in relation to property boundaries (but not proof of ownership), public access ways (but not proof of public right of way), street frontage and other spaces not built over. This can be checked with additional data such as bulk, style and use, age and condition.

Business park   A development of usually separate units for office, laboratory, light manufacturing, assembling or other high-tech uses, often custom-built, in a landscaped setting with high car-parking standards often located adjacent to or visibly close to major edge of town primary roads or junctions.

Capital growth   The property investment term that refers to the increase in, or potential increase in, the value of that investment on the open market.

Capital value   The value of an investment at any particular point in time reflecting general market conditions and the particular qualities of the investment.

Casement (window)   Outward-opening window with hinges on the vertical jamb (edge).

Cash flow   The movement of money, in all its forms, through a business as a measure of its profitability.

Catchment area   The area surrounding a facility (e.g. a health centre or pub) from which its users or customers may be drawn.

Census enumeration districts   The primary area used in the collection of census data whose boundaries coincide with local authority units such as parishes, wards and voting districts. They normally contain on average 200 households or 500 people and a breakdown of census data at this level is available in most local authority offices or libraries. A directory relating them to postal codes is also available.

Concept diagram   Usually a 'bubble' diagram that sketches out the key ideas for a design strategy within which specific options for development can be considered for the study site.

Configured movement   A term taken from the now rarely used verb to configure, 'to fashion according to a model or to put together in a form or figure' (*Shorter Oxford English Dictionary*), hence in this sense a means of movement that is to some extent prescribed.

Conservation status   Parts of urban areas can be classified as Conservation Areas which means they are subject to the strict planning and building controls of the Planning (*Listed Buildings* and Conservation Areas) Act 1990 and its subsequent amendment by the Planning and Compensation Act 1991.

Construction costs   Funding is not all required at the outset since costs rise towards the end of the building period when the shell is being fitted out. It is normal practice in financial appraisals to assume borrowing on the total estimated costs for half the building period.

Containment   Term derived from *townscape* analysis. A contained space or street is one where the buildings form a strong continuous edge and where the ratio of the width of the space or street to the height of the buildings enclosing it is sufficient for the observer to feel that they are in an enclosed space rather than an open one.

Contextual analysis   A study of urban matters at whatever scale showing how they pertain to or derive from their wider urban context.

Contingencies   An estimate entered in valuation calculations and building estimates to cover unforeseen costs that may arise, especially if the project involves refurbishing an existing structure.

Cornice   In the context of the exterior of a building, normally taken to mean a decorative moulding which projects from a wall below the roof or below a parapet.

Covenant (restrictive)   A mutual agreement between two or more persons or parties to do or refrain from specified activities. In law, a restrictive covenant is a legal agreement or a particular clause of such a contract that prohibits stated actions on the property.

Covenant (tenants)   A covenant describes the credit rating and thus the status of the commercial tenant. The better the covenant, the more secure and the more desirable the tenant from an investor's perspective. The building let to a quality tenant will therefore be more valuable.

Daylight and sunlight controls   Controls over building height and floor set-backs through standard calculations of sun height over the horizon on given dates in the calendar year and angles of light casting shadows on adjoining buildings. These used to be strictly applied but are less used now. They come under the general heading of daylight factors.

Density   See *gross density, net residential density, residential density, habitable room, plot area ratios*.

Design brief   Another form of supplementary design guidance. The term has a variety of meanings and is used inconsistently. Different planning authorities use different terms: planning brief, development brief, principles of development, planning guidance, planning framework, as well as design brief. One of the common characteristics of different definitions of briefs is that they provide detailed development guidance for specific sites, distinguishing them from design guides which focus on areas or issues.

Design guides   Design guides are documents prepared by the local planning authorities as additional information and guidance regarding design matters. Design guides, as distinct from development plans, do not have statutory status and are classified as supplementary design guidance. Supplementary design guidance, however, can play a significant role is ensuring good design.

Development   The carrying out of building, engineering, mining or other operations in, on, over and under land, or the making of any material change in the use of any buildings or other land' (Town and Country Planning Act 1990). There are several building operations that are not classed as development. These are defined in Section 55 of the Act. An amendment in 1992 on 'building operations' included as development (for the first time and therefore requiring planning permission) the following operations: A: demolition of buildings; B: rebuilding; C: structural alteration of or addition to buildings; and D: other operations normally undertaken by a person carrying on business as a builder. At the same time the Secretary of State introduced an extra sub-section to Section 55 that to all intents and purposes placed 'demolition' outside local planning control.

Development appraisal   The overall set of assumptions and calculations required to arrive at an estimate of the financial viability of a proposed development. The problems with appraisals do not concern the method but arise from the values attached to the variables in that method.

Development brief   A statement that may be produced by a *local planning authority* or developer setting out guidelines of their view for the development of a specific site or area. It will usually identify the *planning gains* that a *local planning authority* hopes to achieve from the development, and may incorporate a *design brief*. A developer's brief will naturally set out what the developer hopes to achieve and may vary considerably from that of the local planning authority.

Development control   A statutory procedure exercised by a *local planning authority* to ensure a development complies with planning permissions, conditions, enforcement notices and the provisions of approved plans currently in force. This is a complex business and the current law and guidance as well as the local planning authority should be consulted.

Development costs   These may include costs for demolition, construction, infrastructure, landscaping, professional fees, finance (cost of borrowing), letting and sales fees and legal requirements.

Development plan   A generic term used in UK planning legislation for the statutory plan that must be prepared by *local planning authorities* for their entire area and that encompasses unitary development plans, *structure plans*, *local plans* and mineral plans. The current legislation and *Planning Policy Guidance* (PPG) documents should be referred to for details.

Development process   The manner in which the development of buildings and other structures takes place in urban areas to enable the economic prosperity of the inhabitants.

Districts   See *legibility*. Medium to large elements of a city which the observer walks into and which have an identifiable set of characteristics. These might be related to use or to architectural style. A district may be defined by what is exterior to it.

Dwelling unit   A self-contained unit in a dwelling for an individual, a family or a group.

Eaves   Lower edge of a sloping roof which projects beyond walls.

Edge cities   Urban developments around the junctions of major highways just outside existing cities. The term was coined by Garreau (1991).

Edges   See *legibility*. In Lynch's (1960) use of the term, linear elements not used or thought of as routes. They may either join two recognisable areas as a 'seam' or, alternatively, may act as a barrier between recognisable areas. Edges may take the form of intensely busy roads, railway lines, cuttings and canals.

Enclosure   See *containment*.

Environmental control in buildings   Includes the provision of shelter from the elements (the walls and roof), natural lighting (windows), and natural ventilation (windows).

Equities   Stocks and shares not bearing a fixed interest where the prospect of the increase in sale value on the market attracts the investor.

Exposure   A term used by financial managers to

describe those investments held in a portfolio that the market generally considers to be at risk of falling in value, which puts the holder at credit risk.

Façades   The face (elevation) of a building, especially the principal face.

Fanlight   A glazed panel, often decorative, above a door.

Favela   A Brazilian term for areas of land that have been illegally occupied by squatters.

Figure ground drawing   Produced by shading in the buildings in plan form in black, thereby revealing the public and semi-public realms as white.

Financial appraisals   The term used to describe the calculation of the value of an existing or possible property investment or a property development opportunity.

Financial viability   The most commonly used method for appraising the viability of development proposals is the *residual method of valuation.*

Floorplate   Describes the size and shape or layout of the floorspace on any one floor of a building.

Floor space index (FSI)   See *plot area ratio.*

Footfalls   The degree of pedestrian movement passing a given place.

Footprint   The enclosed shape made by the external or outside walls of a building. Spaces at ground level covered by the building at higher levels should be shown as a pecked line within the footprint. Essentially it would be the imprint left in soft sand if the building were to be suddenly swept away.

Forward funding   To sell to an institutional or other investor, before construction starts, the completed development designed and pre-let to a top credit-rated occupier.

Fractal   A term derived from the Theory of Chaos meaning that a form can be similar regardless of the scale at which it is studied. 'Also a way of seeing infinity' (Gleick 1987).

Freeholders   Persons holding the freehold title to land who may occupy the property (owner–occupier), let it out on a short-term basis to a tenant or on a longer term basis to a *leaseholder.*

Functionalism   The theory that only a detailed and scientific analysis of the problems set by a building's needs will lead to the right spatial solution often regardless of the cultural or geographical context.

Fund managers   Those directing large investments such as unit trusts which give a rate of return based on a wide-ranging or specialist group of mixed shareholdings designed to spread the risk posed by any single stock failure. See also *institutional investors.*

Gable   Triangular vertical face of a double-sided sloping roof.

Generative techniques   Methods to assist in the regeneration of an area such as the use of landscaping, the arrangement of buildings around a series of axes and sub-axes, and the urban space itself to form the basis of the composition.

Generic   Another slippage from the biological dictionary meaning having the rank of a genus – a classification below family and divided into subordinate species.

Geographical Information Systems (GIS)   A computer system for capturing, managing, integrating, manipulating, analysing and displaying data that is spatially referenced to the earth (*International GIS Dictionary*, McDonnell 1995).

Gilts   Investments with a fixed interest that will ensure a steady known income to the investor.

Grain   Used to describe an established pattern of built form, including plot divisions, within settlements. Derived from the natural pattern found in processed wood. To cut across this with a new road would be 'to go against the grain' of the settlement.

Grand Manner   A style of city planning and redevelopment used in many north European cities (particularly capital cities) from the seventeenth through to the nineteenth centuries, based on the classical planning principles of ancient Rome.

Green-field sites   Not previously developed in urban use – usually rural and hence the name.

Grid blocks   The block is determined by the convenient public circulation and not by the dimensions of lots. In grid blocks, some lots have indirect access to public streets.

Grid layouts   Urban layouts with grid blocks.

Gridiron blocks   Here the blocks are determined by the dimensions of the lots. In gridiron blocks all the lots have direct access to the public streets.

Gridiron layout   Urban layouts with gridiron blocks.

Gross density   Ratios usually given for cities as a whole which simply relate the total residential population to the total land area of the city.

Gross internal area   The area measured to the inside of the external walls and used by the quantity surveyor to estimate construction costs.

Habitable room   The rooms in a dwelling excluding bathrooms, toilets, and some other spaces. Often used as a measure of density, e.g. habitable rooms per hectare.

Income stream   A property term that refers to the rent received by the landlord after outgoings.

Institutional investors   Insurance companies and pension funds seeking growth and income for longer term security to meet predictable and unpredictable future financial commitments such as bad debts, insurance claims and pension payments.

Investment yield   Describes the financial returns received by the investor in the form of rental income after deductions for maintenance and management.

Landmarks   See *legibility*. Usually a defined simple physical object, such as a church spire, a tower, a dome or a hill. They are not entered into but serve as a point of reference. They may be either distant or local.

Land utilisation   A measure of how land in an area is divided between public and private use. Since most land in public ownership is open space in the form of circulation for pedestrians and traffic, parks and other public open spaces, a high ratio of public to private will be associated with a high ratio of open space to built form.

Leaseholders   Users of property paying for that right on a long-term basis (usually annually) with a guaranteed period of occupancy (in England and Wales, often starting at 99 years, although any period can be agreed; the usual length of time is different in Scotland).

Legibility   Technique pioneered by Kevin Lynch (1960) as a method of categorising elements of *mental maps*, in order to assist dialogue, research and action in urban design.

Liquid asset   An asset capable of being quickly realised by sale or exchange.

Listed buildings   A statutory list of Grade I and Grade II buildings, each with some subdivisions but all subject to stringent regulations of the Planning (Listed Buildings and Conservation Areas) Act 1990. There are deterrent financial penalties should any building operations be carried out on them without the consent of the *local planning authority*. See also *conservation status*.

Local planning authority   The elected local government council responsible for administering the statutory provisions of planning law. There are two tiers of planning authority: county council and metropolitan council for strategic planning; and district and borough councils for local planning. Their functions and responsibilities are set out in detail in the Town and Country Planning Act 1990 and various *Planning Policy Guidance* documents.

Local plans   General term used in a *development plan* for any detailed and usually map based plan adopted by a *local planning authority*, for part or all of an area already subject to an approved *structure plan*. The current legislation and *Planning Policy Guidance* documents should be referred to for details.

Masterplanning   In current UK practice, providing the framework for the physical development of larger parcels of urban land, in terms of layout, land uses, *built form* and phasing of development.

Means of escape   Technical term used in building and fire regulations to describe arrangements made for escape from a building or development in case of fire.

Mental maps   'Map' or other type of representation of a physical area that is formed in an individual's consciousness, i.e. inside their head. See also *legibility*.

Microclimate   Localised conditions of climate immediately around and within a group of buildings, usually characterised by considerable uniformity of climate. May be negative, e.g. a wind tunnel, or positive, e.g. a sun-trap.

Mixed use   Development comprising more than one land use or value on a single plot or within a single building, or an area where sites and buildings of different uses or values are grouped together.

Modern Movement   Architectural movement with origins in the late nineteenth century. Associated with a scientific approach to problems and stylistically with a free flow of space, buildings as objects, white concrete, horizontal windows, flat roofs and buildings raised on stilts.

Morphology, morphological analysis   The study of the shape and pattern of urban structure or urban layout in terms of urban form and the pattern of spaces throughout a study area. Associated with use of *figure ground drawings*, historical studies and an examination of *building types*.

Movement systems   Term encompassing both transport infrastructure (road and rail) and pedestrian routes.

Multiple shops   Distinguished by the Board of Trade Census of Distribution as having five or more branches dealing directly with the public.

Net income   In property terms, it is rental income after responsibility for repairs, maintenance, insurance and any other similar costs have been taken into account.

Net residential density   Normally refers to the ratio of residential population to the area of the site occupied by the residential development. This might include semi-private communal space in blocks of flats as well as outdoor spaces that relate to those dwellings and local access roads and footways on the site. It excludes major areas of open space and non-residential uses.

Net usable space   That space actually occupied for the activity in question and not including foyers, stairwells, corridors and other common space.

Nodes   (1) a transport node is a point of interchange between two or more modes of transport. (2) See *legibility*. A point to or from which an observer might be travelling and which provides an event on the journey. It is characteristically a major junction or interchange. It can also be a meeting of paths; its key feature, unlike a landmark, is that it must be entered.

Parking standards   The number of car parking spaces in a new development is controlled by the *local planning authority*, usually on the basis of a standard set number of square feet or square metres of development per car park space to be provided by the developer.

Paths   See *legibility*. In terms of legibility analysis, paths are routes through which the observer moves, e.g. roads, paths, railways, walkways. They are the means by which people can view the city and form their *mental maps* of it.

Pedestrian desire lines   The route that pedestrians either do take (regardless of the intentions of designers) or would really like to take.

Pediment   Large, classically inspired, triangular moulding or stone facing, set at the roof level of a building.

Permeability   The degree of movement possible or permitted between public outside and private inside or between urban areas, buildings, places and spaces.

Picturesque   A particular tradition within English culture that focuses on sensory and primarily visual experience and (as *Webster's Dictionary* puts it) 'representing the charming in scenes, ideas, etc., without attaining beauty or sublimate'.

Pilaster   Moulding made to look like a column, set against the wall of a building.

Planning gain   A procedure used by *local planning authorities* to ensure that the costs of infrastructure associated with a particular development are met by the developer and landowner, not the taxpayer. New residential estates, for example, may generate a need for more school places or transport improvements which the developer will be legally obliged to provide. The process is supported by government and incorporated in planning legislation as planning obligations (Section 106 of the Town and Country Planning Act 1990) while policy guidance is given in DoE Circular 1/97, entitled Planning Obligations.

Planning Policy Guidance (PPG)   A series of numbered planning topic papers presenting the government's view on policy for each topic.

Plot (or floor) area ratios   Divides the total built floor area by the area of the site to give a common index. A plot ratio of 4:1 (400%) indicates that the amount of built floor space is four times the area of the site. Also known as the *floor space index* (FSI).

Portfolio   Used in property terms to describe a list of shareholdings and/or investments held by a commercial investor.

Pre-let or pre-sale   Refers to the sale or letting of a building to its occupier in advance of its construction. Contrast with *speculative development*.

Present value   The value today of a development that will be completed at some point in the future.

Prime property   Buildings in the 'best' locations, housing the 'best' tenant occupiers with quality and flexibility of design. They are a small minority of the total stock and are rarely traded.

Public realm   The spaces between and around buildings that have unrestricted public access although their mode of access may be severely restricted. Also, generally, that which is in the public as against the private interest.

Quoin   (pronounced 'coin') Stone or mouldings made to look like stone which are set at the corners of buildings and which project slightly from the brickwork.

Regeneration   A term that in the UK implies physical redevelopment; cultural, social or economic measures that promote improvement, or a mixture of any number or all of these.

Render   Two-coat plasterwork on external wall. See also *stucco*.

Rental growth   The current rise or possible future increase in rents achieved. The extent of rental growth will be one of the factors that determines *capital value*.

Rental values   The rent that would be paid by a willing tenant in order to occupy an available building.

Residential density   Sometimes measured in number of dwellings or bed spaces per hectare and, in local plans in the UK, the number of habitable rooms per hectare.

Residual method of valuation   This method has three functions: (1) to determine the value of the land and therefore how much the developer can afford to bid to acquire the land in what is likely to be a competitive process; (2) to calculate the overall value of the completed scheme and the level of profit that the proposal will produce for the developer; (3) to assess the likely level of costs that will be incurred during construction in order to identify a cost ceiling that must not be exceeded if the development is to remain profitable.

Residual value   The result of the *residual method of valuation*.

Residue   The value of land determined by what can be developed on the site, the strength of the demand for space, the availability of alternative space elsewhere and thus the value and cost of the development.

Sash (window)   Windows that slide vertically past each other to form an opening.

Secondary property   The majority of buildings lack at least one of the qualities of prime property, and are thus secondary or worse and are down-valued accordingly.

Serial vision   A notation method developed by Gordon Cullen in *Townscape* (1968) which allows the observer to record the features of the environment that are important to the unfolding view.

Sight lines   Imaginary lines similar to *building lines* but splayed back from road junctions, or entrances from properties on to the public highway, the roadside of which must be kept clear of all obstruction to clear vision by vehicle drivers on safety grounds.

Site utilisation   Calculation sometimes used to limit the proportion of a site that can be built on. A site util-

isation factor of 0.6 means that only 60% of the site may be built upon.

Site value   There can be many different values: the historic price of the last sale; a forced sale or unencumbered sale; the various values calculated by bidders; the owner's expectation; and finally, what the owner actually gets for it. It is used here in the sense that it is the maximum price the developer might bid, on his calculations and assumptions, in order to succeed in his bid for the site.

Speculative development   A development completed without the benefit of being pre-let or pre-sold.

Stakeholders   Any person or organisation with an interest in a particular development or other intervention such as any planning framework or local authority brief that will affect future development.

String course   Externally, normally taken to mean a horizontal band of either stone or brick and *render*, which runs across the *façade* of a building.

Structure plan   The part of a *development plan* that every county planning authority is required to prepare for its entire area, and which has to be approved by the Secretary of State. It is more policy-based than map-based.

Stucco   External coating of concrete or plaster to masonry wall. See also *render*.

SWOT analysis   A common management technique that considers the Strengths and Weaknesses of an organisation, the Opportunities offered and the Threats faced.

Townscape   The visible impact of streets and urban scenes, spaces, façades, enclosures, vistas, vegetation, materials and finishes. Gordon Cullen first advocated the awareness of this aspect of urban design. The term 'streetscape' is also sometimes used. Both are the urban equivalent of the rural landscape.

Unitary Development Plans (UDP)   Prepared by each council (as *local planning authority*) within a metropolitan area or London, comprising Part 1, corresponding roughly to a *structure plan*, and Part 2, *local plans* that are prepared covering all or part of the area. The current legislation and *Planning Policy Guidance* should be referred to for details.

Urban design framework   Sometimes also called an urban *design brief*.

Urban form   The physical shape of urban areas as determined by the relationship to each other and the city region of the basic urban elements such as transport links, land use, *built form*, population settlement and topography.

Urban structure   A term implying an urbanised area but with an understanding of its physical form, shape and structure.

Vacancy rates   The extent to which rented property remains unlet (i.e. vacant) and which can be expressed as a ratio related to time or as a proportion of similar properties in an area.

Village design statements (VDS)   VDSs are based on the concept that the residents of a village have a unique perspective on the character of the place in which they live and that this can be translated into a document to inform planning policy. See also *design guides*.

Yield   The basis of the multiplier (years purchase) used to convert the rental value of a property into its *capital value*, reflecting the location and quality of the building, the status of the tenant and the degree of risk associated with the development.

Zoning regulations   These are more commonly used outside the UK (typically in the USA) by means of a zoning ordinance. This demarcates a city by ordinance into zones (areas/districts) and the establishment of regulations to govern the use of land and the location, bulk, height, shape, use, population *density* and coverage of structures within each zone. A form of this type of control may be used by a *local plan* within the *development plan* system of the UK.

Bibliography

Alcock, A, Bentley, I, Murrain, P, McGlynn, S and Smith, S (1985 and 1993 new edition) *Responsive Environments*, Architectural Press, London, in association with Oxford Brookes University, Oxford.

Aldous, T (1992) *Urban Villages: Concepts for Creating Mixed-use Urban Developments on a Sustainable Scale*, Urban Villages Group, London.

Alexander, C (1966) 'The city is not a tree' in Legates, R and Stout, F (eds) *The City Reader*, Routledge, London.

Alexander, C (1977) *A Pattern Language: Towns, Buildings, Construction*, Oxford University Press, New York.

Arnheim, R (1977) *The Dynamics of Architectural Form*, University of California Press, Berkeley.

Arts Council for England (1996) *Commissioning Art Works*, Arts Council of England in collaboration with Public Art Forum, London.

Askew, J (1996) 'King's Cross: Case study' in Greed, C (ed.) *Implementing Town Planning: The Role of Town Planning in the Development Process*, Longman, Harlow.

Barcelona (1996) *Barcelona: Visions*, Ajuntament de Barcelona, Barcelona.

Barton, H, Guise, R and Davis, G (1995) *Sustainable Settlements: A Guide for Planners, Designers and Developers*, University of the West of England, Bristol/Local Government Management Board, Bedford.

Bentley, I *et al.* (1996) *Responsive Environments: A Manual for Designers*. Butterworth Architecture, Oxford.

Bentley, I (1997) *From Hell Town to Angell Town*, Routledge, London.

Board, C (1997) *High Residential Densities*, MA Thesis, University of Westminster, London.

Booth, P and Boyle, R (1993) 'See Glasgow, see culture' in Bianchini, F and Parkinson, M (eds) *Cultural Policy and Urban Regeneration: The Western European Experience*, Manchester University Press, Manchester.

Boyer, M C (1990) 'The return of aesthetics to city planning' in Crow, D (ed.) *Philosophical Streets: New Approaches to Urbanism*, Maisonneuve Press, Washington, DC.

Bristol City Council (1992) *Draft Bristol Local Plan: Written Statement*, Bristol City Council, Bristol.

Broadbent, G (1990) *Emergent Concepts in Urban Space Design*, Van Nostrand Reinhold, London.

CAE (Centre for Accessible Environments) (1998) *Keeping Up with the Past – Making Historic Buildings Accessible to Everyone*, Centre for Accessible Environments, London (video).

Calthorpe, P (1993) *The Next American Metropolis*, Princeton Architectural Press, New York.

Caminos, H and Goethert, R (1978) *Urbanisation Primer*, MIT Press, Cambridge, MA.

Carmona, M (1998) 'Urban design and planning practice' in Greed, C and Roberts, M (eds) *Introducing Urban Design: Interventions and Responses*, Addison Wesley Longman, Harlow, pp. 39–63.

Comedia (1991) *Out of Hours, A Study of Economic, Social and Cultural Life in Twelve Town Centres in the UK*, Comedia Consultancy, Stroud.

Coupland, A (ed.) (1996) *Reclaiming the City: Mixed-Use Development*, E & FN Spon, London.

Cowan, R (1997) *The Connected City: A New Approach to Making Cities Work*, Urban Initiatives, London.

Cowan, R (1998) 'The people and the process' in Greed, C and Roberts, M (eds) *Introducing Urban Design: Interventions and Responses*, Addison Wesley Longman, Harlow, pp. 188–194.

Cox, S and Hamilton, A (ed.) (1991) *Architect's Handbook of Practice Management*, RIBA, London.

Cullen, G (1988) *The Concise Townscape*, Architectural Press, London (first published 1961).

Cuthbert, A R and Dimitriou, H T (1992) Redeveloping the fifth quarter, *Cities*, 9(3).

CZWG (1990) Masterplan Report, unpublished report of CZWG, London.

Davis, M (1992) *City of Quartz: Excavating the Future in Los Angeles*, Vintage, London.

Dawson, J (1983) *Shopping Centre Development*, Longman, London.

Delafons, J (1992) Democracy and design, *Proceedings of International Symposium on Design Review*, University of Cincinnati, Cincinnati.

Department of the Environment (1976) *Design Guidance Survey, Report on a Survey of Local Authority Design Guidance for Private Residential Development*, Department of the Environment, London.

Department of the Environment (1992) *Planning Policy Guidance (PPG12): Development Plans and Guidance*, HMSO, London.

Department of the Environment (1993) *Planning Policy Guidance (PPG3): Housing*, HMSO, London.

Department of the Environment (1994) *Planning Policy Guidance (PPG15): Conservation Area and Listed Buildings*, HMSO, London.

Department of the Environment (1997) *Planning Policy Guidance (PPG1): General Policy and Principles* (revised February 1997) HMSO, London.

Department of the Environment & Department of Transport (1992) *Design Bulletin 32: Residential Roads and Footpaths: Layout Considerations* (second edition), HMSO, London.

DETR (1998a) *Places, Streets and Movement*, Department of the Environment, Transport and the Regions, London.

DETR (1998b) *Planning for Sustainable Development: Towards Better Practice,* Department of the Environment, Transport and the Regions, London.

DETR and CABE (2000) *By Design, Urban Design in the Planning System: Towards Better Design,* Thomas Telford Publishing, London.

Eade, C (1997) Homeowners are buying flats on the fringes of the City of London faster than foodstores can be attracted into the area, *Property Week*, 20 June 1997, pp. 30–31.

Economakis, R (1993) *Leon Kier: Architecture and Urban Design 1967–1992.* Academy Editions, London.

English Partnerships (1996) *Time for Design: Good Practice in Building, Landscape and Urban Design*, English Partnerships, London.

Essex County Council (1973) *A Design Guide for Residential Areas*, Essex County Council, Chelmsford.

Essex County Council (1998) *The Essex Design Guide for Residential and Mixed Area Uses*, Essex Planning Officers Association: Essex County Council, Chelmsford.

Farnfield, P (1996) *Estates Gazette*, 5 October 1996.

Fearns, D (1993) *Access Audits: A Guide and Checklists for Appraising the Accessibility of Buildings for Disabled Users*, Centre for Accessible Environments, London.

Franck, K and Schneekloth, L (eds) (1994) *Ordering Space: Types in Architecture and Design*, Van Nostrand Reinhold, New York.

Fulford, C (1996) 'The compact city and the market' in Jenks, M (ed.) *The Compact City: a Sustainable Urban Form?* E & FN Spon, London.

Fullick, L (1997) Learning in partnership. Islington is trying to engage all sectors to work together on education, *Local Government Chronicle*, **6742**, 28 February 1997, p. 16.

Garreau, J (1991) *Edge City: Life on the New Frontier*, Doubleday, New York.

Geddes, P (1905) Civics: as applied sociology, *Sociological Papers* 1904, Macmillan, London.

Gehl, J (1987) *Life Between Buildings*, Van Nostrand Reinhold, New York.

Gehl, J (1995) The challenge of creating a human quality in the city, *Town and Country Planning Summer School*, Royal Town Planning Institute, London, pp. 14–17.

Greater London Council (1978) *An Introduction to Housing Layout*, Architectural Press, London.

Greater London Council (1980) *The Design of Urban Space: A GLC Manual*, Architectural Press, London.

Greed, C (1996) *Introducing Town Planning*, Longman, Harlow.

Greed, C (ed.) (1999) *Social Town Planning*, Routledge, London.

Greed, C and Roberts, M (eds) (1998) *Introducing Urban Design: Interventions and Responses*, Addison Wesley Longman, Harlow.

Greenhalgh, L *et al.* (1997) *The Richness of Cities:*

Urban Policy in a New Landscape, Working Paper, Comedia in association with Demos, London.

Hall, D (1997) The voice of the people: citizen's juries offer an opportunity to hear what your community thinks, *Municipal Journal*, 20 June 1997, pp. 18–19 (Islington).

Heath, T (1997) The twenty-four hour city concept – a review of initiatives in British cities, *Journal of Urban Design*, **2**(2), pp. 193–204.

Hebbert, M (1998) *London: More by Fortune than Design*, John Wiley, Chichester.

Hillier, B (1996) The city as a movement economy, *Urban Design International*, **1**(1), pp. 41–60.

Hillier, B and Hanson J (1984) *The Social Logic of Space*, Cambridge University Press, Cambridge.

Imrie, R (1996) *Disability and the City: International Perspectives*, Paul Chapman, London.

Jacobs, A and Appleyard, D (1986) 'An urban design manifesto' in Legates, R and Stout, F (eds) *The City Reader*, Routledge, London.

Jacobs, J (1992, originally 1961 and 1984) *The Death and Life of Great American Cities: The Failure of Town Planning*, Peregrine Books, London.

Katz, P (1994) *The New Urbanism: Towards an Architecture of Community*, McGraw Hill, New York.

Kostof, S (1991) *The City Shaped: Urban Patterns and Meanings Through History*, Thames & Hudson, London.

Küller, M (1998) Windows are a human need, *Swedish Building Research*, **2**, pp. 6–7.

Llewelyn Davies (1998) *Sustainable Residential Quality: New Approaches to Urban Living*, London Planning Advisory Centre, London.

London Borough of Islington (1994) *Unitary Development Plan*, London Borough of Islington, London.

Lynch, K (1960, and new edition 1988) *The Image of the City*, MIT Press, Cambridge, MA.

Lynch, K (1980) *Good City Form*, MIT Press, Cambridge, MA.

Lynch, K and Hack, G (1984) *Site Planning*, MIT Press, Cambridge, MA.

MacCormac, R (1987) Fitting in offices, *Architectural Review*, **181**(9), pp. 50–51.

MacDonald, W (1986) *The Architecture of the Roman Empire, Vol II: An Urban Appraisal*, Yale University Press, New York.

Madanipour, A, Lally, M and Underwood, G (1993) *Design Briefs in Planning Practice*, Working Paper No. 26, Department of Town and Country Planning, University of Newcastle upon Tyne.

Madanipour, A (1996) *Design of Urban Space: An Inquiry into a Socio-Spatial Process*, John Wiley, Chichester.

Madanipour, A (1997) Ambiguities of urban design, *Town Planning Review*, **68**(3), pp. 363–383.

Massey, D (1994) *Space, Place and Gender*, Polity Press in association with Blackwells, Cambridge and Oxford.

MATRIX (1984) *Making Space, Women and the Man Made Environment*, Pluto, London.

Matsukawa, J (1994) Tokyo travel: urban space to move around Tokyo, paper presented to the OECD conference on *Women in the City: Housing, Services and the Urban Environment*, Paris, 4–6 October 1994.

McDonnell, R (1995) *International GIS Dictionary*, GeoInformation International, Cambridge.

Montgomery, J (1997) Café culture and the city: the role of pavement cafes in urban public social life, *Journal of Urban Design*, **2**(1), pp. 83–102.

Montgomery, J (1998) Making a city: urbanity, vitality and urban design, *Journal of Urban Design*, **3**(1), pp. 93–116.

Moudon, A (1994) *Getting to Know the Built Landscape* in Franck, K and Schneekloth, L, *Ordering Space: Types in Architecture and Design*, Van Nostrand Reinhold, New York.

Moudon, A (1997) Urban morphology as an interdisciplinary field, *Urban Morphology*, **1**(1), pp. 3–10.

Moughtin, C (1992) *Urban Design: Street and Square*, Butterworth Architecture, Oxford.

Moughtin, J C, Oc, T and Tiesdell, S (1995) *Urban Design: Ornament and Decoration*, Butterworth Architecture, Oxford.

Mumford, L (1961) *The City in History: Its Origins, Its Transformations, Its Prospects*, Harcourt, Brace and Wild, New York.

Murrain, P (1993) 'Urban expansion: look back and learn' in Hayward, R and McGlynn, S (eds) *Making Better Places: Urban Design Now*, Butterworth Architecture, Oxford.

Newman, P and Kenworthy, J (1989) *Cities and Automobile Dependence*, Gower, Aldershot.

Oc, T and Tiesdell, S (eds) (1997) *Safer City Centres: Reviving the Public Realm*, Paul Chapman, London.

Owen, S (1979) *The Use of Design Briefs in Local Planning*, Department of Town and Country Planning, Gloucestershire College of Arts and Technology.

Palfreyman, T and Thorpe, S (1993) *Designing for Accessibility: An Introductory Guide*, Centre for Accessible Environments, London.

Power, J (ed) (1980) *Handbook of Architectural Practice and Management*, RIBA, London.

Punter, J (1990) *Design Control in Bristol 1940–1990*, Redcliffe, Bristol.

Punter, J (1996) Developments in urban design review: the lessons of West Coast cities of the United States for British practice, *Journal of Urban Design*, **1**(1), pp. 23–46.

Punter, J and Carmona, M (1997) *The Design Dimension of Planning: Theory, Content, and Best Practice for Design Policies*, Spon, London.

Punter, J, Carmona, M and Platts, A (1994) The design content of development plans, *Planning Practice and Research*, **9**(3), pp. 199–220.

Relph, E (1976) *Place and Placelessness*, Pion, London.

Rowe, C and Koetter, K (1978) *Collage City*, MIT Press, Cambridge, MA.

Royal Institution of Chartered Surveyors (1994) *Understanding the Property Cycle*, RICS, London.

RTPI (1990) *Development Briefs, Practice Advice Note, Appendix 2*, The Royal Town Planning Institute, London.

Samuels, I (1995) Better by design, *Planning Week*, **3**(28), 13 July 1995, pp. 18–19.

Scheer, B and Preiser, W (1994) Introduction, *Environment and Behaviour*, **26**(3), May 1994, pp. 307–311.

Shaftoe, H (1998) 'Planning for crime prevention' in Greed, C and Roberts, M (eds) *Introducing Urban Design: Interventions and Responses*, Addison Wesley Longman, Harlow, pp. 178–187.

Sheffield City Council (1997) *Rebuilding the Heart of Sheffield: St Paul's Chambers Planning Brief*, Sheffield City Council, Sheffield.

Sherlock, H (1996) 'Repairing our much abused cities' in Jenks, M (ed.) *The Compact City: A Sustainable Urban Form?* E & FN Spon, London.

Singmaster, D (1998) From loading bay to loft, *Architects Journal*, **207**(23), June, pp. 53–54.

Skjerve, R (ed.) (1993) *Manual for Alternative Municipal Planning*, Ministry of the Environment, Oslo.

Smith, N and Hensher, D (1997) *The Future of Exclusive Busways: The Brazilian Experience*, Institute of Transport Studies, Working Paper ITS–WP–97–11, University of Sydney and Monash University, Australia.

Thompson, A (1990) *Architectural Design Procedures*, Edward Arnold, London.

Thompson, I (1998) 'Landscape and urban design' in Greed, C and Roberts, M (eds) *Introducing Urban Design: Interventions and Responses*, Addison Wesley Longman, Harlow, pp. 105–115.

Tibbalds, Colbourne, Karski and Williams (1990) *City Centre Design Strategy, Birmingham Urban Design Studies, Stage 1*, Birmingham City Council, Birmingham.

Trancik, R (1986) *Finding Lost Space: Theories of Urban Design*, Van Nostrand and Rheinhold, New York.

Tugnutt, A and Robertson, M (1987) *Making Townscape*, Mitchell, Harlow.

Turner, T (1996) *City as Landscape: A Post-postmodern View of Design and Planning*, E & FN Spon, London.

Unwin R (1920) *Town Planning in Practice*, Unwin, London.

Urban Design Group (1998) *Urban Design Source Book*, Urban Design Group, Oxford.

Urban Task Force, The (1999) *Towards an Urban Renaissance*, E & FN Spon, London.

Wates, N (ed.) (1996) *Action Planning: How to Use Planning Weekends and Urban Design Action Teams to Improve your Environment*, The Prince of Wales Institute of Architecture in association with the Urban Villages Forum, London.

Wates, N and the Urban Design Group (1998) Special Report: involving local communities in design, *Urban Design Quarterly*, **67** (July).

Wates, N (2000) *The Community Planning Handbook*, Earthscan Publications, London.

WDS (1998) *Design Guide 8: Designing Out Crime*, Women's Design Service, London.

WDS (1998) *Design Guide 16: Public Surveillance Systems*, Women's Design Service, WDS (1998) *Community Safety: A Community Development Approach*, Women's Design Service, London.

Zukin, S (1998) Urban lifestyles: diversity and standardisation in spaces of consumption, *Urban Studies*, **35**(5–6), pp. 825–839.

Further references and bibliographies

Readers are strongly urged to refer to the RUDI website: *http://www2.rudi.net/rudi.html* which has a wealth of information about resources in urban design. It also has a searchable bibliography, which is updated monthly by Mike Biddulph.

Index of Authors and Other Persons

Index of Buildings and Places

Index of Subjects